**This book is to be returned on or before
the last date stamped below.** 650.13

THE
Job Hunter's
HANDBOOK

**EVERYTHING YOU NEED TO KNOW
TO GET THE JOB YOU WANT**

This edition published in the UK in 2004 exclusively for
WHSmith Limited
Greenbridge Road
Swindon SN3 3LD
www.WHSmith.co.uk

by Pearson Education
Head Office:
Edinburgh Gate
Harlow CM20 2JE
Tel: +44 (0)1279 623623
Fax: +44 (0)1279 431059

The material in this book is sourced from the following titles, all
published by Prentice Hall:
Brilliant CV by Jim Bright & Joanne Earl © Jim Bright & Joanne Earl 2001
Brilliant Interview by Ros Jay © Pearson 2002
Brilliant Selection Test Results by Susan Hodgson © Pearson 2003
Brilliant Career Finder by Josephine Monroe © Pearson 2003
Brilliant Jobhunter's Manual by Angela Fagan © Pearson 2003

ISBN 0 273 675621

British Library Cataloguing in Publication Data
A CIP catalogue record for this book can be obtained from the British Library

10 9 8 7 6 5 4 3 2 1

Edited by Sandra Jones of Write Mode (sandra.jones@writemode.com)
Typeset by Pantek Arts Ltd, Maidstone, Kent
Designed by Claire Brodmann Book Designs, Lichfield, Staffs
Printed and bound in Great Britain by Ashford Colour Press, Hampshire

The Publishers' policy is to use paper manufactured from sustainable forests.

Contents

Introduction

The recruitment process

▶ Working out what you want to do

One of the biggest decisions you'll ever make is what to do with your working life. Maybe you're about to embark on your first job and want to make sure you start off in the right career. Maybe you already have a job but you feel that it leaves you unfulfilled or that it's leading nowhere. Either way, it's time to decide what job to look for, what career to pursue, what sector to work in. Those are some tough decisions, but Part 1 of this book ('Making a Start') will help guide you to make the right choices. Chapters 1–3 help you to discover what kind of a person you are, where your strengths lie and what work environment would suit you best.

So now you've established what you're looking for, but how do you go about finding it? There are so many avenues to explore – recruitment agencies (in the high street and online); job vacancies in newspapers and trade journals; direct applications to specific companies; using old contacts or forging new ones (which is one of the best ways) – it's difficult to know where to start. Chapter 4 examines these issues and points you in the right direction.

▶ What are the steps in the recruitment process?

Once you've pinpointed those ideal jobs and companies you'll be targeting, it's time to sit down and write that all-important job application. And the cornerstone of any job application is the CV. Part 2 of this book, 'Applying for a Job' (Chapters 5–11), looks at how to prepare, construct and present your CV or application form so that it underlines your greatest strengths and plays down your weaknesses. The most important thing is to ensure that in the recruiter's eyes you stand out as a great fit for the job.

The issue of covering letters – what to include and how to structure them – is dealt with separately in Chapter 9, while proforma application forms (including electronic ones) are examined in Chapter 11.

There are no hard and fast rules about how organizations recruit, but the steps described below are fairly typical, though some firms will do things in a different order and some will skip certain steps.

CV/Telephone screening

In this stage, recruiters narrow down the number of applicants by reading through CVs or application forms. The CV is often the first hurdle to that perfect job, which is why, as we said before, you need to devote a great deal of attention to how it's constructed, presented and delivered.

The CV is often the first hurdle to **that perfect job,** which is why you need to devote **a great deal of attention** to how it's constructed, presented and delivered.

Sometimes the initial screening may involve a brief telephone interview with the recruiter before you are asked to submit a CV or application form; sometimes this telephone screening occurs later. You'll need to be ready for that unexpected phone call though; see p. 239 for more on how to handle this contingency.

Don't put off writing applications to other companies or recruitment agencies because you're still waiting to hear from the first one you applied to. Recruiters are notoriously slow at getting back to applicants. Some online employment agencies even stipulate that 'If you don't hear from us within a month, you can assume your application has not been successful.' So just plough on with the applications. It's always worth following up to check they received your CV or letter of application. However, in the case of job applications, the old saying 'No news is good news' certainly does NOT apply. If they liked your CV, they'll contact you fairly quickly to come and attend an interview or a selection test.

In the case of job applications, the old saying 'No news is good news' certainly **does NOT** apply.

Interview

The interview stage may consist of a single face-to-face interview, or it could involve a series of interviews with different people on a single day or over a period of time.

A face-to-face interview is the most common and involves you being asked numerous questions about you as a person, your work experience, qualifications, interests and your goals for the future. Most of all, the recruiter wants to know what interests you in their job in particular, and what you can bring to it in terms of skills, knowledge, abilities and aptitude.

Very often your initial interview will be with just one person – perhaps your line manager or someone from the Human Resources (HR) Department – and if you're through that stage you'll be invited back for a second interview with someone more senior or with a panel. Panel interviews have several people at once interviewing you, with the same sort of questions we just discussed. You'll need to remember to look at each member of the panel in turn as they ask you questions.

In Chapter 12, we'll be discussing how to prepare for the interview in terms of attire, behaviour, and what to take with you on the day. Research has shown that first impressions are all-important and sometimes the interview makes up their mind within the first minute or so of your entering the room whether or not they'll offer you the job. And this initial impression is based upon relatively minor things like how you greet them, whether you look them in the eye, and how you dress. You'll gain an insight into how to win their approval in this chapter.

Sometimes the interviewer makes up their mind **within the first minute or so** of you entering the room whether they'll offer you the job.

Chapter 12 also examines ways to boost your confidence at interviews and provides some preparation exercises and techniques to help improve your performance on the day.

Chapter 13 analyses a whole range of possible interview questions, in particular it focuses on the tough ones like 'What is your biggest weakness?' so that you know what to expect and won't be caught off-guard. It suggests how best to answer these so that you can present yourself in the most favourable light. We suggest that you read through this and that prior to any interview, you enlist the help of a friend or family member to assume the role of the interviewer and fire some of these questions at you.

Presentations

It may happen that, as part of the interview process, you'll be asked to give a presentation. Sometimes you'll be given plenty of advance notice about this (when you receive your interview letter, for example), but sometimes there may be very little notice – perhaps you'll only be told about it once you're actually at the interview. There is a good reason for this approach – the employer wants to see how you cope in a stressful situation and with limited time for preparation.

Giving a presentation can be a nerve-wracking experience even for those who are used to giving them, maybe in their current job. For someone fresh out of college, it can seem a major obstacle in the recruitment process. Don't worry, help is at hand! In Chapter 14 we'll guide you through the issues of what to select as a topic (if it isn't a pre-set topic), how to structure and organize your ideas, how to use notes, how to engage with the audience, and most important, how to overcome those nerves and feel relaxed and confident, which will put your audience at ease too.

Selection tests

Depending on the type of job and the level at which you're applying, in addition to the interview and possibly a presentation, you may be asked to sit one or more selection tests. This is normal practice nowadays for graduate recruitment, for example, when all the candidates may have very good qualifications on paper and so some other method has to be devised to decide who would be best suited to the role and to the company. In this case, personality and work style may determine who gets offered the job as much as academic qualifications. They'll want to make sure you fit in with the company ethos.

Personality and work style may determine who gets offered the job rather than academic qualifications.

Sometimes these selection tests (which may be verbal, numerical, logic, aptitude, personality or any combination) may take place prior to the interview, as a screening tool, and may take up the best part of a day. You may find yourself sitting the tests in an assessment centre, with fifty or more other applicants. Sometimes though they may be quite short and take place immediately before or after the interview proper, with just you in the room. Sometimes the tests will be in the form of questionnaires or booklets to be completed on paper; however, there is a growing tendency nowadays for applicants to complete on-screen computer tests.

All these different types of testing are analysed in Part 3 of this book ('Proving Yourself'). Chapter 15 provides some practice tests so that you can familiarize yourself with what to expect and how best to respond. In Chapter 18 we'll also give you details of useful websites that provide further information on testing, to help you prepare. Some of these websites also offer online test papers.

Offer or rejection

You can expect to hear the outcome of an interview reasonably promptly. Often people have arrived home from the interview to find a voice mail message for them saying 'Congratulations!' Of course this all depends on how many other applicants they have to see after you; sometimes the whole interview procedure can drag on for several weeks. However, if it's a second or third interview they may offer the job to you on the spot.

If you are offered the job, take time to let things sink in before accepting. Most employers will give you a little while to think things over, but don't expect them to give you very long. Often there is a second good candidate waiting in the wings, should you turn them down.

If you're unlucky enough to be rejected, then join the club! You are in the overwhelming majority. Nearly everybody has been turned down for a job at some time or another – Karl Marx, despite holding a doctorate in

Philosophy, was refused a university teaching post, while Steven Spielberg failed to get into UCLA film school! Just remember: 'Quitters never win. Winners never quit.'

Nearly everyone has been turned down for a job at some time … **Just remember,** 'Quitters never win. **Winners never quit.'**

If you do receive a rejection, don't be tempted to write an abusive letter or make an emotional phone call to the recruiter or employer – this is probably a knee-jerk reaction that you'll regret later. In any case, it's highly unprofessional and will risk your reputation with that particular employer and any other prospective employers who get wind of your behaviour. In any case, you may cross paths with the organization or individual later in your career, and it's always worth building up your contacts.

Gain something positive from the experience by thinking about what you could do differently next time so that it's YOU that gets the job offer. Sometimes employers are willing to provide feedback if it's asked for in a polite and positive manner, and if the purpose is to assist you in strengthening future job applications. However, many employers rightly fear that prolonging the dialogue may expose them to legal action or might mislead the candidate. Just remember though, keep writing those applications and look forwards, not backwards.

◗ Negotiating a package

So you did it! All that hard work and preparation paid off and you've received a job offer. The next issue in the mind of almost every applicant is 'What's my salary going to be?'

Sometimes the salary will have been stated in a job vacancy advert; sometimes you'll be asked the salary you're looking for in the application form, or at the interview. Either way, it's unusual not to find some flexibility in the job package if you can persuade them that you're worth it. After all, they picked *you* from all those other candidates, so they must really want you.

Don't get carried away at this point. They may have a very close second candidate who is flexible on salary, and you don't want to price yourself out of the market. It's generally the case that your next salary is constrained to some extent by whatever you earned in your former job, particularly if it's in the same field. It is customary to expect an increase though, unless you're changing careers totally and starting from the bottom again. Chapter 19 outlines some negotiation techniques to ensure that you pitch your salary at the right level and don't undersell or oversell yourself. It explains how to use other variables such as company car, holiday entitlement, bonuses, etc. as bargaining chips.

In the final Chapter 20 we broach the issue of resignation and how best to tackle it – what to say to your current boss; how to phrase your resignation letter; what to do if your boss makes a counter-offer. The objective is to make the resignation go as smoothly as possible without rancour or remorse, so that you can look forward to embarking on your exciting new career.

▶ And finally…

Nothing can stop the man
with the right mental attitude
from achieving his goal;
nothing on earth can help
the man with the
wrong mental attitude.

Thomas Jefferson

Part **one**

Making
a start

Chapter one

What do you
want
from work?

When people start thinking about choosing or changing career, the first thing they need to decide on is which exciting sector they are going to target in their job search. Either they have a clear idea of where they want to go or they have the 'anywhere but here' attitude and believe any job would be better than the one they currently hold.

But as Glinda, the Good Witch of the North, said to Dorothy in *The Wizard of Oz* as she started out on the Yellow Brick Road: 'It's always best to start at the beginning' – and thinking about your next job is not the beginning. To lay good foundations for your career change (and hopefully to avoid another one in the future) you have to start by looking at the job you have now and work out why it isn't making you happy. If you're looking for your first job, you can still do the exercise below – just think of it as prioritizing a 'wish-list'.

Begin by looking at this random list of good things people often say their work gives them. (If you're wondering why there isn't a list of the bad things a job offers, it's because all jobs consist of inconvenience, annoyances and paperwork. Sorry!) Put them in order of importance to you and discard the benefits and corollaries of work that mean nothing to you:

- money
- power
- a sense of purpose
- thrills
- long-term security
- opportunity for growth
- autonomy

- status
- satisfaction
- friends
- challenges
- fun
- creative freedom
- material rewards.

Your list should provide a snapshot of the benefits and rewards you most want your next job to give you. Now, ask yourself how many of these benefits your current job supplies you with. If it isn't very many, it's easy to see why you've been feeling restless and unfulfilled.

But this short, incomplete list doesn't reveal what *really* motivates and drives you at work. The next survey, however, has been designed to uncover your unconscious ambitions for work.

▶ Career motivation survey

The following eight sections of questions will help you discover the things you really want from work. Right now you might be thinking that all you want is a big salary or to do something truly worthwhile – in 20 minutes, though, you might realize that's not really what you want, or it's only part of the story.

The instructions for completing the survey are relatively simple. Each section consists of nine statements; your task is to allocate 15 points among the nine statements. You could give all 15 points to one statement or spread them fairly evenly across the statements depending on how strongly you agree with them. For the results to be accurate though, your total points for each section must be exactly 15. No more, no less.

Right now you may be thinking
that **all you want**
is a big salary or to do something
worthwhile with your life.

When you have completed all eight sections, fill in the category column (categories run from A to I) from the data in the results section at the end. Finally add up the points you have awarded to each category.

Section 1
points | category

i   Wherever I work I always have a prestigious position.

ii   Friendships at work would make it hard for me to move on.

iii   Work should enrich my personal development.

iv   I dislike being a small cog in a big machine.

v   I want all the symbols of wealth.

vi   I want to do something distinctive.

vii   I want my colleagues to look to me for leadership.

viii   I get worried when I can't see where my job is heading.

ix   The ability to make meaningful contributions at work gives me a great deal of satisfaction.

Section 2

i   I'd like a relationship outside work with my colleagues.

ii   Doing meaningful work is more important than a big salary.

iii   I want to be wealthy.

iv   Deciding how to spend my time gives me satisfaction.

v   I want to create things that people will associate with me.

vi   Recognition as part of 'The Establishment' would thrill me.

vii   I want to feel I have worked for my expertise.

viii   I want to be a leader.

ix   Job security is important to me.

Section 3   points | category

i   I want my work to carry my name.

ii   I won't feel a sense of achievement unless I have material possessions.

iii   I prefer being my own boss.

iv   I want public recognition for my work.

v   Work is part of a search to find meaning in life.

vi   I want to feel I will always be all right in the future.

vii   I'd like a role that gives me influence over my co-workers.

viii Professionally, I want an opportunity to demonstrate that I really know my stuff.

ix   Friendship with people at my work is important to me.

Section 4

i   I'd like to be seen as a specialist in my field.

ii   I see my career as part of a search for greater meaning in my life.

iii   I want to use my personal creativity in my work.

iv   I like to take responsibility for my decisions.

v   I want to be able to buy anything I want.

vi   I get satisfaction from working closely with other people.

vii   I'd only ever relax if I was in a secure career.

viii Telling colleagues what to do is important to me.

ix   Status is an important motivator for me.

Section 5

i   I'd find great comfort in knowing how well off I'll be when I retire.

ii   Being close to colleagues is important to me.

points | category

iii   If I believed my job was worthwhile I would devote
      myself to it.
iv   I want to innovate at work.
v   It's important that I have the ability to choose my
      own tasks.
vi   I'd like to be known as an expert.
vii   I want to be able to spend money easily.
viii I like jobs that give me power over how
      co-workers perform.
ix   I'd like formal recognition from others for my
      achievements.

Section 6

i   Having a high status job would give me satisfaction.
ii   I want to do things no one has done before.
iii   Usually, I take the safe option.
iv   I don't want to be watched over too closely by
      my boss.
v   I want to be in charge of people and money.
vi   I want to get to know people through work.
vii   I want to be one of those people with valuable
      specialist knowledge.
viii There's not much I wouldn't do for money and status.
ix   More often than not, I do what I believe is right
      rather than the things that would further my career.

Section 7

i   I want to be creative at work.
ii   It's important that I like the people I work with.
iii   I'd like to influence the people I work with.
iv   Choosing my work myself would bring satisfaction.
v   I want financial security.

points | category

vi   It feels good when people look up to me.

vii Only a high standard of living will give me satisfaction.

viii I want to be the best in my field.

ix   I will only be satisfied if my job delivers real value.

Section 8

i   It would please me if I didn't have to answer to others.

ii   I'm happier in charge.

iii I want the things I produce to bear my name.

iv   Work without meaning is not worth doing.

v   A secure future is attractive to me.

vi   I would enjoy the status that comes with a senior position.

vii High standards of living attract me.

viii I want to be an expert in my field.

ix   If I'm lucky enough to work with friends, nothing else matters.

Results

Match the number of each statement (i–ix) to a category (A–I) as follows:

Section 1
i = D, ii = G, iii = B, iv = F, v = E vi = A, vii = C, viii = H, ix = I

Section 2
i = G, ii = B, iii = E, iv = F, v = A, vi = D, vii = I, viii = C, ix = H

Section 3
i = A, ii = E, iii = F, iv = D, v = B, vi = H, vii = C, viii = I, ix = G

Section 4
i = I, ii = B, iii = A, iv = F, v = E, vi = G, vii = H, viii = C, ix = D

Section 5
i = H, ii = G, iii = B, iv = A, v = F, vi = I, vii = E, viii = C, ix = D

Section 6

i = D, ii = A, iii = H, iv = F, v = C, vi = G, vii = I, viii = E, ix = B

Section 7

i = A, ii = G, iii = C, iv = F, v = H, vi = D, vii = E, viii = I, ix = B

Section 8

i = F, ii = C, iii = A, iv = B, v = H, vi = D, vii = E, viii = I, ix = G

Now fill in your totals for each category below. To check your results are accurate, make sure the total adds up to exactly 120.

A + B + C + D + E + F + G + H + I = 120

☐ + ☐ + ☐ + ☐ + ☐ + ☐ + ☐ + ☐ + ☐

Then check to find out what motivates you if you scored highly in the following categories.

A If you scored highly in this category you are motivated by the opportunity to be creative.

B If you scored highly in this category you are motivated by work that gives you a sense of purpose and offers meaning.

C If you scored highly in this category you are motivated by the chance to exert power and influence.

D If you scored highly in this category you are motivated by status.

E If you scored highly in this category you are motivated by material rewards.

F If you scored highly in this category you are motivated by work where you can be independent.

G If you scored highly in this category you are motivated in jobs where you have a good working relationship with your colleagues.

H If you scored highly in this category you are motivated by the need for security.

I If you scored highly in this category you are motivated by opportunities to use your expertise and specialist knowledge.

▶ How to use the information

The benefits of your results from this survey might not be immediately apparent – after all, what good is knowing that you're motivated by status when you're looking to take an entry-level position somewhere? Well, the information you've just gleaned should help you to identify moves that would be right for you and set you on the right path. At the very least it should stop you choosing the wrong career. For instance, there's no point hankering after a City salary if you've just realized that you hanker after security in your work: in the City your job is only as safe as market performances allow. The survey results might also guide you into the right kind of job – you know you want to have a bit of power, but now maybe you know you'd rather have power over creative output rather than over people.

Looking for a new career is a bit like looking for a new partner; your life goals need to match. But instead of wondering what you have to offer – the way most people write a lonelyhearts ad – looking for work starts with working out which career offers you your heart's desire. For your change of career to be a success, you want to make sure your ambitions for work dovetail perfectly with your ambitions for life (see the next exercise, p. 23).

Looking for a new career is a bit like looking **for a new partner:** your life goals need to match.

Once you've looked at what a career can offer you, you need to look – as you would at a potential partner – at how it will treat you over the years. If you have just discovered autonomy is a major driver for you, then heading into a job where you're likely to get pushed around will clearly not make you happy. Now is the time to work out what you need your job to give you – is it status, camaraderie or an easy commute? Perhaps you are one of those workers who could do a number of jobs but would thrive in, say, a small company or a corporate atmosphere. Environment is often as important as salary and duties. Considering these sorts of factors before you start looking for a new career will guide you in the right direction.

Before we move on to discuss your ideal job, take a few minutes to fill in the Ambitions Chart overleaf. It asks you to fill in your ambitions for every part of your life because satisfaction rarely comes from work alone. For each column, write your goals and aspirations and include *everything*: from your desire for a season ticket at Highbury to a large family or a happy retirement.

Analysing your chart will give you more information about the kind of career you're best suited to. If, for example, under 'home' you described a rural idyll far from civilization, perhaps you might want to reconsider your ambitions to work in city-centred professions like the media or finance. The point of this chart is to highlight the 'must-haves' your new career has to offer you. Each one is a brick in the well-laid foundations of your new life. Building up a profile of a new career brick by brick is a much more organic way of getting the job you want and is far more likely to produce the right result than the 'I think I'll have a go at law today' approach. Focusing on the small essentials is also much less daunting than creating a whole new life for yourself out of little more than thin air.

A good career isn't one that pays brilliantly or **impresses your mates –** it's one that **makes you happy.**

▶ Ambitions chart

Home	Family	Leisure/Travel	Money	Work

Community	Retirement	Status	Health

While this book is about finding work, it's also about finding happiness. To ensure you get both, you need to be certain about the commitment you're prepared to make to work before you begin your career search. A good career isn't one that pays brilliantly or impresses your mates, it's one that makes you happy.

Top Tips **Making a start**

- Think about what you most dislike in your current job.
- Prioritize your 'must-haves' for a future career.
- Discover your prime motivators at work (see pp. 16–20).
- Write down your life ambitions (see pp. 23–24).
- Now pinpoint and target your job sector and career choice to your key drivers.

Chapter two

2

Getting to
know
yourself

There is a concept every sales rep understands implicitly: you have to know your product inside out to sell it effectively – and in job hunting that product is YOU. As you are about to start selling yourself, you need to get to know your strengths and your weaknesses so you know (a) which roles suit you best and (b) which attributes you most want to tell your new employer about.

When you combine the information you collated in Chapter 1 (what you want work to do for you) with the information you'll pull together in this chapter (what you have to offer), then you'll have the best possible starting point from which to launch a new career.

> You have to know **your product inside out** to sell it effectively – in job hunting **that product is YOU.**

The object is to find your perfect career, something ideally suited to you. To do that we need to work through some more exercises to find out what the foundation stones of your career will be – the unshakable qualities you offer and your non-negotiable desires for work.

Some career advisors call this 'establishing your palette', i.e. working out your personal colours from which you can paint your own personal career picture. You might be eager to move straight to the chapters concerning getting a new job, but rest assured, your patience with these early, crucial steps will bear juicy fruit.

◗ What kind of worker are you?

No matter which field you end up entering, most jobs, roles and tasks will be the same. Whether you're in law, nursing or town planning you'll still work with managers, researchers, specialists, assistants, etc., not to mention eccentrics, Luddites, motivators or misery guts. Practically every workplace in the world is made up of the same types of people doing the same types of job. This next section will help you uncover which job types best suit you.

Most of us have worked for a bad manager at some point, or with an over-ambitious junior member of staff. Generally, when we have a problem with people at work it's not because they're bad people, it's because they're in the wrong role. When we work in positions we're not naturally talented at, we make mistakes, we get demoralized, and it affects our relationships with our co-workers. So it's important to work out where your natural talents and abilities lie, as this will help you understand what kind of roles you will flourish in – and therefore be happy in.

Generally when we have
a problem with co-workers,
it's not because they're bad people,
it's because they're
in the wrong role.

Knowing your strengths and aptitudes will help you seek new roles with greater confidence, and that confidence will help you win over new employers.

▶ Discovering the true you

This next exercise has its roots in a couple of well-known and well-used team role and personality tests developed by Dr Meredith Belbin, and Isabel Briggs Myers and Katharine C. Briggs. Detailed and personalized tests are widely available online, and for a small fee and five minutes in the company of your favourite search engine, you can easily get yourself psychometrically tested (see Chapter 18 for more details).

Many tests come to black-and-white conclusions and run the risk of labelling participants as capable of working well only in a narrow field. This one has been structured to give broader results, as most workers are capable of performing many roles in the workplace.

Completing the exercise is relatively straightforward. There are 28 pairs of statements and you must allocate three points to each pair – you can give all three points to one statement and none to the other, or split them 2:1 between the statements depending on how strongly you agree with them. When you've finished, add up the points you've awarded to each letter.

Psychometric exercise

1

When plans change, I'm good at spotting the opportunities
and benefits which the new situation offers.   *A*

I'm good at knowing when people have something to offer ·
and can encourage them to join in.   *B*

2

I can work well with anyone.   *C*

The success of the project is more important than my co-workers
liking me.   *D*

3

I am capable of seeing projects through to the very end. *E*

I produce ideas effortlessly. *F*

4

I have the ability to sense what will work in most situations. *G*

I am fair-minded and suggest proposals without bias if I think
they will work. *H*

5

I come alive in meetings when new ideas are being discussed. *A*

I find it difficult to take the lead. *C*

6

In a meeting, I like to feel every viewpoint has been expressed. *B*

Often I'm too objective about all the options to be enthusiastic
about any one in particular. *G*

7

People sometimes think I'm pushy when I'm just trying to get
the job done. *D*

Sometimes I lose concentration when I get excited about my
latest plan. *F*

8

Colleagues often tell me I'm thinking too much about the detail
and not about the big picture. *E*

I like meetings to be well structured and to stick to the agenda. *H*

9

I am reliable and can be trusted to see all tasks are attended to.   *H*

I'm happier working towards a common goal.   *C*

10

I'm good to have on a project because I spot mistakes that
would otherwise cause trouble.   *E*

I think my colleagues trust my judgement – I have a reputation
for being fair.   *G*

11

I get frustrated when meetings lose direction and I try to bring
them back on track.   *D*

I seem to be good at influencing people.   *B*

12

I like being first with new developments and information.   *A*

I liven up meetings by contributing something unexpected
and original.   *F*

13

I hate leaving loose ends when my projects finish – my
colleagues say I am a perfectionist.   *E*

I'm comfortable holding unpopular views and will challenge
colleagues when I think they are wrong.   *D*

14

Although I like to hear what people have to say, I find it easy
to make up my own mind.   *B*

Getting to know my colleagues gives me pleasure.   *C*

15

I'm capable of seeing how ideas might benefit other
departments and companies.   *A*

I have a talent for sticking to the brief and getting the job done.   *H*

16

I'm good at dousing down outrageous and unworkable
suggestions from others.   *G*

I'm happiest at work when I'm using my imagination.   *F*

17

I find weighing up all the options and possibilities satisfying.   *G*

Meeting new people with something to offer should be one
of the perks of any job I do.   *A*

18

I'm good at finding consensus and a way forward.   *B*

I'm attracted to the unusual option rather than the safe one.   *F*

19

Sometimes I hold up proceedings while I make sure
everything has been done properly.   *E*

It feels good to know I'm building friendships with clients
and colleagues.   *C*

20

I'm open to meetings going off at tangents just to see what
ideas get thrown up.   *A*

My integrity and need to do a job well means I usually
complete projects on time.   *E*

21

I make good decisions under pressure.   *B*

Being able to devote myself to a project gives me satisfaction.   *E*

22

When meetings become difficult, I like to go to the toilet or the
watercooler to work out solutions to problems.   *F*

Sometimes I find it hard to get complex points across.   *H*

23

I am able to influence decisions and outcomes.   *D*

I am pleased when I solve practical problems.   *H*

24

If a project loses direction, I am able to take control and bring
it to fruition.   *D*

I can keep my cool and think straight in difficult situations.   *G*

25

Unless I have a clear goal or task, I find it difficult to get started.   *H*

I am comfortable asking people to do things that I cannot
do myself.   *B*

26

Others may think I lack intuition or imagination.   *G*

I find it exciting to work with brilliant people, even if they are a
bit difficult.   *C*

27

I bore easily and need sparky colleagues to bounce off. *A*

Sometimes I must seem impatient when progress is slow
or disrupted. *D*

28

When everyone's talking in meetings, I find it difficult to get my
point across. *C*

Explaining and clarifying detail is not one of my strong points. *F*

Write your totals for each letter below, making sure the grand total
comes to 84.

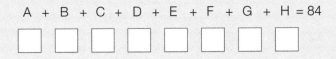

A + B + C + D + E + F + G + H = 84

Then look below to see what type of worker you are.

Category A = INDUSTRIALIST

You are the kind of worker who can get on with tasks unsupervised with
just the sketchiest of briefs. You are a fantastic researcher and can
uncover solutions through inspired investigation and diligence. Your tendency for hard work compensates for shortcomings in imagination and
you keep projects moving.

Category B = TEAM CAPTAIN

You are by nature a collaborator and a decision maker. You understand
the benefits of teamwork and are good at recognizing other people's
strengths. You see the big picture and communicate well with all types
of people. You have the ability to encourage your co-workers and gain

their respect. Your weakness is that you do not do well on your own as you lack flair.

Category C = MIDFIELDER

You are great at following the plan. You are practical and have a systematic approach to work. You are known for your common sense and discipline and generally find a place for yourself in most teams. However, you do not cope well with change and can become flustered and demoralized when plans change or the goalposts are moved.

Category D = GARDENER

Your speciality is taking someone else's idea and bringing it to fruition. You grasp concepts easily and also have the intelligence to improve ideas. Although you may not be vocal in meetings, when projects are finished they clearly bear your stamp as you have a talent for influencing the people around you. Your natural drive and self-confidence are often responsible for getting complex projects off the ground. While you are invaluable, you are not necessarily well liked as you can be snappy with slower colleagues if you think they are being obstructive.

Category E = PERFECTIONIST

It is your attention to detail that often saves colleagues and projects from ending up in the mire. You are fastidious – your perfectionism often bores colleagues who think you are holding them back – and well suited to detailed work and ensuring deadlines aren't forgotten. You are the sweeper and you make sure nothing gets past you. Even though you are incredibly valuable to any team, you do not make friends easily as you are seen as self-controlled and intolerant of flamboyant co-workers.

Category F = INVENTOR

You are the kind of worker who is almost useless for most of your working day. However, you are responsible for the ideas that drive companies forward and your moments of inspiration transform projects, teams and results. You are happier working on big headline projects and enjoy problem solving. You are independent, imaginative and intelligent but have a tendency to think all your ideas are fantastic and you need co-workers to calculate their true merits. You can be impractical and co-workers may think you are a dreamer.

Category G = ANALYST

You can process and evaluate data, situations and problems and have the ability to weigh up several options. You bring balance and a level head to most situations. Your colleagues may see you as a bit of a pessimist as you can spot where projects will go awry. While they may also see you as critical, it is just your critical thinking that ensures success. You may find it difficult to have many social relationships with co-workers.

Category H = PRAGMATIST

You are the Doubting Thomas of any team. You need proof that something will work before you are confident about moving forward, but once you have that confidence, you are good at implementation and sticking to the brief. You prefer communication to be in black and white rather than proceed on a nod and a wink. You have self-control and buckets of common sense, but you can come across as unenthusiastic and inflexible.

▶ How to use the results

Identifying your strengths

Most respondents find that they score highly in one category while three or four tie in 'second place', with just a few points between the remaining categories. Fairly obviously, your leading category is the one you are most naturally suited to. But as we might already be working with a Team

Captain, we sometimes seek out another role for ourselves within the work environment to avoid conflict – and this is when we work well in any of our second-place categories.

On the surface, some of the categories – such as Team Captain, for example – seem more glamorous than others. However, every category is equally valid and companies cannot be successful unless they employ people in every category. In this instance though, you are not looking to create the perfect team (the reason why most employers submit their staff to similar tests) but to find out where your natural talents lie. Happiness comes from playing to your strengths and the information you now have will help you identify roles you would thrive in. Of course, job ads never read 'Perfectionist required to balance out Inventor-heavy team' and the purpose of the survey is not so you can say 'Right, I'm going to be a Gardener' but to learn more about your strengths. If, for example, it's becoming clear that you don't have great communication skills but you still crave a senior position, perhaps you'd be happier in a role where you manage data rather than people. Or if your natural talent is for creativity, you should start looking for work that will let you express it.

Happiness
comes from playing
to your strengths.

Hopefully the results of your survey will have confirmed things that you 'kind of' knew about yourself already and will give you the confidence to tell prospective employers that you are excellent at idea generation, paying attention to detail, or being trusted to follow the brief. Any candidate who can be sure of what they have to offer is attractive to employers. Even though someone else might have more relevant work experience, you'll have the edge if you can convince an employer of your worth. If you're not worth anything, you won't be valued. Therefore knowing and communicating your worth puts you in a strong position.

And identifying your weaknesses ...

Your survey results might also have revealed something about your weaknesses – perhaps a tendency to overlook details or an unwillingness to embrace new ideas. This is still information you can use to guide you away from unsuitable positions. Simply knowing that you have a tendency to be dogmatic or flamboyant might help you recognize that there are times when enthusiasm and caution are called for. This knowledge will help you perform better and get more job satisfaction.

If you've just learned that you're a born leader but you have no leadership experience, then you've just discovered a weakness undermining a strength. If you want to seek a leadership role in the future, you'll need to address the hole in your work experience. It's not enough to believe you should be in control – you're going to have to prove your aptitude and ability to cope with the associated pressure. You should be examining your career so far to find examples of times when you've taken the lead. Maybe it was just in one meeting, or when you volunteered to organize the Christmas party, but start looking for ways of illustrating your innate talents. No matter what strengths you've just uncovered, HR departments and employers will disregard them if you can't back them up with a few facts.

This survey won't have uncovered all your shortcomings, of course, but part of knowing yourself well is coming to terms with the things that are just beyond you. Preparing for a new career means eliminating the weaknesses that keep you and your dream job apart. Your next task involves assessing your shortcomings and then addressing them.

Preparing for a new career
means eliminating the weaknesses
that keep you and your
dream job apart.

If you already know what field you want to work in, or what kind of job you'd like to do, then the next exercise examining recruitment ads will be a little easier. But if not, don't worry as most recruitment ads ask for the same thing anyway.

▶ Recruitment ads

For job hunters, looking at recruitment ads can be dispiriting – no one ever seems to be offering a job they're interested in or one that requires their skills. We've known for a long time that looking for a job in the Situations Vacant column can be frustrating as employers seek amazingly well-qualified candidates for remarkably small salaries.

However, recruitment ads can be very valuable to career changers as they act as signposts down unfamiliar paths. By analysing their content, you can identify what employers are looking for. The idea of this exercise is to compare what employers seek with what you offer, to enable you to iden-tify the holes in your professional repertoire. The aim is to address as many of your professional weaknesses as possible before you head too far down an unsuitable road.

Gather together all the publications you have lying around your home or your office that carry recruitment advertising. If you're desperate to enter a particular field, go out and buy the trade publication for your desired profession and include the recruitment advertising from that. If you're open-minded about what path you'll take next, choose from a broad spectrum of publications.

Find between 10 and 20 adverts for jobs that you would consider doing – these do not have to be jobs you are qualified for or that are in your field or have any bearing on what you've done so far. In a sense you are creating a beauty pageant of desirable jobs. Some of them might even be roles you don't hope to apply for until much further down the line.

Create a beauty pageant
of desirable jobs ...
and identify the obstacles
that stop you from getting them.

Examine them closely to see whether they're looking for a particular qualification, a certain type of work experience, or desirable qualities that ideal candidates should be able to demonstrate. Now, ask yourself which of their demands you cannot meet. These are the weaknesses that might stop you getting your dream job.

Don't be disheartened though – if you're honest, you have given yourself the best opportunity to address your weaknesses, deal with them and eliminate them. While you might be several years away from applying for some of the positions you've just scrutinized, you now know what skills, qualifications and experience you need to acquire to be able to reach your desired goal. In the meantime, knowing your desires, your strengths and your weaknesses will lead you in the right direction.

▶ Skills and opportunity

Although you might be years away from some of the positions you've just scrutinized, you might not. Many skills are transferable and it's worth having a closer look at how your skills might offer opportunities. The best careers are the product of the confluence of skills and opportunity. Wherever the skills fit the opportunity, you'll find a motivated worker who takes home satisfaction along with a pay packet.

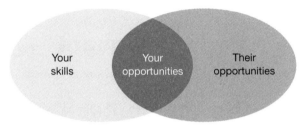

Wherever the **skills fit the opportunity,** you'll find a motivated worker who **takes home satisfaction** along with a pay packet.

As this diagram shows, you are not qualified for every job advertised, nor will all your skills be utilized in every job, but where your skills do match the jobs advertised – the opportunities – that's where you'll find a job match. Obviously, the bigger you can make the dark shaded area, the greater number of jobs you can go for.

Take those 10 or 20 job ads again. Now make two lists, one of the qualities and skills the advertisers are looking for and another of the skills and attributes you offer. For example:

They want	I offer
Ability to work under pressure	Reputation for meeting deadlines
Easy-going personality	Flexibility
Shift work	Ability to get on with colleagues
Qualification in business	Extensive computer skills
No fear of technology	Hardworking nature
Familiarity with accountancy practice	Two years' management experience
Analytical skills	Proven problem-solving ability

There is a near match between this candidate and this position, in fact it's just really a business qualification the candidate is lacking. But the candidate has two years' management experience, which may compensate for the lack of a formal qualification. With a well-crafted application it's plausible that this opportunity moves from the lightly shaded area to the dark shaded part of the diagram.

Look carefully at the job adverts you've selected. With a little bit of persuasion and a recrafted CV, how many could you shift into the dark shaded area?

Very often, there is one thing that stops career changers moving advertisers' opportunities into their shaded area – and that's specialist knowledge. If you keep coming up against this obstacle, you need to find a way to persuade employers this isn't the barrier they think it is. Perhaps you're a fast learner, a voracious reader (who could acquire knowledge quickly) or you could bring something else to the bargain in compensation. The crucial thing at this stage is not to rule out dream jobs because your skills don't perfectly match those in the job spec. It's quite likely that the advertiser doesn't expect candidates to be able to tick every box – they were simply advertising their wish-list. A good application can compensate for most shortcomings.

Don't rule out dream jobs because your skills don't perfectly match those in the job spec.

Hopefully, you can see that by making a creative application – or by acquiring just one new skill – you'll be able to move a whole swathe of jobs into your dark shaded area. At this stage you should realize how 'nearly qualified' you are for a range of jobs you had previously considered beyond your grasp. By spotting the barrier – often something that can be overcome through part-time study or making the most of your current position – you can make yourself even more marketable.

Top Tips Getting to know yourself

- Get to really know your sales product – that's YOU.
- Work out your natural strengths – and weaknesses.
- Identify what weaknesses might stand in the way of you and that perfect job.
- Set about addressing those weaknesses.

Chapter three

Working out what
you
want to do

▶ Career clarity

Most of us don't have a smart answer to the question 'What do you want to do?' If you do happen to know what kind of work you want, congratulations, you are very rare and very lucky. Very few people ever have a clear idea of what career they'd like to follow and their lack of clarity often stops them from moving forward. The purpose of this chapter is to turn hunches, dreams and possibilities into career reality. Because if you find a career you really, really want, you will look four times as hard for your next job. And the harder you look, the more you increase your chances of finding the work you were born to do.

If you know
what kind of work you want,
congratulations,
you are very rare and very lucky!

One of the dangers with the 'What do you want to do?' question is that it implies you have to stick to something for the rest of your life. That's one reason why so many people find it so hard to answer. Another danger is that it forces you to choose one option over another – few of us are so driven that we have only one thing that really matters to us. The question can produce better results if we take some of the implied pressure out of it and rephrase it as 'What do you want to do today? Or for the next few years?' You might also find it's easier to work out what you want to do if you broaden the question to 'What are some of the things you really want to do with your life?' By breaking down the big questions into manageable sizes, this chapter hopes to elicit some genuine answers from your subconscious.

If you've ever had any career counselling, it's possible you've filled in questionnaires about your abilities and aptitudes which have enabled profiling software to probe your subconscious to suggest a career as a pottery glazer or a livestock auctioneer. It never fails to amuse just how specific these programs are – they don't just suggest you look for work as a designer but seem to know you'd *really* enjoy designing costume jewellery! As they never ring true and book printing technology doesn't allow for such interactivity, there are no tests of that ilk here. If you want to try one, however, there are plenty online, some you have to pay for, some you don't. Try *www.cascaid.co.uk* for a potted version of a software program favoured by UK career counsellors. Another good free one is at *schoolfinder.com* – it's been designed for Canadians looking for colleges, but it's still relevant to the UK career market and it's good fun. You have to register your details first but that doesn't take long.

Part of the problem with the results of such career profiling tests is that it's very difficult to feel that you would enjoy jewellery design unless you have some experience or knowledge of it. The software could throw up 20 suggestions, but unless you understand what a career in that area involves, it's impossible to be enthusiastic. It's a bit like shopping for clothes with your mother: she keeps on holding up jumpers you can't see yourself wearing while saying 'What's wrong with this one?'

A far more effective way of uncovering the field and position that's right for you is to let the certainties you know about yourself and what you want from work guide you to a natural conclusion. The exercises and devices in this chapter are designed to propel you to that conclusion a little faster.

Let the certainties **you know about yourself** and what you want from work guide you to **a natural conclusion.**

▶ A vine-ripened career

If you're wondering why we're taking such a basic approach, talk to any gardener you know. They will tell you the fruits and vegetables they grow themselves taste better than anything you can buy in the supermarket. It may not be because they actually *do* taste better, but because the gardener gets pleasure from reaping what he sows – anything you've tended with care and worked hard for always tastes good because it tastes of satisfaction.

By taking control of your career, by making decisions that will make you happy, by accepting responsibility, you will be tending to your career like a gardener does his produce. And the fruits of your labour will be even sweeter if you don't harvest your decision too soon – some things taste better when they've been left to ripen on the vine. So rest assured, this methodical approach to career finding will pay handsome dividends in the long run.

Over the next few pages, we're going to put all your potential careers in the greenhouse, germinate the seeds, weed out the seedlings that don't feel right, and tend to those that have a future. We're then going to hothouse them until we're left with career options that excite and satisfy you.

▶ Asking the right questions

So if asking 'What do you want to do?' doesn't work, what questions *are* the right kind to ask? Generally, they're the ones that make you analyse how you feel about specific options, that force you to answer in concrete terms rather than vaguely, and that make you consider the same problem from a slightly different angle. This chapter has several sections of questions all designed to prompt slightly different responses to myriad employment options. As you work through each section, you should start to build up a list of things you're good at, things you want and things you enjoy. Keeping all this information in mind, you'll then move on to a series of questions designed to help you discover career paths you might not have considered before.

This book can't tell you what career is right for you – there isn't a magic formula – so it's up to you to look carefully at your answers to spot the patterns and clues that will lead you to a natural conclusion.

There are no prizes for answering these questions quickly and experience tells us that your first answer is not always your best – it's generally the one you're used to giving. So take your time to break habits and consider unconventional responses – there are no wrong answers.

Let's start with a series of questions that, in a roundabout way, replace the dreaded 'What do you want to do?':

1   What comes naturally to me?

2   How hard am I prepared to work?

3   What do I enjoy doing?

4   What aspects of work have I enjoyed the most?

5   What do I find most meaningful about the world?

6   How much risk can I tolerate?

7   What kind of workplace best suits my talents, personality, values, passions and lifestyle?

8   What's important to me?

9   What do I most value?

10   What gives me most satisfaction?

Take your time to think about your answers as they might provide clues to your new career. They might also help you put your new career into perspective: while you fathom out what your new career might be, you are giving it a disproportionate amount of attention and it's easy to lose sight of what really matters. If your answers indicate that work isn't the be-all and end-all of your life, you might want to consider looking for a career or working pattern that allows you to concentrate on the activities that bring you pleasure and satisfaction.

The next set of questions is designed to get you dreaming. Whether or not we ever achieve our dreams, they are important as they inspire us and inform our choices. They act as a marker on the horizon and are something to head towards – you make much faster progress if you're aiming for a specific destination. And who knows what you'll discover on the way? As you read these questions, let your imagination run wild – this is not the time to dismiss outlandish ideas or half-baked fantasies, this is the moment to imagine yourself attaining your heart's desire.

Whether or not we achieve our dreams, **they are important** because **they inspire us and** inform our choices.

1   When I was a child, what did I think I would grow up to do?

2   What did other people think I would grow up to do?

3   What work do the people I most admire do?

4   In the movies, which jobs seem the most exciting to me?

5   If all jobs paid the same, which area would I choose to work in?

6   What kind of people would I like to work with?

7   What would I wear to my ideal place of work?

8   If I could get up tomorrow and do any job at all, what would that be?

9   How do I see work fitting into my life in a year's time? Five years' time? Twenty years' time?

▶ What do you enjoy?

While your answer to the above question should be a massive clue to a career that would give you pleasure, it's incredibly hard to answer. It's one of those nightmare interview or dinner party questions, isn't it? 'So, what do you enjoy doing then?' Should you mention your love of newts and Stoke City or should you lie and mention opera and voluntary work with disadvantaged kids? A bit like the 'What do you want to do?' question we encountered earlier, it's one of those posers for which few of us have a neat answer. Most people um and er and answer vaguely. The truth is, most of us enjoy doing pretty ordinary things like spending time with our families and shopping for new clothes/gadgets/toys – not the kind of information that indicates a future career option.

The way to get meaningful information is by asking the question in ways that demand specific responses. See how you get on with these:

---

1   I was happiest at work when...

2   Do I prefer spending my free time reading the paper and doing the crosswork or am I happier outdoors playing sport or doing exercise?

3   Do I prefer my own company or big crowds, seeing friends one to one or in a gang?

4   I notice I start talking quickly and loudly whenever the conversation gets on to the subject of...?

5   Do I enjoy arguing the toss or am I happier just to listen?

6   Am I happier going to see a show or putting it on?

7   Do I enjoy being the centre of attention?

8   What events in my diary help me leap out of bed?

9   What makes me so excited I can't get to sleep?

Another way of uncovering what you enjoy doing the most is to look at the choices you make in your day-to-day life. For instance ...

1 When you are buying a newspaper, what stories or special offers persuade you to buy a particular paper?

2 When you read a newspaper, which sections do you enjoy reading the most?

3 When you're looking through the TV listings, what sort of programmes attract you?

4 Which subjects make the most interesting documentaries?

5 If you were in a doctor's surgery, what sort of magazine would you pick up while you were waiting?

6 What would be an ideal way to spend a holiday?

7 If the weekend was three days long, what would you do on the third day?

8 If you were to study at night school for pleasure, what would you like to learn?

By taking your time to answer these questions thoughtfully and fully, you should be starting to build up a list of areas that interest and excite you, as well as the kind of activities and encounters that bring out the best in you. The aim is for you to discover:

- what you like
- what you want
- what environment you're suited to
- what roles you're happiest playing.

▶ The work style questionnaire

The following questionnaire will give you an idea of your work style and may help you build on knowledge you already have about those working situations in which you are most effective and those which you find more difficult. Look at each of the statements below and rate them on a scale of 1 to 5.

1 = Strongly disagree

5 = Strongly agree

	Statement	Rating	
1	I am happiest when I can implement my own ideas.		IND
2	I don't like working on my own.		SOC
3	I am often the one to come up with new ideas.		CRE
4	I like paying attention to detail.		REL
5	I don't like a predictable work routine.		CRE
6	I work most effectively if there are ample opportunities to share ideas with colleagues.		CO
7	I like to have the freedom to try out new ideas, even if there is a risk that they may be unsuccessful.		IND
8	I believe that colleagues would describe me as a reliable person to work with.		REL
9	I never have trouble coming up with suggestions.		CRE
10	I like taking decisions at work.		INF
11	I work most effectively if I am left to get on with my tasks without interference.		IND
12	I seek out opportunities to take responsibility.		AMB
13	Having good working relationships with my colleagues is very important to me.		SOC

	Statement	Rating	
14	I am often the one to organize an event such as a leaving do or an office outing.		SOC
15	Having work which offers plenty of opportunities for advancement is important to me.		AMB
16	I am always prepared to try a new approach.		CRE
17	I encourage other people to contribute suggestions and ideas.		CO
18	I dislike having to complete tasks in a hurry.		REL
19	Being respected by colleagues is very important to me.		PER
20	I expect my own efforts to be rewarded financially or with promotion.		AMB
21	I find it difficult to deal with confrontations at work.		UC
22	I work hard and I expect to gain promotion rapidly.		AMB
23	It really matters to me that family, friends and colleagues value the job I do and the progress I make.		AMB
24	I only thrive if my work is frequently praised.		UC
25	I get a lot of satisfaction from persuading someone to see a problem from my point of view – I like winning an argument.		INF
26	I listen carefully to what others are saying.		CO
27	I don't usually offer an opinion at work unless it is deliberately sought.		UC
28	I can usually motivate other people by being enthusiastic myself.		INF
29	I pay great attention to details like punctuality and time keeping.		REL
30	I find it difficult to accept criticism.		UC

	Statement	Rating	
31	I thrive on change and on being asked to do something new or get a project started.		CRE
32	I shall only be happy when I get to the top in my chosen profession.		AMB
33	I like following things up and researching information.		EVA
34	Even when working in a team, I still like to have the ultimate responsibility for decisions.		IND
35	I think I can easily spot and take advantage of new opportunities.		CRE
36	I don't mind being unpopular if it leads to good results.		CT
37	I can often persuade people to do something in a different way from the tried and tested.		INF
38	I think colleagues may sometimes view me as rather forceful.		CT
39	I do not make careless mistakes with my work.		REL
40	I believe people are motivated by feeling encouraged.		CO
41	I am probably a bit of a perfectionist.		CT
42	I can influence the decision making process effectively, even when I don't take the decision myself.		INF
43	I enjoy analysing problems and situations and looking at all the options.		EVA
44	I like being given difficult tasks, I see them as a challenge.		VAR
45	I do tend to get bored easily and then my attention to detail may slip.		VAR
46	I often find that colleagues confide in me.		SOC
47	I like working to targets, but I like to set them myself.		IND
48	I find I settle into a new job quickly and easily.		VAR

	Statement	Rating	
49	I will sometimes give in even if I don't agree just to avoid falling out with people.		UC
50	I never put off difficult tasks – I like to deal with them straightaway.		PER
51	I enjoy those working days where you just never know what is going to happen next.		VAR
52	To me the best part of work is forming good relationships with customers and colleagues.		CO
53	I take advantage of any training opportunities that are on offer.		PER
54	I enjoy seeing other staff develop and improve.		CO
55	If I am having a problem with a colleague, I try to address it straightaway, rather than letting a problem build up.		SOC
56	I never find myself doing things at the last minute.		CT
57	If I have got a problem with something, I don't mind admitting it.		PER
58	I am prepared to work hard to see something through.		PER
59	I think regular appraisals at work are very important.		CT
60	I keep pretty calm in a crisis.		REL
61	I view work as the most important part of my life.		AMB
62	I could never stay in a job where I felt bored.		VAR
63	I need to be able to use my professional knowledge and skills.		PER
64	I like integrating and managing the efforts of others.		INF
65	I need to see the results of my work.		EVA
66	I cope well with constantly changing demands.		VAR
67	I plan a job carefully before I make a start.		EVA

	Statement	Rating	
68	The idea of routine really depresses me.		VAR
69	I really enjoy gathering information and data.		EVA
70	If I say I will do something, then I do it.		REL
71	I take opportunities to train and teach other members of staff.		INF
72	I often socialize with colleagues outside working hours.		SOC
73	I really hate it if I upset somebody at work.		UN
74	I believe people work most effectively if they are told exactly what to do.		CT
75	I try hard to encourage quiet colleagues to contribute to discussions and meetings.		CO
76	I am usually the first to arrive and the last to leave.		CT
77	I prefer the idea of becoming a specialist to that of becoming a general manager.		PER
78	I really need to take responsibility for organizing my own workload.		IND
79	I like to have all the stages of a project clearly mapped out.		EVA
80	I would really rather run my own business than work for someone else.		IND
81	I will often check out my ideas with a colleague before I raise them with a larger group.		UC
82	I believe that time spent thinking before taking action is time very well spent.		EVA
83	I really enjoy striking up new relationships with customers and clients.		SOC
84	I sometimes come up with unusual suggestions and I don't mind being laughed at, if it helps people try a new approach.		CRE

To obtain your score, add up the scores for each group of questions which have the same symbol and enter them below:

Symbol	Score
AMB	
CO	
CRE	
CT	
EVA	
IND	
INF	
PER	
REL	
SOC	
UC	
VAR	

Add an extra 5 points to your top score – this helps distinguish what is most significant for you, especially if you have produced similar scores across several of the characteristics. Here are the profiles for each characteristic.

AMB – Ambitious

Success in professional, financial and status terms is a key factor for you and is likely to influence how you operate at work. Your drive and energy are very useful for seeing projects through and making sure targets are met. Your focus on your own success is likely to have a downside too – you may not pay as much attention to the views and ideas of colleagues as you could.

CO – Co-operative

Co-operative people are very focused on the team and on getting the best out of other people, as well as themselves. As a co-operative person, you will often be the one who helps teams to gel, as you are likely to be able to encourage even the quieter members of a team to bring their ideas and suggestions to situations. If there is a downside, it may be that you become more interested in the team functioning as a successful unit, than in the end goal.

CRE – Creative and imaginative

Creative people bring ideas to the workplace and their infectious enthusiasm can often rub off on the whole team. As a creative person, you are likely to have imaginative ideas about how problems should be solved or how a new direction can be pursued. If you have a fault, it is that it is sometimes difficult for you to accept realistic restraints, such as resource implications. You may be keen to come up with plenty of ideas, but are a bit more reluctant when it comes to seeing them through by paying attention to detail and concentrating on the job in hand.

CT – Controlling

The controlling people are exactly that – they need to feel that everything is under control and in good order and this generally applies as much to their own work as it does to the work of those around them. You're likely to be very concerned with detail and procedures and although this sounds dull, it can actually be very useful, especially in ensuring that important procedures are followed or that a project doesn't get lost because no one is paying attention to the more routine aspects of the work. Of course, the downside is that you can lose sight of the greater vision and you can be extremely irritating to colleagues and rather difficult to work for if you're in a management or supervisory position.

EVA – Evaluative

Evaluators are often the calm, rational members of a work team, unlikely to go off on some of the wilder tangents pursued by their creative colleagues. You are likely to be good at researching and gathering information, weighing it up and making constructive suggestions about what is likely to work and what might not. Of course, there is the possible disadvantage that you may be determined not to act until you have all the appropriate information to make the best possible decision and you will argue for the most commonsense course of action – occasionally losing the opportunity for something more risky, but perhaps more successful.

IND – Independent

Independent people value autonomy at work above all things – freedom to implement their own ideas and in their own way. If this is you, then you're likely to have a lot of energy and enthusiasm, so long as you are left to do things in your own way. Like your creative colleagues, you may bring new and imaginative ways of looking at a problem. You may find it hard to work co-operatively and your colleagues may be annoyed because you seem to get away with things that they can't. You tend to pass by some of the constructive suggestions made by other people.

INF – Influencing and persuading

These people are very good at persuading others to buy something or do something. They are not simply good at the 'hard sell'; they enjoy bringing subtle influences to bear too and can often have a very strong impact in a team. If you are an influencer, you may not always come up with the ideas, but once you are convinced that an idea really is a good one, you are likely to affect its chances of being implemented. Managers like to have you on-side and if you are a manager, you should not have too hard a time keeping your team interested and involved. For you, winning an argument can occasionally become more important than the actual merits of that argument.

PER – Persistent Professional

These people work hard and their real interest is in building up specialist knowledge and expertise and being able to apply this. If this is you, then you're likely to work hard for success, but see this in terms of professional development and respect from colleagues, rather than in straightforward terms of financial reward or promotion. You may tend to distance yourself from some of the day-to-day activities in the department, but you'll always be happy to give advice.

REL – Reliable

Reliable people keep businesses functioning, and reliable does not equate with boring. If you are reliable, you're likely to be trusted and valued by colleagues and managers. You get on with things and will see a project through to the end without showing the obsessive qualities of the controller. You can sometimes get passed by for promotion on the grounds that other people have decided you are quite content where you are.

SOC – Sociable

Sociable people are not necessarily the same as co-operative people, though it is more than possible to be both of these. Sociable people will not stay in a job if they don't like the people and/or the environment, so they are usually a cheerful and positive influence around the office. If you are sociable, one of your real strengths is making new relationships with other departments, customers or clients and you're always the first to welcome new members to the team. You can tend to get so interested in organizing office outings or chatting to people to find out what's going on, that work gets put on the back burner.

UC – Under-confident

Under-confident people are by no means under-competent, though they sometimes tend to feel that this is the case. If this is you, you probably have plenty of good ideas, but you are unwilling to express them. You'll find that colleagues trust you and may well seek you out to test their own ideas on someone, so you tend to use these opportunities to get your ideas drawn into the team and the system. You run the risk of being viewed as disinterested.

VAR – Variety and risk

People who score highly here need variety and some unpredictability in their work in order to thrive. If this is you, then you're often very valuable at times of change, because where other colleagues may see this as a source of stress and anxiety, you'll see it as an opportunity or a challenge and some of your positive attitude will rub off on others. You are willing to have a go and if things go wrong, you'll not lose too much sleep over it. Of course, you do get bored quickly and you will often resist carrying out the more routine aspects of your work and find yourself working in a slightly chaotic way.

The balanced worker

Of course, everyone is a mixture of all the above to various extents and there are also many other dimensions that make up the working you: your experience so far, how important a role work plays in your life and, crucially, the people you are working with in any team or department at any one time – all these are powerful influences. If some of the above does ring true for you, use it as a learning experience. If there are things you would like to change, consider ways in which you could achieve this. If you are quite happy with the way that you work, then continue as you are.

▶ Getting specific

Hopefully these questions are helping you to understand yourself better and to reconnect you with the attributes and desires that are unique to you. They are also designed to widen the scope of what you consider work to be, as well as put your search for work into a wider context. What they don't do, however, is suggest possible career routes that aren't connected to your present job. By contrast, these next questions are designed to prompt specific responses so you can work out how you feel about specific careers.

1   Scroll through your address book and answer the question: 'What do my friends do for a living?'

2   Which of these friends enjoy their work?

3   Would you like any of your friends' jobs? If 'yes', then think about why.

4   Who seems to get the *most* out of their job? Why is that?

5   What makes you envious about other people's jobs? (Salary, conditions, co-workers, room for growth, etc.)

6   Looking at all the departments in your company, which would you most like to work in?

7   Who has the best job in your current place of work? Why is that?

8   Flick through a newspaper and see who is featured (consider everyone from the man in the street asked for his opinion to professionals quoted in articles to people selling their stories about illicit nights with footballers or celebrities) and see what jobs they do. Which sound the most interesting to you?

9   Ignoring salaries, level of opportunity etc., which sectors of job opportunities interest you the most (e.g. agriculture/ environment; banking and finance; sales and marketing; crafts and trade; voluntary and government, education; engineering,

surveying/ architecture; health, beauty and fitness; information technology; recruitment; social sciences; travel and leisure)?

10   Buy a newspaper on a day it's packed with a variety of recruitment adverts. Ignore for a moment your suitability and qualifications – which jobs sound the most desirable?

What makes **you envious** about **other people's** jobs?

If you've answered these questions thoughtfully, you should now be in possession of a batch of fields and positions that interest you. Hopefully you will consider that a few of those options are worth investigating further. If you're still feeling a bit clueless, perhaps your answers to the next list of questions will stimulate some more possibilities.

Do you want to work ...

- with computers?
- with children or animals?
- with creative people?
- with disadvantaged people?
- in a big office?
- for a small company?
- in a smart suit?
- in casual clothes?
- for yourself?
- abroad?
- on practical projects?

- on creative projects?
- outdoors?
- alone?
- in a city centre?
- from home?

▶ How to use this information

By now you should start to have a clear image of yourself in your next job. You should be able to close your eyes and visualize what sort of clothes you wear to work, what kind of office you work in, how you fit in with the people around you, and the kind of work you do. You should also be starting to understand how your new career will make you feel – positive, satisfied and enjoying each day. If work felt like a grey drudge before, it should now be a colourful kaleidoscope of opportunity and possibility.

The next stage is to take this information and turn it into viable career options through careful research. Think of yourself as a career detective following up leads – there may be some very obvious lines of enquiry, but it may be the long shots or glossed-over clues that help to solve your career dilemma. At this stage you don't want to rule out any options – keep your mind open and your research as wide-ranging as possible.

Think of yourself as
a career detective
following up leads.

If you've discovered that your natural talents and abilities are leading you towards a field of which you have little knowledge or experience, you need to start investigating that field as soon as possible. After all, when you're ready to look for work, you'll be competing with people who do have experience of that sector. Your research will be the pole you use to vault over the competition and attain that perfect job.

A good place to start your research at this stage is the recruitment section of relevant trade publications. While you're unlikely to land a job through an advert (very, very few people do, especially career changers), it's the easiest way of seeing what kinds of positions are available in your new field. You may find of course that none of the jobs advertised appeals at all. Just because you've found a career that is theoretically perfect for you on paper, it doesn't mean it actually exists – it might turn out that your only way to get that career is to create it yourself. If employers aren't offering the opportunities and benefits you want, you should come to terms with the possibility that you may have to (temporarily) leave the PAYE nest and freelance to get the career that's right for you.

Hopefully, now that you're looking in the right areas, you'll find a range of jobs you could see yourself performing, so use the recruitment adverts to see what employers offer and what skills they're looking for.

Top Tips Working out what you want to do

- Put yourself and your lifestyle preferences under the microscope.
- Think about what you enjoy doing the most with your time.
- Take a look around you – what jobs and fields inspire you?
- Narrow down the field you'd like to work in.
- If it's a field you're unfamiliar with, do some research on it.
- Use recruitment ads in trade journals to see what jobs are on offer.
- Consider ways of adding to your skills set.

The best career changes take place where the skills fit the opportunity. At this stage you want to be looking at opportunities that are right for you. If you really can't see a way into your desired profession, now's the time to work out how you can add to your skills-set, your professional repertoire, and look for ways to make sure your talents fit the opportunities that are out there.

> # The best careers advice
> # to give to the young is:
> # Find out what you like doing best,
> # then get someone to
> # pay you for doing it.
>
> **Katherine Whitehorn**

Chapter four

Finding
and making
job
opportunities

When thinking about where to find a new job, most of us would first turn to job adverts and/or recruitment agencies. These are by no means the only routes to finding that dream job, but let's take a look at them first, before considering other options.

▶ Job advertisements

There are, of course, plenty of places to find advertised jobs – your local job centre and local newspapers will contain a broad range of opportunities, if you are set on working in a particular region. If you know what industry you want to work in, especially if you are willing to consider a wider geographical area, your best bet is to look at national newspapers and the trade press.

Newspapers

Broadsheet newspapers carry weekly supplements on major areas of employment, such as media, law, charities and medicine. One of the motivations for newspapers to invest in such specialist journalism is the income these supplements generate from recruitment advertising. This means there are two reasons for picking up a broadsheet on the day it features your field – news and vacancies. Generally, newspaper articles carry great weight in the industries or sectors to which they relate. If you don't know what's making the news in your sector, you'll seem incompetent and out of touch. It really is essential reading, so it's worth annoying your newsagent and flicking through the broadsheets to make sure you're not missing out on vital information.

If you don't know what's making **the news in your sector,** you'll seem incompetent and out of touch.

Even on days when the papers don't carry specialized sections, it's still important to keep abreast of general news. The business pages are full of job leads every day – companies expanding, old contacts moving to positions of power, or changes in policy or direction that might create opportunities.

Trade press

Whether you want to be a professional cricketer or a marine biologist, there will be a trade publication for your industry. Trade magazines and newspapers are the noticeboards for their fields and carry a broader range of stories, most of which are too specialized to make it into national newspapers. New appointments, new technology, annual reports and industry events are all given prominence, making trade magazines a job hunter's information goldmine. Even the adverts in trade magazines can provide useful leads for things like websites and seminars that can help further your research.

It's important to read the relevant trade publications regularly. Over time you will build up a sense of the problems facing your industry or sector, the people whose star is on the ascendant, and areas to be avoided. It's the best source of information for identifying suitable companies and finding out the names of people to approach within companies. If you read about someone interesting, or with whom you agree or disagree, don't be afraid to get in touch. Send them an email congratulating them on their award/promotion/point of view. It's a good means of adding to your contacts book and of increasing the ways you'll hear about job vacancies.

Trade magazines are
a job hunter's information
goldmine.

Avid reading of trade magazines – some industries have several – is the best way of compensating for lack of professional experience in your chosen sector. You can pick up knowledge, contacts and tips through reading, and often the information you absorb is more relevant and up to date than information you get at college or in books. Reading is the homework you can't fake.

As there are so many trade publications, not many are stocked by newsagents – even large city-centre branches carry only a narrow selection. The best way of getting hold of them is by subscription, although many are given away free (they make their money through recruitment advertising) at industry events and in the lobbies of key companies. If you're not sure of the name of the magazine for your sector, have a look at the website for the Audit Bureau of Circulations (*www.abc.org.uk*) or a magazine retail site like Cheapest Magazines (*www.cheapest-magazines.co.uk*). Alternatively, flick through the latest media yearbook at your local library or bookshop.

Specific companies and organizations

If you can put together a shortlist of employers you'd like to work for, it's worth checking out their websites for job adverts within that company. Most companies and organization websites have a section headed 'job opportunities' or 'vacancies' or similar. if you don't know the name of the company's website, here are a few tips (also useful if you want to read up more about a potential employer):

- just type the company name into your browser;
- type the name into *www.google.com* and hit 'I feel lucky';
- type the company name plus **.co.uk** or **.com**;
- if the name is more than one word long, try (a) no space between words, (b) a hyphen between words, (c) an underscore between words: **boggswidgets, boggs-widgets, boggs_widgets**;

- if it's an internet or computer-related firm, try adding **.net**;
- if it's a government body or department, add **.gov.uk**;
- if it's a trade organization or other body, try **.org** or **.org.uk**.

These days you don't even need to type **http://** or often even **www**. Your browser will work this part out for itself. (Note that some addresses don't begin with **www** anyway).

▶ Recruitment agencies

Understanding recruitment consultants

The role of a recruitment consultant is perhaps one of the most misunderstood and under-utilized resources available to job hunters in the UK.

Recruitment agencies in the UK are part of a booming multi-billion pound industry covering a multitude of skills and experience across all sectors of the market. No matter what role you're seeking, there's bound to be a recruitment organization that can help you.

No matter what role you're seeking, **there's bound to be** a recruitment organization that can **help you.**

For the job hunter, the recruitment industry is an invaluable tool that should not be overlooked. Providing a wealth of experience with direct access to many unadvertised jobs and vital contacts across a range of industries, the right recruiter can save you time and effort and, more importantly, help you find the job that's right for you.

The recruitment industry makes its profit by a number of different methods dependent on the type of assignment. Briefly explained, recruitment organizations operating in the permanent market will charge their client a fee for finding and placing a suitable candidate in their vacancy, while recruitment organizations operating in the temporary marketplace will charge their client a fee based on an hourly rate. The important factor for job hunters to note is that they will not be charged for the agency's assistance or role in helping them to secure a new position.

Let's start by taking a look at the three main types of agency operating in the recruitment marketplace:

- high street recruitment
- specialist recruitment
- executive search recruitment.

These three operate within specific sectors of the market, often depending upon the type of employment you are seeking and the salary banding of that position.

Executive search recruitment

Normally operating at the top end of the market, these companies (also known as headhunters), consist of recruiters paid by clients who hire them specifically to fill a position.

Organizations may find it impractical to advertise a vacancy openly in the media or the internet and often rely on executive search firms to tap into the market discreetly and identify suitable individuals. Some executive search firms specialize in specific industries, while other generalist firms operate across a broad range of industries.

Executive search companies normally operate their fees in two different ways: either on a retainer or on a contingency basis. Essentially, a retainer is when the client company hires an executive search company to search for a suitable candidate and is paid an agreed fee regardless of whether or not a suitable candidate is found. A contingency search fee is paid only when a candidate is hired. Fees are normally based on a percentage of the first year's salary including any benefits.

As an executive job hunter, you should be aware that executive search companies are working primarily on behalf of their clients and ensuring that their best interests are served – after all, they are the paymasters! Your search for a new role may be a time-consuming business as executive search firms will concentrate on their current vacancies, ensuring they are filled before perhaps having the time to search out a role for you, the job hunter. For this reason you should multiply your chances: approach a number of different search firms who are likely to have a number of different vacancies with numerous clients.

Multiply your chances: approach **a number of different** search firms who are **likely to have various vacancies** with **numerous clients.**

As a job hunter, decide what firms you will approach – an initial telephone call will often indicate whether they can be of help to you. For advice contact the Association of Executive Search Consultants at *www.aesc.org.*

Some organizations ask for your permission prior to sending your CV to an interested client, while others ask you to rely on their discretion as professionals. These types of search organization are recommended for experienced professionals looking for their next career move, as they can offer advice, discretion and complete confidentiality that is vital in a high-profile move.

High street recruitment

High street recruitment agencies are the types you would expect to come across while out shopping in your local town. They are normally identifiable by their appearance as shopfront locations and often advertise their current vacancies as part of the window display you would see in any high street store. Their vacancies tend to cover a range of difference jobs and are normally driven more by salary bracket (junior to £30K) than by individual specializations.

High street agencies generally fall into one of two main categories:

- local
- national.

Local agencies are often part of a small branch network and are normally operated by local recruitment professionals. Local agencies have often been in the town for a number of years and are likely to have built up a reputation and close business relationships with local companies. It is often the case that local high street agencies will have clients different from those at national high street agencies and it is worthwhile for the job hunter to register with both in order to reach a greater number of vacancies.

Local agencies are likely to have **built up a reputation** and close business relationships **with local companies.**

National high street agencies are identifiable by their presence in the high street. They tend to be recognizable by their brand names, for example

Adecco, Manpower, Kelly Services. These types of agency operate in most major cities in the UK and have the added advantage to you, the job hunter, by providing access to many national organizations operating at a local level.

Specialist recruitment

The main differences between high street and specialist agencies are their locations and the types of vacancies they deal with. Specialist agencies tend to operate within specific sectors of the market, for example IT or sales across a range of salary bands, and their locations tend to be in office blocks away from the hustle and bustle of the high street. In common with high street agencies, specialists fall into both local and national categories with similar advantages and disadvantages.

▶ Using the internet in your job search

A recent survey by Oftel discovered that over 11 million homes in the UK have internet access. It is therefore not surprising to discover that over 50 percent of UK companies now use online recruitment as part of their strategy for attracting workers. If you are a serious job hunter, you cannot ignore the internet. Use it as a valuable resource to search for jobs, post your CV, get some career tips, and find out more about the companies you're interested in.

Fifty percent of UK companies use online recruitment as part of their strategy **for attracting workers.**

Finding the right job site for you

With the number of UK job sites growing every day, it is often difficult to decide which one is right for you, how many you should register with and – for the first-time user – to understand how they work.

Briefly, there are a multitude of job sites available on the internet servicing the UK marketplace. These may be roughly categorized as follows:

- industry specific, e.g. IT jobs
- skill specific, e.g. SAP programmers
- location specific, e.g. jobs in Scotland
- recruitment agency specific, e.g. Adecco
- company specific, e.g. IBM.

With such a wide array to choose from, it is little wonder that many of us can become confused when embarking on our job search. To further add to the confusion, you'll discover, as I did, that many sites share jobs, which can become a little frustrating when attempting to identify which site is best suited to your needs.

When choosing who to place their vacancies with, employers and recruitment agencies will often look at the number of vacancies in their specific sector as well as the proportion of overall traffic visiting the site before deciding upon the site that will attract the type of individual they need to fill their job roles. The number and type of jobs carried on a site is a useful indicator of their relevance to you the job hunter in deciding whether or not to register with them.

The Association of Online Recruiters (AOLR) is an industry body established by online recruitment companies which aims to regulate the online recruitment industry. Membership requires all sites to adhere to a code of ethical conduct that includes a commitment to the security of a candidate's personal information and the provision of meaningful traffic figures to advertisers. If you are embarking into online recruitment for the first time, I would suggest that you only register with sites that are members of AOLR to give you added confidence in their professional conduct. That said, there are many reputable and very successful sites that have chosen, for whatever reason, not to join AOLR, while still conducting their affairs in a highly professional manner.

Most useful are the sites held by the big search engines (see Altavista Careers or Excite Careers, for example). These have useful links to other related sites. To search the web for yourself, use terms like 'jobs' + 'UK'. Or go to *www.askjeeves.co.uk* and just type in 'IT jobs' or 'secretarial jobs', or whatever field you're looking in, and you'll be given links to a host of relevant sites.

For some resources to help you in your job and advertisement research, you may like to check out the sites detailed below. The first is a list of sites specializing in particular fields, although many of the general sites (also listed below) offer the facility to type in your specific area of interest to narrow the search.

Trade specific

www.education-jobs.co.uk	Education
www.justengineers.net	Engineering
www.cityjobs.co.uk	Finance
www.jobinga.com	Games industry
www.ITJobPages.co.uk	IT
www.nescogroup.com	IT
www.technojobs.co.uk	IT & Engineering
www.Personneltodayjobs.com	Personnel
www.jobsgopublic.com	Public sector
www.marketingjobsite.co.uk	Marketing
www.marketing-jobs-recruitment.co.uk	Marketing
www.mtselect.co.uk	Motor trade
www.NewScientistJobs.com	Science

www.secsinthecity.com	Secretarial, admin, PA
www.Communitycare.co.uk	Social services
www.TravelWeeklyjobs.com	Travel industry

General recruitment sites

www.gojobsite.co.uk

www.jobsguardian.co.uk

www.jobsearch.co.uk

www.jobserve.com

www.planetrecruit.co.uk

www.manpower.com

www.monster.co.uk

www.pricejam.com

www.stepstone.co.uk

www.topjobs.co.uk

www.totaljobs.com

www.unsystem.org (UN website)

www.worktrain.gov.uk (UK Government site)

ww.jobability.com (UK job site for disabled people)

A more detailed listing is provided opposite.

This table was correct at the time of printing. Unfortunately, many websites are not maintained and may be out of date. On the other hand, new websites continue to appear.

▶ How do online job sites operate?

In general the job sites operating in the UK marketplace will offer varying levels of service including:

● CV posting

● personal job search agent with email notification

Site name	Web address	Updates	Post CV	Career advice	Post jobs	Company info
America's Job Bank	www.jobsearch.org		✓		✓	
CareerBuilder	www.careerbuilder.com	✓		✓	✓	
Careermart	www.careermart.com		✓		✓	✓
Careermart Hi-tech	www.careermarthi-tech.com		✓		✓	✓
CareerPath	www.newcareerpath.com		✓		✓	✓
Excite Careers	www.excite.co.uk/directory/ Business/employment	✓	✓	✓	✓	✓
Fairfax General Employment	www.mycareer.com.au	✓	✓	✓	✓	✓
FastCompany	www.fastcompany.com		✓			
Hot Jobs	www.hotjobs.yahoo.com		✓		✓	✓
Job options	www.joboptions.com	✓	✓		✓	✓
Jobs at Microsoft	www.Microsoft.com/jobs		✓		✓	✓
Guardian Unlimited	http://jobs.guardian.co.uk	✓	✓		✓	
JobSearch UK	www.jobsearch.co.uk		✓		✓	
Jobsite UK	www.jobsite.co.uk		✓	✓	✓	✓
Manpower	www.manpower.com		✓	✓	✓	
Monster	www.monster.co.uk	✓	✓	✓	✓	✓
Oz search	www.ozsearch.com.au	✓	✓	✓	✓	✓
Price Jamieson	www.pricejam.com		✓		✓	
Recruiters Online	www.recruitersonline.com		✓		✓	
Top Jobs On The Net	www.topjobs.co.uk		✓	✓	✓	✓

- CV management
- message boards
- privacy options
- expert advice on job hunting from resident career counsellors
- newsletters.

As a job hunter, you can decide how many or how few of the services on offer you want to use. If, for example, you are looking for a new job while still employed, it would be wise to consider whether or not to post your CV onto the site (dangerous if your current employer happens also to use the site). The privacy options included on many of the sites will give you control over exactly what happens to your details after registration.

Most large organizations in the UK market will have their own website, specifically designed to provide information on their organization as well as providing details of any vacancies. If there is a specific company you are interested in, it would be wise to view their website in order to gain a fuller understanding of their business. If you do not have their web address, then use a search engine to help you find it (for example, *www.google.co.uk*).

▶ Applying for jobs online

Before you start job hunting online, ensure that you have a copy of your CV available on your computer or on a floppy disk. Many sites (e.g. *www.jimbright.com*) offer a facility to compile a CV on your behalf using their software. I would always advise using your own well thought-out and researched CV to create a more powerful document. It also gives you the advantage of standing out among the other people using that site who have chosen to use a predetermined format. Tailor you CV each and every time to the job you are applying for in order to highlight your key skills and achievements and, more importantly, to focus the employer's eye on your suitability. If you are not applying for a specific job but intend to post your CV online for employers to see, then spend some time researching the common skills and phrases that employers use to describe the type of role you desire. Then use that same language in your CV.

Employers and recruitment agencies are increasingly using software designed to screen applications for identifiable key words relating to the advertised role as well as trawling job boards for suitable candidates. Before replying to an advertised post or posting your CV onto a job board, take some time to consider the language that is used by employers and agencies when seeking to fill a particular job. Identify and use key words in your online CV to increase your chances of web-screening software choosing your details from all the other job hunters.

Use **key words** in your online CV to **increase your chances** of webscreening software **choosing your details** from all the other job hunters.

When you have identified a job that fulfils your criteria, it is as easy as following the instructions on screen to make your application directly to the employer or the recruitment agency. The instructions will normally guide you to your email screen and ask you to enclose your CV as an attachment to the main document.

▶ Dos and don'ts of email etiquette

Email etiquette is often harder to judge when deciding what information to include in your covering letter/email. Email has now become such a norm when communicating with family and friends that many people fall into the trap of becoming overly familiar when using email to apply for jobs. Think of an email when used in conjunction with a job application in exactly the same way as you would a hard copy covering letter (see Chapter 9).

Top Tips Writing emails

- **Check your email for spelling and grammatical errors** – use a spellchecker if you have one. Ensure that grammar is appropriate to the country you are applying to, e.g. UK English or US English.

- **Reread your email and covering document prior to hitting the send button.** Their very convenience of speed can also be their downfall, as no sooner have you hit the send button than your eye catches a glaring mistake as it wends its way to your intended recipient.

- **Be concise.** Ensure that your message conveys your point. Long emails can be boring and irritating for the reader.

- **Ensure that your email address is professional.** Names such as *HotDan99@freemail.com* or *guesswho@freemail.com* are likely to be viewed not only as unprofessional but potential virus carriers that may be deleted on receipt.

- **Include a subject box** as it will indicate to the recipient straight-away which position you are applying for. An email that arrives with 'No Subject' may never be opened as it does not indicate its subject and could be viewed as spam.

- **Sell youself.** Make sure that the most important selling points appear within the screen window. The recipient may not bother to scroll down their screen to read the part where your information starts to get interesting.

- **Don't include photographs with your email.** Not only may they be used in a discriminatory way, but their main failing when transmitted by email is that they are likely to hit a firewall installed by the intending company and may be deleted on receipt.

- **Don't use unfamiliar abbreviations** that may make perfect sense to you but leave your addressee in complete bewilderment.

- **Don't write in capital letters.** It amounts to SHOUTING at your recipient!

> ● **Don't use fancy fonts or different coloured backgrounds** in your email. Keep to a business format using a recognized business font, e.g. Times New Roman.

▶ Advice for career changers

Recruitment agencies and HR departments

A problem all job hunters face is how to get past the CV sifters in recruitment agencies and HR departments. Understanding how they work will therefore help you in your quest.

A problem all job hunters face is **how to get past the CV sifters** in recruitment agencies and HR departments.

Employers often turn to their personnel department or outside agency only as a last resort – their first choice is almost always to hire someone they know or someone who has been recommended. If you imagine a conversation between a manager looking for a new sales exec and someone from the company's HR department, it might go something like this:

Manager: I just want someone bright, who can pick things up quickly and get on with the clients.

HR: If I put that in an advert, I'll get half the population applying. We'll have to narrow it down a bit.

Manager: OK.

HR: Do you want someone with experience of widgets?

Manager: That'd be nice, but widgets aren't rocket science.

HR: What software do you use?

Manager: Sage and Excel.

HR: Presumably you don't want a teenager?

Manager: I guess the average age of the department is 24.

HR: (making notes): That'll be a second jobber then. Now, what's the most valuable thing a new recruit could offer?

Manager: In an ideal world? New sales leads I guess, anything that helps the department perform better.

The HR exec then goes away and writes an advert that reads: '*Acme Corp seeks experienced sales exec to join their widget department. Must be literate in Sage and Excel, have transportable client portfolio and at least three years' experience in the field.*'

The advert is then placed in a newspaper and lots of people whom the sales manager would have considered are put off applying. The HR exec then collates and filters the applications from people who haven't been put off and weeds out candidates who don't meet the specified criteria. The HR exec then hands the sales manager the cream of the crop – maybe only ten CVs from which to select even fewer candidates for interview.

Clearly, then, the traditional recruitment procedure fails career changers on two fronts: (a) adverts are often filled with discouraging wish-lists rather than essential criteria; and (b) to make life easier, HR departments usually filter out candidates whose CVs don't tick every box. What's also clear is that career changers greatly enhance their chances of job success by avoiding recruitment adverts and impersonal personnel departments.

If, for example, a career changer wanted to get a job selling widgets, their best bet would be to make direct contact with the sales manager. If you can get hold of the right person, convince him or her of your love of widgets and your ability to sell them – maybe on a commission-only basis at first to prove that you can do it – then the next time a vacancy comes up, you can bet the sales manager would rather call you than their officious HR exec. To successfully change careers you need to avoid traditional recruitment procedures.

To change careers successfully you need to avoid traditional recruitment procedures.

▶ Non-traditional methods of finding jobs

There are three main ways of finding jobs through unconventional means:

1 Personal contacts

2 Using research to spot opportunities

3 Persuading companies to create a job especially for you.

Getting and using contacts

Contacts are just about the most valuable career currency you can carry. The more contacts you have, the richer your career will be. If you think you're a little poor in the contacts department, here's a sure-fire way to achieve overnight wealth – just redefine your notion of what a contact is. A contact isn't just someone influential who can make things happen; a contact is just about anyone you've ever met!

You need to start seeing yourself at the centre of an ever-growing contacts web and realize that your contacts have contacts of their own. If you have five people you can call on for a favour or information, it's quite likely that they also have five people they can call on. That means you're just a phone call away from 25 people who could be useful to you in any manner of situations.

If you can rekindle old acquaintances, you can also add to the entries in your phone book. Getting in touch with people you haven't spoken to for some time can be difficult, if not embarrassing. But it's much easier if you're getting in touch for a reason, and it's possible your career change could be that reason. If you've heard, for example, that someone you went to college with is now in the profession you covet, calling them up for some advice or help might be easier than just calling up for a chat.

As a contact is one of the most likely ways that you are going to find the job you want, it's imperative you make every contact you have count. So if that means asking a mate to put you in touch with someone useful they know, or using *www.friendsreunited.co.uk* to hook up with old schoolfriends, that's what you have to do.

A contact **isn't just** someone influential who can make things happen; a contact **is just about anyone you've ever met!**

Even people who you think are at the other end of the useful scale are worth getting in touch with because you don't know who *they* know. As soon as you know where you want to get to, you should be telling as many trusted people as possible just in case they know someone who knows someone.

You should also be starting to network and adding new contacts to your address book every week. You can network at social events, but you'd do better targeting your 'contact gathering' at industry events. If you bother to show up at a seminar or conference in the right field, you're guaranteed to meet people who can help you. It can be scary going to a conference if you're new to the profession and don't know anyone, but the following tips should help turn a nerve-wracking experience into a fruitful one:

- **Introduce yourself.** Always make a point of introducing yourself whenever you're in a new environment, be that a friend's dinner party or visiting the waste disposal department in your company for the first time. The more people know who you are and what you do, the more they can think of you for opportunities that might arise. Shyness, unfortunately, is not an option, so make sure people know who you are.

- **Circulate.** Make the effort to go to conferences, parties or exhibitions and always wear your name badge. Delegates attend these events to meet people – it's perfectly acceptable to walk up to a stranger in this environment because you recognize them from an article in the trade press, or you're interested in their company or you heard them speak.

- **Get introductions**. Make the organizers of seminars and conferences work for their money. It's their job to match-make, so if you recognize a name in the guest book, ask one of the hosts to introduce you. And when you're talking to contacts and they happen to mention someone else, ask for an introduction – the act of introduction acts as an endorsement and helps create an air of professionalism.

- **Always carry a business card.** If your current position does you no favours whatsoever, get private cards printed stating your name, number and email address. Of course, there's no point having cards if you don't use them, so make sure everyone you meet at an event gets a card before you part.

- **Maintain your network**. Always find a reason to keep in touch with people you meet whom you think might be useful. If you read an article about them, send them an email to give them feedback. Or if you hear about a promotion, send an email congratulating them. Alternatively, if you read something that you think a contact might be interested in, send it to them. It's crucial to keep finding ways to remind people not only that you exist but that you're thoughtful, on the ball and available.

Obviously the influential contacts, perhaps people who have the power to hire, are the best to have. But nearly as good to know are the people who just know about vacancies. Contacts don't have to be chief executives – they are anyone who can give you information you can't get elsewhere. That information could be about job opportunities in their organization, or it might be simply that their company is changing direction slightly – and that might be enough for you to create your own role in that company.

Naturally, we'd all prefer it if a contact would phone us up and say: 'I've put your name forward for this fantastic position that's just come up.' Sadly, this is about as likely to happen as an alien invasion, but you can absolutely guarantee it won't happen if you don't tell people what your plans are. You need to communicate your needs, let people know that you're in the market, give them some idea of your capabilities. After all, there's little point having contacts if you can't make them work for you.

Communicate your needs, **let people know** you're in the market.

Some of your contacts may not even know that much themselves, but they may be able to help you access information that's unavailable to your rival job hunters. The kinds of things even poorly connected contacts can do for you are:

- Pass you copies of in-house newsletters so you can see internal adverts and exclusive news
- Get you a password to access company websites, often good sources of company news and vacancies
- Put up an advert offering your services on the company noticeboard.

The point is, whatever someone does, if they do it in the right place then they are a contact you want to nurture ... and then exploit.

Spotting opportunities

The next best way for career changers to leapfrog conventional job candidates is by spotting opportunities *before* they are advertised. With careful and dedicated research, you can always make sure you're in the right place at the right time.

To do this you need to keep reading trade magazines and talking to contacts, constantly looking for clues to potential opportunities. For instance, if you read that a company is setting up a new division, there's a chance that it will need new staff. If the article mentions the name of the new division head, send that person an email.

The kinds of information that suggest opportunity might be around the corner include:

- a company expansion
- a change in legislation
- the launch of a company
- the launch of a rival company
- a new boss (this is often the trigger for a wave of resignations that makes way for new blood)
- the launch of a new product
- the development of a new technology
- a merger or acquisition.

Just sending your CV is unlikely to get you an interview. If you think of it from the new division head's point of view, yours is probably one of a handful of CVs they've been sent since the article appeared. Sending an email saying 'Hi, I believe you're expanding and here's my CV' makes you seem arrogant and opportunist. When you make contact with a potential employer for the first time, it's important that you come across as a serious candidate. The more time you spend writing your covering letter or email, the more serious you will seem. (See Chapter 9 for guidance on how to write and set out a covering letter.)

All correspondence should be professional, not overly friendly, spelt correctly with good grammar and presented soberly – gimmicks involving fancy paper and unusual fonts are more likely to irritate than entice. Make absolutely sure that the person you're writing to knows how to get in touch with you – always add your contact details (home phone, mobile, email, address).

The same procedure works if someone tells you about a new development that might lead somewhere. If you can't persuade your contact to make the introduction for you, approach the relevant person in the same way, knowing full well that the very fact you know about the development makes you look good as you seem well connected.

Persuading companies to create a job for you

This is perhaps harder than the other methods of finding work outlined above, but it is more likely to bring about results than relying on recruitment adverts and agencies. Although it sounds bold, the procedures aren't much different from the advice in the 'spotting opportunities' section above. The big difference is that instead of just expressing an interest in the new venture or direction, you are explicit about how you could help.

For instance, if a company is moving into an area in which you have some skills, contacts or knowledge, perhaps you could help it through the transition. Or if you can see that an existing company could expand into an area with which you are familiar, that's an opportunity to put yourself forward as someone to lead the business in a fresh direction.

Wherever you feel you can add something to someone's existing business, you should feel comfortable about suggesting a mutually beneficial arrangement. Most business owners and managers are willing to consider suggestions that make their company – or more probably just them – look good. The equation is pretty simple ...

You + company = more successful company

... and wherever you can create success, you create a job opportunity for yourself.

Career changers can make this method work to their advantage if they are encouraging a company to move towards the field they are hoping to leave. Your track record in your current profession could give you the credibility a new employer will look for. You then use your new job as a bridge between two fields and look to complete your journey in a few years' time.

▶ So what are you waiting for?

In this first part of the book, you've completed a real voyage of self-discovery – examining your strengths and weaknesses, your motivations and ambitions both at work and in life generally; the way in which you like to work; the environment that you're happiest in; the sectors and jobs that interest or inspire you. Hopefully you should by now have a much clearer idea about what makes you tick as an individual and what will really give you satisfaction in your new job. So you've got to know the product that is YOU, and which you'll be marketing in your job application, and the sector or kind of job you'll be targeting.

We've also examined the various avenues open to you today as a job hunter – the more traditional ones like high street agencies, newspaper ads, and personal contacts but also the plethora of online recruitment agencies and jobsites available through the internet. This also makes it easier to look for jobs further afield, in other cities and even abroad.

So what are you waiting for? You're ready to start marketing yourself in that all-important CV. In Part 2 we'll be looking at what to include (and what not), the best way to present it, and your covering letter.

One secret of success in life
is for a man to be ready for
his opportunity when it comes.

Benjamin Disraeli

Part two

Applying for a job

two

Chapter five

Preparing

your

cv

Getting a job today can involve several steps, starting with a CV, followed by psychological tests and interviews. The CV is the only step where you have control over the information that you present. In every other step, the employer decides what questions to ask, what information to collect. The CV is your vital opportunity to present yourself at your best.

▶ Why do you need a CV?

Before you do anything else, ask yourself why you are preparing a CV. The answer to this question is going to vary from one person to the next, but here are our top ten reasons for writing a CV:

1 You have seen a job advertised in the paper that appeals to you.

2 You want to market yourself to win a tender or a proposal, or be elected to a committee or organization.

3 You have seen a job on the internet job site that appeals to you.

4 Your friends/family told you of a job going at East West Ltd.

5 You want to work for East West Ltd and thought that sending a CV to them might get their attention.

6 You've seen a job advertised internally at work.

7 You're going for promotion.

8 You're about to be made redundant and want to update your CV to be ready for any good opportunities.

9 You're feeling fed up, and writing down all your achievements will cheer you up and might motivate you to look for a better job.

10 Oh, so that's a CV! I've never done one. I suppose I ought to try to remember what I've been doing with my life!

All of these certainly are good reasons to write a CV, but the CV serves many different purposes. One way of seeing the differences is to ask yourself who is going to read the CV in each case?

CVs 1 to 5 are going to be read by potential employers who probably do not know you. A CV for 6 or 7 is likely to be read by your boss or other people who know you. CVs 8 to 10 are really for your own benefit and should not be considered as suitable for sending out to employers.

The right mix

Have a think about the list of reasons again. How else can you divide up these reasons?

A most important difference is that, in some cases, you'll have a good idea of what the employer is looking for because you have a job advertisement in front of you and can tailor your CV accordingly. For others, you have no idea what the reader might want to see.

It's always worth updating your CV from time to time so you don't forget important details, but remember, the result of that process will not be a winning CV. It will be a useful list of tasks and achievements.

CVs are like baking cakes. You need all the right ingredients: flour, butter, eggs and so on. It is what you *do* with the ingredients that makes the difference between a great CV (or cake) and failure. Keeping your CV up to date is like keeping a stock of ingredients in the pantry – potentially very useful, but don't imagine that is the end of it!

Think about what the employer is looking for and **reflect that in your CV.**

If there is a most important piece of advice to give you, it is that you must think about what the employer is looking for and then reflect that in your CV. This advice was the most common tip from a large sample of recruitment managers.

▸ What do I put in my CV?

You should tailor the information in your CV to the main points in the job advertisement. Okay, that sounds fine, but how do you do it?

Get as much information about the job and the company as you can. When you've got that, go and get some more! The main source of information about a job is normally from:

- a job advertisement
- a job description
- a friend in the company
- the media
- gossip and rumour
- someone already doing the job or something similar.

There is no substitute for experience. Talking to someone who does a job similar to the one you wish to apply for in the same company may well provide you with a good picture of what the job is really like. Bear in mind, of course, that this source of information is not always reliable. You may react differently to your friend, and therefore their experience of a company may be very different to yours.

Get as **much information** about the job and company as you can. **Then go and get some more!**

However, a friend with reliable information can be a golden opportunity. Make sure you don't waste the chance to get some information. If you have friends who can provide valuable information – use them!

The main source of information about an employer's company is normally from:

- the media
- annual reports/company brochures
- industry/trade magazines or journals
- the internet
- industry directories
- gossip and rumour.

There are many other sources of information about companies and if you're serious about knowing more about a potential employer (and you should be), then it's worth a visit to your local library. Ask a reference librarian to assist you with your search. It will help if you outline to the librarian that you are looking for information on a specific company for a job search.

Top Tips How to research a company

Get as much information as you can about the company you're applying to via the following avenues:

- trade journals and newspapers
- annual reports
- library resources (ask the librarian for guidance if necessary)
- the internet for both:
  - company websites: these generally give details of the company's Board of Directors, its mission statement, organizational structure, contact/location details etc. plus often offering the facility to download their annual report
  - newspaper websites: For example, *www.guardian.co.uk*, *www.telegraph.co.uk*, *www.timesonline.co.uk*, or *www.independent.co.uk* will keep you in touch with what is happening both

within the company and within the sector. Try using their 'search' facility for recent press articles (some give access to archived articles too, although may charge for this service)

- personal contacts (someone who works in the same company or same field).

Look out for press reports of any possible mergers or takeovers that might affect the company or its competitors. Is the company expanding or contracting in terms of numbers of locations and staff?

This information will be very useful both in your initial application but also in case you are called for interview. If you can mention some major change that was only announced recently, this will demonstrate not just your keen interest but also your ability to keep up with the latest events. It shows a dynamic approach.

▶ Reading the job ad

Job advertisements and descriptions should be treated as clues. Job advertisements are usually reliable sources of information and should be taken seriously. Employers can be found to have broken the law if they put misleading or incorrect information in advertisements.

Information from other sources can sometimes be invaluable, but sometimes it can be grossly inaccurate. The same principles apply whatever the source of the information.

Here is a typical job ad. Below it are our tips for reading the ad. After reading the job advertisement, the seven questions below will assist in breaking down the job ad successfully. Remember, reading an ad properly is the first crucial step to preparing a successful CV.

Training Manager
Handle Sisters Pharmaceuticals

Would you like to join the world's 3rd biggest pharmaceutical company, currently expanding rapidly in the European market? We require a manager to join our training division, where you would be responsible for the delivery of training programmes to our sales staff.

A dynamic, results-focused team player, you will have excellent communications skills, and will be able to handle pressure and work to deadlines. With several years of solid experience in a multinational, you will be accredited in NLP and will have a basic understanding of training evaluation techniques. Reporting to our Regional Manager, you will be required to provide input into the marketing strategies for the European region by training our sales staff to improve market share.

Handle Sisters are Equal Opportunities employers.

Please forward your CV to: Linda Spark, Personnel Dept, Handle Sisters Pharmaceuticals, 58 Boundary Street, London EC1 2LP.

▶ The seven job advertisement interrogation questions

1   What don't you understand about the job ad?

2   What type of industry/company is it? What's happening in the company or industry? Is it restructuring or expanding? Does it operate with low overheads and high profit margins?

3   What is the main purpose of the role being offered?

4   Why is this role important to the company? How will this role affect the company's bottom line?

5   What types of skills do they want? What other skills might be needed, given the job's purpose?

6   What personal qualities do they want? What other personal qualities might be needed, given the job's purpose?

7   What types of knowledge/training do they want? What other knowledge or training might be needed, given the job's purpose?

Now that you've read the questions, we'll take you through them one at a time.

1 What don't you understand about the job ad?

Here are some definitions to help you understand our example.

- **Equal Opportunities employer** refers to a company that has policies of non-discrimination in the workforce on the basis of gender, ethnicity, sexual preference, age or other factors (see Chapter 18 for website address of relevant organizations).

- **Neurolinguistic programming (NLP)** is a controversial training technique that is intended to improve both verbal and non-verbal communication.

A general clue to the significance of these jargon terms can be gleaned from their positions in the ad. If the jargon words appear next to descriptions of qualifications required, it's a good bet that the words refer to skills you will need (such as NLP in this case). If the words appear towards the end of the ad where the contact details appear, or near a description of the company, then it is likely that these words refer to general conditions of employment or company policy (such as Equal Opportunities employer).

If you're still stuck, you could try contacting the Office of Fair Trading about the phrases that may have legal meanings, like 'Equal Opportunities employer'. You could always contact the employer directly and ask, but if you think this may create a poor impression, get a friend to call instead.

If the terms are likely to refer to a technical aspect of the job, it may be worth visiting your library for books on the subject, or contact the relevant professional association or trade union (such as the Transport and General Workers Union, the Association of Chartered Accountants or the Publishers Association).

Other than standard reference works like dictionaries, thesauruses and encyclopedias, logging onto the internet is a very powerful way to search for information. If you use the internet, you can use a search engine like *www.google.com* or *www.lycos.com* to search for a particular keyword or phrase that you do not understand. Another good idea would be to try out some of the job websites we recommended in Chapter 4 (see pp. 79–81). These contain explanations of work-related terms, and some carry profiles of different employers and company sections.

Logging onto the internet is
a very powerful way
to search for information.

2 What type of industry or company is it and what's happening currently?

Some of this information can be gleaned from the job ad. In our example, the company seems to operate on a global scale as it refers to the 'European division' and asks for experience in multinationals. Secondly, it gives the impression it is expanding in that part of the world. However, this doesn't mean that it is expanding everywhere, and it doesn't say whether Europe includes the UK. The job may involve overseas travel, or it may be based overseas. It is not possible to tell whether the company is restructuring or what its profitability is.

Information about companies can be gleaned from many different sources; don't forget our earlier tip to visit your local library. Here you can review any existing information in such publications as the *Financial Times Top 500 Companies*. Ask a librarian how best to conduct your search as it's easy to miss huge chunks of information.

Do you know anyone who works for the company? If so, talk to them. Could they get hold of any company brochures, newsletters or advertising material for you? In our example, you might ask if there is anything in the latest pharmaceutical trade journals.

If you're keen to work for a large company, start reading the business pages of the newspaper to see if there are any stories about the company. If it's a public company, you could always ask for a copy of the Annual Report. This may tell you whether the company is growing or not, how profitable it is, and whether any redundancies are planned.

In our featured ad, because this company sells pharmaceuticals, it might be worth going to a pharmacy to ask about the company, or asking a doctor. Then you might be able to find out if this company sells medicinal products. Also check out the supermarkets to see if this company sells domestic products such as soap powder. Take the job ad with you, so you can match the logo and address with the products on the shelf.

3 What's the main purpose of the role?

In this case, it's fairly clear that the main duty will be to conduct training of sales staff. Duties are likely to be fairly well known by job applicants, as the role needs somebody with experience and qualifications. However, training itself is a broad role that may involve many responsibilities. It may be that the company specializes in an industry that has very specific training needs. For example, a petroleum company may have to adhere to occupational health and safety (OHS) requirements for using chemicals. Alternatively, training may involve stress management techniques in a high-pressure work environment. It is well worth finding out what particular needs a company may have over and above those in the job advertisement.

4 Why is this role important to the company?

The role is important because the company wants to increase sales of its products. To do so, it thinks it needs better-trained sales staff. The company will be looking for someone who can demonstrate an impact on sales through improved training.

5 What types of skills do they want and what other skills might be needed?

The company wants someone who can teach NLP. Other than that, you will need to be able to gauge whether the company's training programme is successful or not (evaluation). Other skills required are good communication skills. In this job, this involves being able to talk to groups of trainees, to produce clear training materials, and to be able to write reports and present them to management. Because the company is linking the job to strategic planning, it will be important that you are able to demonstrate general business and commercial awareness. Be sure you can find your way around a balance sheet.

6 What personal qualities do they want and what other qualities might be needed?

They want someone who is 'dynamic' – meaning somebody who can motivate the sales staff and conduct interesting training courses, and generally make an enthusiastic addition. 'Communication' and 'team player' skills mean you need to get on well with others, speak (in public) well and write well.

7 What knowledge and training do they want and what other knowledge/training might be needed?

A degree in Psychology, Business or Commerce may be helpful. Any evidence of business-related experience is probably very useful. Experience in a similar job would be good. The ability to speak a relevant language, such as French, German or Spanish, or experience working in European cultures, should improve your chances.

You can see already how, in answering these questions, we are building up a picture of the type of job on offer, and the sort of qualities the candidate should possess. Therefore, we are increasing the chances of a good fit.

Having read and interpreted the job ad, and gathered all the rest of the information you need on the company, you should have a much clearer idea of what the company wants. Armed with the idea of what an ideal candidate would be like, it's time to tailor your application to make that person YOU!

Top Tips **What to look for in job ads**

Before you do anything else, look carefully at the ad to determine:

● the type of company it is

● the purpose of the role (and the department)

● the skills required

● personal qualities they're looking for

● knowledge/training needed.

This will help you decide if the job is a good 'fit' with your own skills, qualities and experience and where there may be any gaps that you'll need to address.

▶ The applicant–employer fit

If you hang around with recruitment consultants for long enough (about two minutes is usually adequate!), you'll hear them talking about 'fit'. The way that they see recruitment and the way many firms think about it is in terms of getting a good 'fit' between the employer and the employee. Opposite is a diagram that illustrates this concept of fit.

As you can see from the diagram, fit is all about matching a candidate to a particular job. The best candidate for the job will be the one who who matches all the requirements of the job. Employers tend to think about 'fit' in terms of four different qualities:

1 **Knowledge:** which refers to the experience and qualifications that you possess.

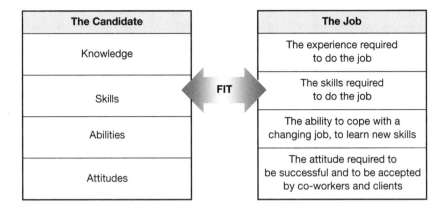

2   **Skill:** which refers to the demonstrated skills you have (perhaps evidenced by your qualifications).

3   **Abilities:** which show your potential to carry out a range of different tasks beyond your immediate skills or knowledge, and the degree to which you can take on new tasks successfully or be trained in new methods or equipment.

4   **Attitudes:** which indicate your personality, and the degree to which you are enthusiastic, flexible and positive in approach.

It's clear when you look at the diagram that merely setting out your life history on a CV is highly unlikely to offer the best fit. That's why it's vital to tailor your CV to the particular position – to improve the fit between you and the job.

It's vital to tailor your CV to
your particular position –
to improve the fit
between you and the job.

The following chart illustrates this point. Below are three candidates who have applied for a sales job. From reading their CVs, the employer has listed each candidate's knowledge, skills, abilities and attitude on a grid, next to the job requirements. Which candidate fits the job best?

We think that Tim is the weakest candidate. He has the best academic qualifications, but these are unnecessary for the position offered. Although Tim could easily learn new skills and accommodate to changing demands in the job, the comment in Tim's CV, 'I am a strong-minded person who is not afraid to stand my ground in disputes', gave an unfortunate impression of someone who might be argumentative with the public.

Applicants for a sales assistant job in a chemist

	Job requirements	Tim	Liz	Jane
Knowledge	Knows how a cash register works. Knows procedures for dealing with customers	*Degree in English, worked part-time in a burger bar for 18 months*	*Worked in father's hardware store for 10 years*	*Worked in a shoe store for 3 years*
Skills	Numeracy Good communication skills	*Easily able to handle cash and card transactions*	*Easily able to handle cash and card transactions*	*Easily able to handle cash and card transactions*
Abilities	To learn to process charge cards, electronic transactions	*No difficulties learning new skills*	*No evidence of learning new skills*	*Probably able to deal with new payment methods with some training*
Attitude	Polite, punctual, trustworthy, calm	*Strong-minded, self-confident, assertive*	*Honest, a bit aloof at times*	*Calm, honest, level headed*
Degree of fit		**POOR**	**AVERAGE**	**GOOD**

Liz clearly has a lot of experience in retail, but in a very different area. There could be some concerns about her ability to deal with customers sensitively. There did not appear to be much development of new skills over the ten years, and little evidence that she would adapt to new payment processes easily.

Jane looks the strongest candidate to us. She has the necessary experience, and should be able to adapt to most new processes with training. She is not over- or underqualified for the job and seems the best prospect.

In this analysis you might think we have been terribly unfair to one or other of the candidates. Perhaps we have, but the point of this exercise was to illustrate the sorts of processes that recruiters go through in making decisions to shortlist applicants.

▶ Improving the fit

When you set out job requirements as clearly as this, it's easy to see how you can start to mould your CV to match the job. Each of the candidates above could probably make themselves look the best candidate by altering their CVs. Below we offer some advice on how to do this.

Tim could turn that negative remark about standing his ground into a positive one, by rephrasing it: 'I am a confident person, and I enjoy talking to customers, and helping the customer reach the right decision.' Tim could also put more emphasis on his retail experience and less on the education. Perhaps a 'career objective' statement outlining what Tim hopes to achieve would help persuade the recruiter that this was a serious career move for Tim.

Liz needs to make far more of her ten years' experience. There must have been many achievements during that time, and new skills that she has learned. These need to be stressed in the CV. Jane looks pretty good already, but perhaps she could try to emphasize her abilities, or her potential to learn more, by providing examples of new skills she has learned over the past three years.

▶ Making you fit

Applying for a job can be very competitive, especially if the company has a good reputation, or the position is particularly exciting – both things you are looking for in a new job. It doesn't pay to overestimate your skills beyond your abilities, but nor can you afford to be overly negative. It constantly amazes recruiters when they receive, all too commonly, covering letters that begin: 'Dear Sir, first of all can I point out that I don't have the required experience, but ...'

It doesn't pay to overestimate your skills beyond your abilities, but nor can you afford to be overly negative.

Of course, nobody likes to appear big-headed, and it can be hard to describe your own abilities and not feel this way. The point is that a potential employer wants to know what you can do, and playing down genuine abilities will not present you in the proper light.

▶ Who are you?

Now we've briefly examined what the ideal candidate should look like, how do you go about listing *your* skills? Here are our tips to help you describe yourself.

When it comes to describing themselves, many people forget potentially vital details, or think that some achievements are probably irrelevant to their CV. Then again, there are some people who play down their achievements. Finally, there are those people who just cannot see that 'played in the under-sevens soccer team' is not as important as 'was elected as Prime Minister'!

In our research we found that those candidates whose CVs focus on outcomes and achievements are more likely to be shortlisted by recruiters than CVs that describe the duties and responsibilities of each previous job.

The four most common faults here are:

- forgetting some potentially impressive achievements
- thinking some achievements are not relevant
- playing down your achievements
- including every boring irrelevant detail.

CVs that focus on outcomes and achievements are more likely to be shortlisted.

You'll be saying to yourself at this point, 'Hang on, they're telling me not to exclude relevant stuff and in the next breath they're saying not to include irrelevant material. That's really helpful!'

We're going to introduce you now to some exercises that will assist you in determining what is important and what is not.

To complete the exercises, you'll need a list of your past activities and your achievements. We suggest that to ensure you do not omit anything by accident, you should try to list your past in as much detail as possible. At this stage do not attempt to decide whether the information is relevant or not.

We have developed some forms to help you get all the relevant details down in some order. Some people may find it easier to jot things down as they come to them, which is just fine. But you may wish to put all the information onto our templates when you've finished.

▶ Building a personal history

Divide your life into the following sections where applicable:

Stage of life	Use this template
Secondary school (typically 11 to 16 or 18 years old)	Template 1
Vocational training (16–22 years old)	Template 1
University (usually 18–21 years old)	Template 1
Any postgraduate training (typically in your 20s)	Template 1
Jobs held in the first 5 years after completing your training/education (between 20 and 30 years)	Template 2
Jobs held in your 30s	Template 2
Jobs held in your 40s	Template 2
Jobs held in your 50s and so on	Template 2
Life achievements/awards/community work/sports and hobbies	Template 3

Of course, many career histories will vary from the one shown. Here are a couple of other models.

For people without formal qualifications:

- jobs held between 15 and 20
- jobs held 20 – 30
- jobs held 30 – 40
- jobs held 40 – 50 and later

You should use Templates 2 and 3.

For people who joined the workforce later in life:

- what you did before starting training/joining the workforce
- any training
- first 5 years of work
- next 10 years
- the next 10 years, and so on

You should use all three templates, but it may be that Template 3 (the Life template) could be the most important.

You can see the general pattern we are suggesting is to divide up your life into sections which you might think of as:

- early work and training
- early jobs post-training
- mid-career jobs
- later career jobs.

When you have settled on a way of dividing up your life that suits you, use our templates to guide the process.

Template 1: Training template

For each place you did any training, complete the following details.

Secondary/ Tertiary	St Custards	Dates attended	From 1979	To 1985
Subjects studied	Results	Teams or clubs	Achievements	
Latin	C	Basketball club	I played in the cup-winning team in 1981. I captained the team in 1983 and we came second out of 20 teams.	
Home Economics	A			
Sports	D			
English	B			
Maths	C			
Spanish	U			
Geography	D			

Template 2: Jobs template

Employer Name and Address	Old Joe Pigtail And Associates 2 Railway Cuttings East Cheam Trumpton-On-Peas	Dates attended		From 1987	To 1991
Reason for leaving		To get broader experience with mega media international			
Job title	**Dates**	**Key duties**	**Achievements/promotions**		
Junior Accounts Consultant	1987–88	Assisting Accounts Consultant	I was the first employee to be promoted to Accounts Consultant within one year, and also the youngest person to have held that position in the company's history		
		Analysing sales figures	I redesigned the client reports to provide a clearer picture of year-on-year progress		
Accounts Consultant	1988–91	Preparing client monthly reports on sales and promotions activities			

Training undertaken	Instructor/ organisation	Date	Description	What I learned
Effective management	Lars Toeplast Peak Managers Blue Mountains	1991	Wilderness course on team work and delegation	Taught me to set clear goals and listen to others in a group

Template 3: Life template

Activity	Dates	Description	Achievements/ personal development	Possible relevance to job
Community work	1990 to date	Bookkeeping for local branch of Oxfam	Satisfaction of giving something back to local community	Shows energy to use my accounts skills outside of normal areas
Hobbies/ interests	1992 to date	Breeding pedigree Welsh Springer Spaniels	Won best of breed, best overall at County Show	To be a breeder requires responsibility/ commitment and maturity
Sports	1979 to date	Basketball, at school, and now for the Randwick Ragers	Social life, helps keep me fit	Helps me be a team player Reduces stress
Other	1994	On the organising committee of the Festival of Food, a two-week festival aimed at promoting the local restaurants and raising awareness about diet		Good organisational skills

On **Template 1** try to list the following:

● any training you undertook
● the institution
● everything you studied (the correct titles of the subjects)
● the results you got in each subject
● the overall result
● how that training was/could be useful to you in your work.

On **Template 2** list:

- all the jobs you've held
- the names of the companies
- the title of your jobs
- your responsibilities
- your reasons for leaving
- your achievements (which we'll discuss in more detail)
- any promotions.

On **Template 3** include any extra-curricular activities:

- sports
- committees
- interest groups (for example, amateur drama)
- training courses (such as wine appreciation, motor mechanics)
- charitable work
- hobbies.

The following tip may seem a little harsh, but remember this is from the horse's mouth: Do a lot with your life so that there is good interesting material to include in a well-presented CV!

Do a lot with your life
so that there's good, interesting material to include in
a well-presented CV!

Employers talk a lot about their employees 'making a contribution' and if you can demonstrate this in your CV, you'll be a more attractive candidate.

The more time you spend away from passive activities like watching the television, the more likely it is that you'll have positive things to say on your CV. Think for one minute how society views people who do nothing but watch television in their leisure time – they are called 'couch potatoes', or worse. This is especially damning for younger people.

List your achievements for each part of your life

It is surprising how quickly some people can forget what they have achieved or play down their role in successes. Sometimes this is because you are not feeling too good about yourself. You may have lost your job, been unemployed for a long time, or you've been out of the workforce for a long time. You must learn to recognize the symptoms if you are playing down your achievements. It is amazing, but we have seen countless university students who hold excellent degrees, even Masters or PhD degrees, who say, 'But I haven't really achieved anything ...'

Look closely at all the activities you've listed in each period of your life. Now think really carefully about anything that you might have achieved during this time. Our 'Gestalt Rule of Proximity' states that people will credit you with an achievement if you were sufficiently close to it. For example, if you were a member of a team that saw sales increase 20 percent annually, you should claim it as an achievement, even if you can't say for sure exactly how much of that outcome was directly related to your efforts.

▶ Achievements and facts – a balancing act

If you look at our templates, you will see that they are divided roughly down the middle. On the left-hand side are the dates and jobs and hobbies. On the right-hand side we have the achievements, the promotions, the personal development.

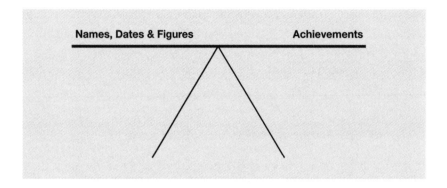

Strike a balance on the information side. It is our experience that people are great at loading the left-hand side of the seesaw while they tend to forget the right-hand side. Why is this?

Some reasons why people focus on 'names, dates and figures' are:

- they are easier to remember
- people are taught to be modest
- names, dates and figures are easier to confirm
- some people get lazy, letting the names and dates speak for them
- writing them out doesn't take much thinking.

We believe that achievements are extremely important. You can see from the 'seesaw' diagram that excluding achievements will lead to an unbalanced CV. This leads us to the next two golden rules:

1 CVs exist to tell the world what you have achieved. Achievements count.

2 Everybody has achievements, some are just better at hiding them than others.

Everybody has achievements; some are **just better at hiding** them than others.

Here are some examples to help you. Check our list of possible achievements:

- promotions
- increasing sales figures
- running a project to change something in your company
- being part of a team that ... (what did your team do?)
- winning an award or prize (no matter how trivial, list it)
- good results in exams or assessments
- gaining qualifications (like a degree, advanced driving qualification, heavy goods vehicle licence)
- employee of the month award
- customer service/quality awards
- outside work achievements – raising money for charity, being elected to a committee
- winning a league, a race, captaining a sports team
- long periods without absence from work (such as no sick days in three years)
- running a marathon or a fun run
- helping to paint a school/community centre
- implementation or design of systems or processes
- improving efficiencies or overhauling processes.

At the end of this chapter you should have three completed templates, and they should look well-balanced. That is, the right and left sides of them should both have plenty of information.

Well done! You now have most of the ingredients you require to build a top CV. Before we do that, let's consider the final ingredient – you!

▶ Character or psychological traits

Let's face it, work takes up a major part of our time, so it stands to reason that people want to work with colleagues who are pleasant and easy to get along with. If you had to choose between two equally talented workmates – one whom you hated, and the other whom you liked – would there really be any decision to make? Increasingly, companies are becoming aware that their employees' personal habits and their work personality not only influence the harmony of the workforce but may directly influence the quality of the work done too.

Many job ads these days list the personal qualities companies believe are important to be successful in their organizations. Many companies take this information very seriously and some will use quite sophisticated psychological tests to measure your ability to work in teams, or how quickly you might lose your temper. Other companies will invite you to join a group of other applicants to assess how well you interact with others.

Generally this sort of information is collected after reading your CV – in interviews and so on – but it is a good idea to emphasize in your CV that you will fit the company's desired 'personality'.

Below we highlight some of the most common 'psychological' traits that employers look for, explain what they mean, and demonstrate how to emphasize your strengths in these areas.

▶ What personal qualities are employers looking for?

From a consideration of job advertisements, the following is our list of the eight most popular qualities desired:

1   communication skills, verbal and written
2   team skills/team player
3   attention to detail

4   energy/dynamism/drive

5   initiative

6   ability to handle pressure

7   enthusiasm

8   leadership.

Let's consider each of these skills in turn.

Communication skills

This is so common that you should assume that every job requires them – and recruiters say so too! There is a mountain of evidence from research on employment interviews that candidates demonstrating good communication skills tend to get the highest ratings. There's no reason why you can't demonstrate these skills in your CV.

Candidates demonstrating **good communication skills** tend to get the **highest ratings at inverview.**

The type and degree of skill will depend on the type of job you are going for. The job might involve communicating with:

- people in your team or unit
- other units in the same organization
- other organizations, or with the public
- special groups such as the young or elderly
- influential or senior clients such as corporate sponsors
- lawyers
- government officials
- senior managers.

What difference does it make who you communicate with? Different situations make different demands on you and you should be aware of what sort of communication you may need. While an employer might tolerate the odd gruff tone or mildly sarcastic remark in the confines of the office, a very dim view will be taken of such behaviour in front of clients.

Look at the job ad or description and try to establish the people you might be communicating with the most.

The skills required may range from being able to understand and relay telephone messages clearly, to writing an extensive report or proposal, or presenting a sales pitch to customers.

Questions to ask yourself are:

- Do I speak clearly in English?
- Can I write clearly?
- Am I able to understand what people are saying to me on most occasions?
- Can I explain things to people clearly?
- So how do I demonstrate these skills on my CV?

You could draw on your work history. For instance, passing a typing test might suggest you can spell accurately, as would shorthand skills. Work as a telephonist, or as a sales representative, suggests that you can communicate verbally and effectively. Giving presentations to clients, or other public speaking experience such as toastmasters' courses, looks good.

Team skills

All this means is that you're happy and effective working in groups with other people. You're happy to work together, share information, help out team members when they are struggling. You tend to like people, and are reasonably well liked.

It sometimes seems that 'team player' is added to just about every job going without any real reason. As a general rule, it's code for saying: 'Do you get on with other people, or are you self-centred and arrogant?'

Some people think the expression 'team player' refers to membership of sporting teams. Generally this is not the case, and it is better to use examples of your team skills drawn from work experience. Of course, if you cannot think of any convincing examples from work, then you might consider using some limited example from your hobbies.

Attention to detail

Many jobs request this skill. Just because this quality is not included in an advertisement, don't assume it's not important. Making silly mistakes in some jobs such as an accounts clerk, where large sums of money may be involved, can lead to very expensive outcomes!

In a study we conducted, where we deliberately included spelling mistakes on some CVs but not on others, we found that even one error reduced the chance of the candidate being shortlisted by between 30 and 45 percent. Think about it – just a minor error can reduce your chances of being interviewed by almost half!

Even **one spelling mistake** on your CV can reduce the likelihood of being shortlisted by **between 30–45 percent.**

Spelling errors and typos, bad grammar and poor phrasing were some of the most frequently mentioned problems with CVs by the recruiters we interviewed. Here are just a few of their tips on the subject.

If you are going to claim that you have good attention to detail, then demonstrate it on your CV by making sure it is completely free of mistakes. The most obvious lapse in attention to detail is spelling. It is essential that all spelling and grammar are correct.

One recent example of a CV we saw from a student read: 'I have excellent attention to deatail'! Not only does this sentence undermine itself, it sends out warning signs – what other weaknesses does this candidate have?

Energy, dynamism, enthusiasm, drive and initiative

Nobody wants to employ somebody who slumps in their seat, seems to take forever to carry out the most trivial tasks, and sighs deeply every time they are asked to do something.

Most organizations are looking for someone who is alert, gets on with work quickly without unnecessary complaint, and who (within reason) will find solutions to problems rather than find problems with solutions.

You're only human, so it's okay to feel lousy from time to time – there is nothing more irritating or downright suspect than the person who is always ecstatically happy. Do remember though that the CV is not the place for a display of negativity!

Ability to handle pressure

Pressure varies from job to job, but the request for this ability is an indication that things might get very busy from time to time. Certain types of job rely on a cool head, for example, work in a fire brigade or with the police force, where lapses of concentration or failures of nerve can have potentially fatal outcomes. What the employer wants to see is evidence that you will respond to the challenge and perhaps work faster or longer hours on occasion to meet deadlines or reduce the backlog. What they're saying is they don't expect you to lose your temper or take sick leave at the first sign of pressure.

Pressure in some jobs will be immediate, such as a long queue of irritated customers. Or it could be longer-term stress, such as the pressure to build The Dome in time!

Leadership

Leadership is one of those qualities that tend to get thrown into a job ad without much justification. For a start, nobody can agree what makes a good leader. However, if you can demonstrate that you managed a team of people successfully, either by length of time in the position (this says that if you were not a good leader you would have been moved on quickly) or by tasks achieved by a group under your management, this may be the sort of thing the employer is looking for. Equally, being elected to a chairperson's role or similar would suggest that you command the confidence of others. Be careful not to confuse strong-mindedness with leadership. The person who charges off from the social group in one direction, only to see the rest of the group subsequently set off in another direction, is demonstrating their hot-headedness and not leadership.

▶ How do you rate against the list of important qualities?

Here are a few questions that might help you think about these qualities and skills in relation to yourself. Use these questions to trigger ideas about your personal qualities.

- Do you tend to get details right more often than not or do you find details irritating?

- Do you prefer working in a team of people or on your own?
- Do you like to be a leader or a team member?
- Are you punctual for work?
- Would you say you're outgoing, like meeting people and going to parties, or do you prefer your own company, or just a few trusted friends?
- Do you tend to be cheerful and positive or do you easily get depressed?
- When people make a lot of demands on you, do you tend to remain calm or do you find yourself losing your temper?

All of the above questions are commonly asked of candidates by employers because they are regarded as important qualities in successful employees. You may be thinking that to any or all of those questions your answer is 'Sometimes yes, sometimes no', or 'It depends', or 'It's not as simple as that'. That is a perfectly reasonable response. The point is, if these are the qualities sought by employers, the more you can demonstrate them through deeds, the better.

▶ Exercising your skills

The following exercises should help you address these 'personality requirements' of employers more easily.

Communication skills

List the people or group of people you commonly communicate with. Next to each person or group of people write down how you communicate. Is it face-to-face, in writing, or on the phone? What is your presentation style? Then write down how you know that what you're communicating has been successful. Take a look at our example, then try to fill out the table yourself.

Communication exercise

Who	What	Success?
Managing director	Face-to-face question	Body language, no clarification needed
Unit leader	Presentation of monthly reports	Performance appraisal requested to coach others

Team work and leadership

List examples of your ability to get on well with co-workers. Here are a few examples to guide you:

- 'The restructuring of the company motivated my new team, and we all took on extra duties to ensure that we accomplished our goals, which we actually exceeded every month.'

- 'Five of us were assigned to investigate why our customer service ratings were down. We divided the tasks up into different product areas, and decided on weekly team meetings. We soon discovered that there were some common problems, and our recommendations when implemented proved very popular.'

- 'I took on an ex-colleague's duties to ensure a smooth service before a replacement was recruited for our team.'

- 'I was voted most popular employee twice last year.'

Remember, many jobs will be fairly clear whether they want a leader or a team member (or both). Looking like a leader when a team member is called for will have recruiters thinking this person will not take direction and will question decisions. Equally, if a leader is required, looking too much like 'one of the boys' might be interpreted as being a poor leader.

The following are some sample statements showing leadership:

- 'I reorganized the way payments were processed. This involved reassigning several staff, some job enlargement and the redundancy of three staff members.'
- 'Under my management, the group has shown record profits in the past eight quarters.'

Statements showing team membership are similar to those suggesting good relations with colleagues.

Take time **every couple of months** to update your skills and achievements list. That way you **won't forget anything.**

Try writing your own statements to show you are outgoing, like meeting people, going to parties, or that you prefer your own company or that of just a few trusted friends. Some examples follow:

- 'I enjoy public speaking.'
- 'I am the staff social representative.'
- 'I enjoy dealing with my customers.'
- 'I enjoyed my five years in sales.'

There are few jobs that would openly seek people who are not outgoing, but they do exist. Any job where contact with other employees or the public is not frequent would be a case in point. Such jobs include machine operators, back-room processing jobs, or jobs where people are out 'on the road' alone like truck drivers, or people working from home. Inadvertent statements that may make you look a little anti-social would be:

- 'I have learned to be very self-reliant.'
- 'I worked in sole practice for 20 years.'
- 'I enjoy the challenge of myself against the elements on orienteering holidays.'

Attention to detail

List work tasks or preferably results where your attention to detail has been demonstrated. For example:

- 'I have never had documents I have typed sent back to me with factual or grammatical errors in them.'
- 'During my time in this post, I reduced the amount of internal mail that was incorrectly addressed by more than 30 percent.'

Energy, enthusiasm and initiative

Try writing your own statements after reading these samples:

- 'My project required me to identify better ways of doing things in the Accounts department to increase productivity and customer satisfaction. Mustering the talent of our Finance Department, I solicited employee ideas and persuaded Management to award the best idea a £500 incentive. These ideas resulted in savings of over £500,000 to the company.'
- 'I was given the task of reorganizing client files to better improve storage and retrieval. Although this was an area in which I had limited experience, I contacted my colleagues in other parts of the company and by sharing ideas with them and working long hours, I implemented a new system within two weeks (three weeks earlier than my manager had expected).'

Pressure

Statements that show your calm temperament, or ability to handle pressure, might look like this:

- 'My current role regularly involves having to produce briefing reports at extremely short notice. It is satisfying to get the job done against apparently impossible odds.'
- 'A key skill is my ability to calm down angry passengers whose flights have been delayed.'

If there was a time when a job had to be finished by a deadline and you worked overnight or over the weekend to complete it, then write down the details next to the relevant job on your life history.

Finally, reflect on the places you have worked, the times you have worked (such as nightshifts or overtime) and the bosses you have worked for. Are there any things that stand out as particularly good or bad?

▶ The essential ingredients

So now you know what the employer's ideal candidate looks like and why 'fit' is important. You should also now be aware which of your achievements and which of your personality or character traits make you suitable for the job. These essential ingredients all need to be played up in your CV. We'll examine how to do this in the next chapter.

Chapter six

6

Constructing

your

cv

▶ How do I set out my CV?

There are several ways of writing a CV. Different approaches work for different people. We'll be examining here four different CV styles:

- chronological CV
- functional CV
- hybrid CV
- structured CV.

▶ Chronological CV

This CV is the style many people use without thinking. It lists your training and jobs in order of the dates you commenced each of them. Typically, people list their most recent training or jobs first and proceed back to the first things they did. This is called the 'reverse chronological' CV.

The components of this CV are in order:

1 personal and contact details
2 qualifications
3 professional development/training courses
4 employment history, including:
   - employer
   - dates of employment
   - positions held
   - achievements.
5 interests.

Here is a quick example of the chronological CV.

Bob Brown

| Address: | 10 Elm Ave |
| | London, SW2 4UL |

Contact details:	(H) 020 8311 3111
	(W) 020 8222 2222
	(M) 07700 10000
	email: b.brown@hotmail.com

| Personal: | Date of birth – 19 June 1965 |
| | Nationality – British |

Qualifications

| 1983–85 | BA in Management, University of London |
| | Majoring in Accounting and Commercial Law |

Professional development

I have attended training courses in the following:

- Consultative selling
- Analytical skills
- Negotiation
- Time management
- Business management
- Executive development programme.

Employment history

Jones Bros Ltd

Jones Bros is a large national company which owns a range of goods transportation systems. Next Day Freight provides distribution systems for a broad customer base including a range of major UK companies.

Regional Manager for Next Day Freight   *3/00 to present*
Reporting to the General Manager.
My major responsibilities in this position include acting as a change agent reshaping the business into a professional and profitable organization with a strong emphasis on customer service. The bottom line responsibility of

this position is a £50 million business unit employing 350 people in Sales, Administration, Operations, Marketing, Customer Service, Quality and Security. My major achievements in this position include:

- creation and implementation of a regional business plan addressing major shortfalls in the business
- a successful merger with a £10 million business unit
- restructuring of the entire sales force
- negotiation and implementation of a new enterprise agreement
- complete management restructure
- introduction of new Management Information Systems
- negotiating the outsourcing of £2.5 million p.a. of casual labour
- coordinating the building of a major new depot facility
- implementation of a quantifiable quality improvement programme
- development of a new marketing strategy
- development of a major strategic industrial relations plan to create greater incentive for the workforce
- leading the business unit to its best profit performance.

National Petroleum Ltd
National is a major petroleum company that owns refineries nationally, as well as having a major franchise network of petrol stations.

National Distribution Network Manager   *3/95 to 2/00*
Reporting to the National Planning Manager. In this role, I was responsible for the strategic development and network rationalization of the wholesale distribution business worth over £80 million p.a. to company profit. I was responsible for maintaining primary trade and developing an environment for improved profit performance based on best practices, operating efficiency and optimum capital investment.

Major milestones in this role included:
- comprehensive review of the sector and development of an integrated business plan for the next century
- development of a new network process to contain the best demographic mix of distribution and marketing
- development and implementation of a merchandising-based franchise package
- implementation of a business planning process for independent distributors

- strategic business review of a £300 million subsidiary
- management of the wholesale investment budget to achieve corporate objectives
- successful rationalization and restructuring of the distributor business to improve the return on investment.

Regional Finance Manager   *3/93 to 2/95*
Reporting to the Regional Manager
My major responsibilities in this role were the financial performance of the dealer and distributor businesses within the area, and entailed the management of profitability, franchisee selection and administration.

Senior Reseller Area Manager   *1/91 to 2/93*
Reporting to the Wholesale Network Development Manager
Responsible for bottom line profit, achievement of volume targets, financial management and credit control, tendering for new business and network development.

Marketing, Planning and Economics Officer   *2/89 to 12/90*
Responsible for SWOT analyses, forecasting and preparation of cost submissions.

Transport Distribution Manager   *2/88 to 1/89*
Consulting to wholesale fuel distributors.

Rundle and Smith Chartered Accountants   *1/86 to 1/88*
Team audit work for a range of companies.
Reason for leaving: to pursue a marketing career.

Interests
Swimming, tennis and bike riding, competitive squash, share dealing.

Referees
Available upon request.

▶ Functional CV

This is a style that emphasizes the skills of the individual and their achievements. It is often used when the applicant lacks formal qualifications, or their qualifications are judged obsolete or irrelevant. If you have had many different jobs with no clear pattern of progression, or a lot of gaps in your work history, some people recommend this approach. After all, you don't want to present your career as a drunken stagger through the world of work!

Bob Brown

Address:	10 Elm Ave London, SW2 4UL
Contact details:	(H) 020 8311 3111 (W) 020 8222 2222 (M) 07700 10000 email: b.brown@hotmail.com
Personal:	Date of birth – 19 June 1965 Nationality – British

Qualifications

1983–85	BA in Management, University of London Majoring in Accounting and Commercial Law

Skills, knowledge, attributes and abilities

Communication skills

In my role as Regional Manager for Next Day Freight I am required to liaise across a broad cross-section of employees. In order to keep employees abreast of company direction and anticipated changes, I implemented briefing sessions held across all shifts once a month. Here I was able to communicate directly with the staff myself and field any questions. Employee satisfaction regarding communications improved from 2.5 to 4.3 over a 12-month period.

Business management

I have a sound knowledge of business management principles. Having completed studies in Management at the University of London, I have continued to keep myself up to date with recent trends and developments by subscribing to journals and magazines. I have also attended several training courses, including the London Business School Executive Development Programme and specialist management courses. Over the past three years, I have implemented ideas gained from my knowledge to restructure our sales force, supervise the implementation of a new Management Information System and quality improvement programme.

Selling skills

As National Distribution Network Manager for National Petroleum Ltd., I was responsible for developing a merchandising-based franchise package which aimed at converting successful franchisees with other companies to National Petroleum. I developed a programme which targeted the top 100 successful franchisees and by interviewing a cross-section, identified reasons most would convert. I then developed a selling kit for representatives to use and conducted selling-skills training courses for representatives to develop better levels of skill. I dealt with the top three clients personally and all three converted. Of the remaining 97 franchisees, 70 percent converted.

Negotiation skills

In my capacity as Regional Manager for Next Day Freight, I have been required to address numerous issues regarding workforce planning. This included outsourcing £2.5 million worth of casual labour, implementing a staff incentive programme and developing a new enterprise agreement. These represented major changes for our existing and often volatile workforce. By developing a committee (which I chaired) involving employee, management and union representatives, we have been able to successfully introduce the required changes without any lost time. Employee satisfaction with working conditions has risen from 1.8 to 4.0 over the past three years.

Tenacity

On my appointment to the position of Regional Manager Next Day Freight, I quickly identified potential cost savings in merging our business unit with our sister company's (Parcel Pick Up) business unit worth £10 million. The project to merge the two units was finally realized last month after planning and negotiations spanning more than three years. Anticipated cost savings as a result of the merger are likely to be in the vicinity of £5 billion.

Summary of employment history

3/00 to now	Jones Bros Ltd	Regional Manager Next Day Freight
3/95 to 2/00	National Petroleum Ltd	National Distribution Network Manager
3/93 to 2/95		Regional Finance Manager
1/91 to 2/93		Senior Reseller Area Manager
2/89 to 12/90		Marketing, Planning and Economics Officer
2/88 to 1/89		Transport Distribution Manager
1/86 to 1/88	Rundle and Smith Chartered Accountants	Team audit work for a range of companies. Reason for leaving: to pursue a marketing career.

Interests
Swimming, tennis and bike riding, competitive squash, share dealing.

Referees
Available upon request.

▶ Hybrid CV

This is an increasingly popular approach that combines the best of both the chronological CV and the functional CV. A hybrid CV retains much of the fixed order of the chronological CV but there is a lot more emphasis on skills and achievements – sometimes in a separate section.

The hybrid approach is the one that we recommend to most people because it produces an excellent clear structure but requires the candidate to really think hard about their achievements and what they have to offer. Obviously there is a limit to how long your CV should be. If you decide to use a hybrid style, you may wish to leave out the detailed responsibilities section and just emphasize the skills, knowledge and abilities.

Bob Brown

Address:	10 Elm Ave
	London, SW2 4UL
Contact details:	(H) 020 8311 3111
	(W) 020 8222 2222
	(M) 07700 10000
	email: b.brown@hotmail.com
Personal:	Date of birth – 19 June 1965
	Nationality – British

Qualifications

1983–85	BA in Management, University of London
	Majoring in Accounting and Commercial Law

Professional development

I have attended training courses in the following:

- consultative selling
- analytical skills
- negotiation
- time management
- business management
- executive development programme.

Skills, knowledge and abilities

Communication skills

In my role as Regional Manager for Next Day Freight I am required to liaise across a broad cross-section of employees. In order to keep employees abreast of company direction and anticipated changes, I implemented briefing sessions held across all shifts once a month. Here I was able to communicate directly with the staff myself and field any questions. Employee satisfaction regarding communications improved from 2.5 to 4.3 over a 12-month period.

Business management

I have a sound knowledge of business management principles. Having completed studies in Management at the University of London, I have continued to keep myself up to date with recent trends and developments by subscribing to journals and magazines, I have also attended several training courses, including the London Business School Executive Development Programme and specialist management courses. Over the past three years, I have implemented ideas gained from my knowledge to restructure our sales force, supervise the implementation of a new Management Information System and quality improvement programme.

Selling skills

As National Distribution Network Manager for National Petroleum Ltd., I was responsible for developing a merchandising-based franchise package which aimed at converting successful franchisees with other companies to National Petroleum. I developed a programme which targeted the top 100 successful franchisees and by interviewing a cross-section, identified reasons most would convert. I then developed a selling kit for representatives to use and conducted selling-skills training courses for representatives to develop better levels of skill. I dealt with the top three clients personally and all three converted. Of the remaining 97 franchisees, 70 percent converted.

Negotiation skills

In my capacity as Regional Manager for Next Day Freight, I have been required to address numerous issues regarding workforce planning. This included outsourcing £2.5 million worth of casual labour, implementing a staff incentive programme and developing a new enterprise agreement. These represented major changes for our existing and often volatile workforce. By developing a committee (which I chaired) involving employee, management and union representatives, we have been able to successfully introduce the required changes without any lost time. Employee satisfaction with working conditions has risen from 1.8 to 4.0 over the past two years.

Tenacity

On my appointment to the position of Regional Manager Next Day Freight I quickly identified potential cost savings in merging our business unit with our sister company's (Parcel Pick Up) business unit worth £10 million. The project to merge the two units was finally realized last month after planning and negotiations spanning more than three years. Anticipated cost savings as a result of the merger are likely to be in the vicinity of around £5 billion.

Employment history
Jones Bros Ltd 3/00 to present
Jones Bros is a large national company which owns a range of goods transportation systems. Next Day Freight provides distribution systems for a broad customer base including a range of major UK companies.

Regional Manager for Next Day Freight
Reporting to the General Manager, my major achievements in this position include:

- creation and implementation of a regional business plan addressing major shortfalls in the business
- a successful merger with a £10 million business unit
- restructuring of the entire sales force
- negotiation and implementation of a new enterprise agreement
- complete management restructure
- introduction of new Management Information Systems
- negotiating the outsourcing of £2.5 million p.a. of casual labour
- coordinating the building of a major new depot facility
- implementation of a quantifiable quality improvement programme
- development of a new marketing strategy
- development of a major strategic industrial relations plan to create greater incentive for the workforce
- leading the business unit to its best profit performance.

National Petroleum Ltd
National Distribution Network Manager   3/95 to 2/00
Reporting to the National Planning Manager, my major milestones in this role included:

- a comprehensive review of the sector and development of an integrated business plan for the next century
- development of a new network process to contain the best demographic mix of distribution and marketing
- the development and implementation of a merchandising-based franchise package
- implementation of a business planning process for independent distributors
- a strategic business review of a £300 million subsidiary

- management of the wholesale investment budget to achieve corporate objectives
- successful rationalization and restructuring of the distributor business to improve the return on investment.

Regional Finance Manager   *3/93 to 2/95*
Reporting to the Regional Manager, my major responsibilities in this role were the financial performance of the dealer and distributor businesses within the area, and entailed the management of profitability, franchisee selection and administration.

Senior Reseller Area Manager   *1/91 to 2/93*
Reporting to the Wholesale Network Development Manager.
I was responsible for bottom line profit, achievement of volume targets, financial management and credit control, tendering for new business and network development.

Marketing, Planning and Economics Officer   *2/89 to 12/90*
Responsible for SWOT analyses, forecasting and preparation of cost submissions.

Transport Distribution Manager   *2/88 to 1/89*
Consulting to wholesale fuel distributors.

Rundle and Smith Chartered Accountants   *1/86 to 1/88*
Team audit work for a range of companies. Reason for leaving: to pursue marketing career.

Interests
Swimming, tennis and bike riding, competitive squash, share dealing.

Referees
Available upon request.

▶ Structured interview CV

This is an idea that might work for some people, although it's less traditional than the chronological, functional or hybrid CV. In a structured interview, the job applicant is asked a series of questions in a set order. In a structured interview CV, the candidate sets out a series of questions and provides the answers to them. Increasingly, these types of questions are being asked on web-based job application forms, so setting out your CV in this manner may elicit a positive response from the recruiter. This approach emphasizes skills and competencies over formal qualifications. The following questions can be used to make up a structured interview CV.

Communication skills

● What types of proposals have you written?

● What are some of the most difficult groups you've had to present to?

Business management

● How does your experience in business management match our role requirements?

Selling skills

● What has been the toughest selling assignment you have ever had?

Negotiation skills

● What do you believe are the successful outcomes of a good negotiation process?

● When have you best demonstrated your negotiation skills?

Tenacity

● Describe a project or work assignment that best demonstrates your tenacity.

Structured interview example

Let's look at our sample CV, presented as a structured interview.

Bob Brown

Address:	10 Elm Ave London, SW2 4UL
Contact details:	(H) 020 8311 3111 (W) 020 8222 2222 (M) 07700 10000 email: b.brown@hotmail.com
Personal:	Date of birth – 19 June 1965 Nationality – British

Qualifications

1983–85	BA in Management, University of London Majoring in Accounting and Commercial Law

Employers

1995–2000	National Petroleum Ltd.
2000 to present	Jones Bros Ltd (Next Day Freight)

Professional development

I have attended training courses in the following:

- consultative selling
- analytical skills
- negotiation
- time management
- business management
- executive development programme.

Skills knowledge, attributes and abilities

Communication skills

What types of proposals have you written?

I have written a wide range of proposals, in terms of significance and audience. Proposals have included change in marketing strategy proposals for presentation to Board of Directors; Industrial Relations proposals for presentation to Board of Directors and Union representatives; a prospectus for potential franchisees; merger recommendations for presentation to our Board of Directors and to the Board of Directors of proposed merging company.

What are some of the most difficult groups you've had to present to?
Although I have had no 'difficult groups' as such, I have needed to present to some quite sceptical and cautious groups. These have included union organizers, potential franchisees and the board of directors of a company we were proposing to merge with. All groups were significant stakeholders with a lot to lose from a poor decision, and consequently there were a lot of questions to field and I was forced to think quickly. Presentations were designed to address the audiences' primary concerns in a style that they were most comfortable with. In the above examples my presentations contributed to successful outcomes in all three cases.

Business management
How does your experience in business management match our role requirements?
Over the past nine years my roles have primarily focused on business management. I have a broad background in most aspects of general management including finance, sales, marketing, distribution, business development and, most recently, human resources, in my role as Regional Manager. My experience is complemented by formal studies in Accounting and Commercial Law, demonstrating that I can successfully convert theory into practice. I have the necessary breadth and depth of experience to fulfil or exceed requirements as the Regional Manager for Overnight-Now.

Selling skills
What has been the toughest selling assignment you have ever had?
The toughest selling assignment has been converting existing successful franchisees to change to National Petroleum. Already proven to be successful with GDP Petrol, these franchisees had more to gain by converting to National Petroleum, but naturally some were sceptical. I set about finding the franchisees' most frequent source of dissatisfaction with GDP and structured a package that addressed these concerns. Since there were 100 franchisees to convert, I could not handle all of these myself. By training our representatives, 97 franchisees were approached, of which 70 percent converted. I managed the relationship with the top three franchisees personally, and all converted.

Negotiation skills

What do you believe are the successful outcomes of a good negotiation process?

A genuine win–win result for both parties. I think it is important to go into a negotiation with a clear understanding of what I want to achieve, as well as being prepared to listen to what the other party wants. At the end of the negotiation there needs to be a set of outcomes agreed to and honoured by both parties.

When have you best demonstrated your negotiation skills?

During our enterprise agreement negotiation at Next Day Freight. Management was keen to introduce significant changes to the types of skills, shift rosters and duties performed by employees to deliver maximum workforce flexibility in our 2000 negotiations. These changes represented significant cost savings to the business as well as ensuring longer-term business viability. Without these changes, it was likely that the business would need to retrench many of its current permanent workforce and outsource functions to contractors, By creating a committee of employee, management and union representatives, we were able to successfully identify what each group wanted to achieve. All three groups reached agreement on the issues that were key to their concerns, and conceded on smaller, less important issues. There was no time lost as a result of the negotiations and employee satisfaction rose significantly.

Tenacity

How tenacious are you? Give an example that demonstrates you at your most tenacious.

Of course, I am very tenacious, as can be demonstrated by the successful merger between Next Day Freight and Parcel Pick-Up. Parcel Pick-Up was a family business passed down through three generations and was suffering badly from the high cost of its overheads and a downturn in its speciality service – small parcel delivery. I met with the then Managing Director in 2000 to discuss the possibility of a merger, and it was clear that he was not prepared to concede. It took almost a year of regular meetings and negotiations to build his confidence in our business. In 2001, we successfully merged, retaining all existing staff, combining support functions and sharing overheads.

Employment history
Jones Bros Ltd 3/2000 to present
Jones Bros is a large national company which owns a range of goods transportation systems. Next Day Freight provides distribution systems for a broad customer base including a range of major UK companies.

Regional Manager for Next Day Freight
Reporting to the General Manager. My major responsibilities in this position include acting as a change agent reshaping the business into a professional and profitable organization with a strong emphasis on customer service. The bottom-line responsibility of this position is a £50 million business unit employing 350 people in sales, administration, operations, marketing, customer service, quality and security.

My major achievements in this position include:

- creation and implementation of a state business plan addressing major shortfalls in the business
- a successful merger with £10 million business unit
- restructuring of the entire sales force
- negotiation and implementation of a new enterprise agreement
- complete management restructure
- introduction of new Management Information Systems
- negotiating the outsourcing of £2.5 million p.a. of casual labour
- coordinating the building of a major new depot facility
- implementation of a quantifiable quality improvement programme
- development of a new marketing strategy
- development of a major strategic industrial relations plan to create greater incentive for the workforce
- leading the business unit to its best profit performance.

National Petroleum Ltd
National is a major petroleum company that owns refineries nationally, as well as having a major franchise network of petrol stations.

National Distribution Network Manager   *3/95 to 2/2000*
Reporting to the National Planning Manager.
In this role, I was responsible for the strategic development and network rationalization of the whole sales distribution business worth over £80

million p.a. to company profit. I was responsible for maintaining primary trade and developing an environment for improved profit performance based on best practices, operating efficiency and optimum capital investment.

Major milestones in this role included:

- a comprehensive review of the sector and development of an integrated business plan for the next century
- development of a new network process to contain the best demographic mix of distribution and marketing
- the development and implementation of a merchandising-based franchise package
- implementation of a business planning process for independent distributors
- a strategic business review of a £300 million subsidiary
- management of the wholesale investment budget to achieve corporate objectives
- successful rationalization and restructuring of the distributor business to improve the return on investment.

Regional Finance Manager   *3/93 to 2/95*
Reporting to the Regional Manager.
My major responsibilities in this role were the financial performance of the dealer and distributor businesses within the area, and entailed the management of profitability, franchisee selection and administration.

Senior Reseller Area Manager   *1/91 to 2/93*
Reporting to the Wholesale Network Development Manager.
Responsible for bottom-line profit, achievement of volume targets, financial management and credit control, tendering for new business and network development.

Marketing, Planning and Economics Officer   *2/89 to 12/90*
Responsible for SWOT analyses, forecasting and preparation of cost submissions.

Transport Distribution Manager   *2/88 to 1/89*
Consulting to wholesale fuel distributors.

Rundle and Smith Chartered Accountants   *1/86 to 1/88*
Team audit work for a range of companies. Reason for leaving: to pursue a marketing career.

Interests
Swimming, tennis and bike riding, competitive squash, share dealing.

Referees
Available upon request.

▶ What if I want my CV to look different?

Our extensive work has found that recruiters prefer CVs that look conventional. This has been found in studies throughout the world. Most recruiters are conventional people, and they have a clear idea of what they expect to see in a CV.

Research has shown that
recruiters prefer CVs
that look **conventional.**

Reading a CV is a bit like walking into a restaurant – we know what to expect. In a restaurant, we know that there will be tables and a menu, that we will be asked for our order and we will have to pay for the food. We might even expect to leave a tip! Receiving an unusual CV would be like walking into the restaurant and seeing no tables or serving staff. We might work out that there is a food vending machine to use, or alternatively we might just walk out. Similarly, we might persevere with an unusual CV, or we might just reject it (see 'Wacky CVs', p. 180).

Let's now take a look at the essential components of your CV.

◗ What to include in your CV

The following are the basic headings you'll need to cover:

- contact details
- education and training
- work history
- achievements
- interests and extra-curricular activities.

We'll be looking at all of these areas below. In the next chapter we'll also be looking briefly at a few tricky issues: how many personal details to provide in your CV and the issue of prejudice; whether to enclose a photograph; and whether to gives names of referees in your CV.

Top Tip for CVs

Use our 4-S rule – keep it Simple, Structured, Succinct and Significant.

Contact details

Always include your:

- full name
- home address
- telephone number
- mobile number
- fax number
- email address.

Only give contact details for places where you are prepared to be contacted by prospective employers. If receiving a call or an email at your current workplace might lead to embarrassing questions from your boss, do not give work contact details. Of course, if you want to include an email address, it is now very easy to get a free email account on the web from companies like Hotmail (*www.hotmail.com*) or Yahoo (*www.yahooo.co.uk*).

Remember that you must always put your name, home address, telephone and mobile numbers plus email address on the first page of your CV.

Always put your name, home and email addresses plus telephone and mobile numbers on the **front page of your CV.**

Education and training

If you don't have any formal education, obviously you omit these elements and should be thinking of using the functional or the structured interview CV.

What qualifications is our potential employer looking for? These qualifications are the ones to focus on.

Don't bore the reader by listing every qualification you have obtained – keep it to the relevant and impressive stuff. Go through the list of qualifications you have made and determine which are relevant to the job. List these in order, together with the name of the institution and year you obtained the qualification.

Some qualifications, like a university degree, are regarded as relevant information in most circumstances. Other qualifications, such as a first aid course, may be seen as useful for some jobs, but would look odd being listed for others.

Your age will also help you decide what to include and what to leave out. For people in their first five years of work, education is very important and should be listed in reasonable detail. After those first five years, be a bit more selective about what you use.

Some qualifications become outdated quickly, so claiming to be a computer expert on the basis of a computing degree obtained 15 years ago will not look very convincing. In this case, evidence of recent work in the field will count for a lot more.

Having said that, a degree shows evidence of critical thinking and intelligence and should not be discarded altogether.

The order in which you list qualifications is normally:

- highest postgraduate qualification – Masters or PhD, the subject, and the university at which the degree was taken
- highest undergraduate qualification – the degree, the subject, and the university at which the degree was taken
- secondary school qualifications.

This point may not apply to many people at all, but should you have a PhD, bear in mind that the title of PhDs can often appear to be so obscure or trivially narrow as to detract from a great achievement. Believe us, we have heard the sniggers that sometimes accompany PhD award presentation ceremonies! If you have a very specialized title that is not going to be directly relevant to the job applied for, then stick to the subject discipline name (such as Chemistry, Physics, English, or Psychology).

Don't bore the reader by listing every qualification you have obtained – keep to the **relevant and impressive stuff.**

If you have a degree, it's probably not too important to go into detail about your secondary school results unless they are exceptional. If you have a degree, most employers will credit you with a certain amount of intelligence. What might be useful is to list a few subjects you covered at secondary school, to give an indication of your versatility. For instance, if you have an arts degree, it is probably worth listing 'Mathematics, Chemistry, Statistics' or other numerate subjects studied at secondary school, as this gives an indication of rounded abilities. The opposite applies for science graduates, who might list English and History if applicable.

List any extra languages that you speak, particularly if you're applying to any international companies.

If there is any special thesis topic or aspect of your studies that is particularly relevant to the job, then mention it here.

With all qualifications and abbreviations, do not assume that the reader will understand what they are. For instance, what do the following mean?

- HSC
- SNVQ
- GSCE
- O-level
- A-level
- cum laude
- Honours
- ACA, RIBA
- Baccalaureate
- City and Guilds
- Grade point average or GPA.

Chances are, some of the above will be a mystery to you. If you are applying for a job in the same country in which you were trained and the qualification system has not changed in the last ten years, it's safe to assume the employer will understand the meaning of your qualifications. Otherwise, do not assume anyone else will understand your qualifications – if in doubt, explain what they mean.

If you gained your qualifications overseas, say what the local equivalent qualification is and, even better, get your qualifications assessed by the relevant government department. If in doubt, contact the local immigration department for assistance.

Look at the following grading systems. You cannot be sure that 75 percent from one course is equal to a 'B' in another. A good example comes from UK and Australian universities. In the UK, a 'First' or 'A' is often awarded for scores above 75 percent, whereas that score in Australia is often a 'two-one' or 'B'. The educational standard is probably not too different, it is just the way people use the scales.

You can be sure that if an employer has any doubts, they'll tend to think the worst.

When applying for a job in another state or country, don't assume employers will understand what your qualifications mean. Explain your grades in the employer's local system.

Your work history

Go back to the lists that you have made and try to pick out what in your work history either matches the ideal candidate you have constructed, or looks impressive in its own right.

Your work history is the most 'wordy' part of the CV. This is where you have the most scope to influence the reader through your writing style, the words you use, and the way you describe yourself.

Generally list your most recent job first, and then move on to the previous one and so on. If you have a long work history with many different jobs, then we would recommend you restrict listing full details of the positions held in the past ten years. If there are some earlier jobs that are particularly relevant to the application, then these should be included.

For each job you should list:

- dates (in years) of employment
- job title
- employer's name and city location if appropriate
- your responsibilities (keep it brief)
- your achievements in the job.

Tailor the CV to suit **the requirements of the ad and** include achievements (not just duties), because this **is what will sell you.**

The last point on this list is possibly one of the most important. Just providing a job description is not enough. If many applicants have similar backgrounds, then the recruiter will be bored to tears and may not even read your CV. What makes you different, more employable, are all of your achievements. Always emphasize your achievements in each job.

Top Tips **What to include in your CV**

- **Contact details:** name, home address, phone number, mobile number, email address.
- **Academic qualifications:** List the highest first (e.g. postgraduate or university degree if you have one, A Levels, GNVQ or GCSE etc.) and include the name of the university, college or school where you obtained the qualification and the year.

- **Work history:** Start with the most recent job and then work backwards. If you've had numerous jobs, consider listing only the most recent/relevant ones. Include job title, employer's name and address and your reponsibilities. Ideally, you should also provide dates for each job, but be prepared to explain any gaps later if this should come up at interview.

- **Achievements:** For each job, remember to include a list of your major achievements in the role.

- **Interests and extra-curricular activities:** Include the ones that highlight the personal qualities required in the role you're targeting. For example, playing in football team might indicate that you'd be a good team player; serving on a committee or PTA might show strong communication skills; helping out a charity on a volunteer basis might show good people skills and commitment.

In a study we conducted, recruiters were shown two CVs that were identical except that one described only duties in the job history and the other described achievements. The CV that included achievements was rated much more highly by the recruiters. They were far more impressed with the candidate.

The following is a typical job history.

Employment history

What does this company do?

Trinity Mutual Ltd

Executive Director, Trinity Mutual Master Trust – 3/1998 to present
Key responsibilities include all aspects of the Master Trust, with 25 staff across tour departments including marketing, client administration, systems and accounting.

President Mutual (1984–98)

Any achievements?

Marketing Manager (1996–97)
Key responsibilities included product development and maintenance, marketing and communications of the entire product range of the division.

Assistant General Manager, Financial Products (1995–96)
As above.

Senior Investment Manager, Operations (1991–95)
Key responsibilities included the day to day operations of President Funds Management and 'unusual' investments such as leveraged leases, junk bonds, etc.

Fund Manager, Life Fund and Insurance Bonds (1990–91)
Key responsibilities included managing the £3.5 billion Life Fund and the £1.5 billion Insurance Bond Fund, including asset allocation, general management and 'unusual' investments.

Fund Manager, Insurance Bonds (1987–90)
Key responsibilities included managing the new Insurance Bond Fund, including asset allocation, general management and 'unusual' investments.

Actuarial and investment roles (1984–87)
In this period I was engaged in a number of actuarial roles and investment positions within President Mutual.

The achievement focus

Here is the same job history, but this time there is an emphasis on achievements.

Employment history

Tells you what the company does

Trinity Mutual Ltd (3/1998 to present)

Trinity Mutual is a major insurance agency which operates Europe-wide.

Executive Director, Trinity Mutual Master Trust (31/1998 to present)
Key responsibilities include all aspects of the Master Trust, with 25 staff across four departments including marketing, client administration, systems and accounting. Major achievements included successful relocation of the administration, accounting and systems areas from external suppliers to head office.

President Mutual Ltd (1984–98)

Clear set of achievements

President Mutual is a major insurance agency which operates UK-wide.

Marketing Manager 1996–1997
Key responsibilities included product development and maintenance, marketing and communications of the entire product range of the division. During this time sales rose by 14 percent, compared with a 5 percent rise average in the area.

Assistant General Manager, Financial Products (1995–96)
As above.

Senior Investment Manager, Operations (1991–95)
Key responsibilities included the day to day operations of President Funds Management and 'unusual' investments such as leveraged leases, junk bonds.

Fund Manager, Life Fund and Insurance Bonds (1990–91)
Key responsibilities included managing the £3.5 billion Life Fund and the £1.5 billion Insurance Bond Fund, including asset allocation, general management and 'unusual' investments. The fund outperformed all the indexes.

Fund Manager, Insurance Bonds (1987–90)
Key responsibilities included managing the new Insurance Bond Fund, including asset allocation, general management and 'unusual' investments. Major achievements included growing the Fund from £5 million to more than £1 billion.

Actuarial and investment roles (1984–87)
In this period, I was engaged in a number of actuarial roles and investment positions within President Mutual.

Turning responsibilities into achievements

What has this person achieved?

General Manager, Merchandise and Marketing

The major responsibilities in this role included:

- overall accountability for the product, merchandising and promotions for the 100 stores Europe-wide
- product sourcing
- financial control of the sales budget
- managing the team of 12 buying and merchandising staff
- ongoing liaison with state management
- control and accountability of the advertising and marketing needs of the stores.

What would you look for? Where might there be places where achievements could be emphasized?

The first thing to catch the eye is the overall accountability for 100 stores. Can the applicant point to any financial improvements in the stores' performance? What about the sourcing of the products – any reduction in costs there, or sources of novel products?

The role is a coordinating one – is there any evidence of achievements in organizing the systems the applicant controls? Did the applicant introduce any new marketing strategies or just carry on where their predecessor left off? (That is, did they show initiative?)

The above description could be enhanced by referring directly to achievements that answer these questions. Remember, the CV is supposed to answer questions, not raise them in the minds of the recruiter. The improved version is below.

General Manager, Merchandise and Marketing

The major responsibilities in this role included:

- overall accountability for the product, merchandising and promotions for the 100 stores Europe-wide
- product sourcing
- financial control of the sales budget
- managing the team of 12 buying and merchandising staff
- ongoing liaison with state management
- control and accountability of the advertising and marketing needs of the stores.

Major achievements included:

- restructuring of the buying department, resulting in increased productivity and lower costs
- changes to the supply chain, resulting in a 4 percent increase in margins
- development of reporting systems, resulting in enhanced financial planning
- introduction of new offshore merchandise resources
- development and implementation of marketing strategies
- involvement in new stores and refurbishments
- establishment of quality management functions.

You can see that adding the major achievements gives a much more favourable impression of the applicant.

Try to **find achievements** for each of the responsibilities you held in your jobs.

So what constitutes an achievement? Here is our list of criteria for job-related achievements:

- completing something successfully
- an outcome that can be attributed at least in part to you
- something that is measurable (profits, turnover, savings, words per minute)
- something that you can prove to have happened or that can be verified
- making a change or a difference.

Examples of achievements are:

- winning a customer-service award
- improving profits
- introducing a profitable product
- increasing the number of cars serviced per week
- reducing the number of customer complaints
- reducing the turnaround time for orders
- increasing the reliability of a service.

You have now re-written your CV using more positive language, emphasizing all your achievements, so it's time to see if you have passed the CV fitness test!

Employers think about fit in terms of **knowledge, skills, abilities** and **attitudes**, as we saw earlier (pp. 108–9). Have you worked out:

● what experience is required for the job?

● the skills needed to do the job?

● the abilities that will be required?

● the sort of person/attitudes the employer expects?

Have you included in your CV:

● relevant knowledge?

● relevant skills?

● demonstrated compatible abilities?

● demonstrated compatible attitudes?

If the CV passes the fitness test, you should now apply our Gestalt test! The next set of rules is not ours but comes from respected Gestalt psychology. These well-established rules were used to describe visual perception, but they apply equally well to CVs.

▶ The Gestalt rules of CVs

1 **Similarity:** people will group together, as roughly the same, similar jobs and experiences.

2 **Proximity:** people will assume that things that are close together belong together. In other words, if you were part of a team that had a success, the success will be associated with you personally.

3 **Closure:** people look for closure on projects and activities – can you demonstrate that you finished projects you started?

4 **Continuity:** people will assume that things that follow on closely in a similar pattern are part of a longer-term logical development.

If you were **part of a team** that had success, then that success will be **associated with you.**

Similarity

This can be used effectively on your CV. By emphasizing the similarity of your previous jobs to the one you're applying for, you increase the fit between you and the job. Equally, similarity may govern which previous jobs to include or leave out of a CV. If you have a long work history, it may be sensible to concentrate on listing only those jobs that you have done in the past five to ten years, especially if these are closest to the one you are going for.

Here is an example of the similarity effect:

Employment history

1983–84	Receptionist, Blue Blot Ink Co.
1984–86	Secretary, Blue Blot Ink Co.
1986–92	Sales Assistant, Jeans R Us
1992–93	Secretary, Hercules Music Company
1993–99	Call Centre Operator, Big Brick Phone Co.
1999–2000	Personal Assistant to CEO, Big Brick Phone Co.
2000–Present	Personal Assistant to CEO, Slender Phones Pty

What skills would you describe this person as having? Most people would get the impression from this history that the candidate was a secretary. This is because the terms 'receptionist', 'secretary' and 'personal assistant' all conjure up ideas of similar jobs, whereas 'sales assistant' and 'call centre operator' seem dissimilar. The power of this effect can be seen when you add up the number of years doing the various jobs. This person spent more time (13 years out of 18) *not* being a secretary!

Closure

Closure is something that many employers will be looking for. They want evidence that you can see things through, that you don't quit when the going gets tough. Can you give examples where you completed a project successfully at work? Closure can also be demonstrated by showing that you moved to the next job because your work was completed in the old job, or that you had gained all the personal development likely: 'I moved on because I needed a new challenge having mastered my old job.'

Employers want evidence that you **don't quit** when the **going gets tough.**

Proximity

This is a powerful effect. If you were 'close' to some outcome, you will be associated with it. It is a bit like being at the scene of the crime – you automatically become one of the witnesses (and sometimes a suspect). Consider the following two work histories.

- **Negative grouping:** 'I started in the commodities team, and moved on to sales when the team was disbanded. The sales were outsourced in 1995, when I joined the merchant division.'

- **Positive grouping:** 'I was part of the commodities team that broke all the market records, and then moved to sales, where the group achieved a 25 percent improvement. This led to my current position in the merchant division.'

You can see the power of proximity here. The first example gives the impression of a loser and the second of a winner, despite the lack of evidence to suggest the candidate was responsible for any of the successes or the failures.

Continuity

This relates most obviously to gaps in career history. We'll spend some more time considering this later. However, it is worth pointing out here that most employers want to see continuity in employment. Continuity has two aspects. Firstly, have you been continuously employed over the years and, secondly, does your work history combine to tell a logical story or does it appear random? The following examples illustrate this point:

Continuous employment, but discontinuous types of job

1983–84	Receptionist, Blue Blot Ink Co.
1984–86	Assistant Chemist, Blue Blot Ink Co.
1986–92	Sales Assistant, Jeans R Us
1992–93	Product Packer, Hercules Music Company
1993–99	Stores Administrator, Big Brick Phone Co.
1999–2000	Sales Representative, Big Brick Phone Co
2000–Present	Glazier, Heritage Doors Ltd

Continuous employment, and reasonably continuous types of job

1983–84	Receptionist, Blue Blot Ink Co.
1984–86	Secretary, Blue Blot Ink Co.
1986–92	Sales Assistant, Jeans R Us
1992–93	Secretary, Hercules Music Company
1993–99	Call Centre Operator, Big Brick Phone Co.
1999–2000	Personal Assistant to CEO, Big Brick Phone Co.
2000–Present	Personal Assistant to CEO, Slender Phones Ltd

From these examples, it can be seen clearly that the story of the first candidate's working life is a very confused and mixed one. It doesn't create a great impression. The second candidate's history tells a story of steady advancement (and therefore achievement) in the secretarial area. It's a much more positive story.

Now you know all about the Gestalt laws, so use them to guide what goes into your CV and what does not, how to word your job history and how to present your CV.

Our work is
the presentation
of our capabilities.

Edward Gibbon

7

Some tricky cv issues

et's look briefly now at a few tricky issues regarding what to include in your CV.

▶ Dealing with prejudice

One of the most commonly asked questions when writing a CV is what to do about bias. This is a difficult one to answer and there would be no point in denying that prejudice often plays a part in the recruitment process, although it may not be that obvious. Bias might pertain to any number of variables: a person's age, ethnicity, religion, political beliefs, regional accent, height, weight, sexuality, even colour of hair, etc.

Legislation exists in the UK to prevent certain forms of discrimination, such as sexual, racial and disability discrimination (see web addresses of Equal Opportunities organizations in Chapter 18 for further information). There is, however, no legislation currently in place to prevent an employer screening for anyone over the age of 50, say. Generally in the UK things are improving; anti-ageist legislation is due to be introduced in 2006, for example, in line with a European Union directive. The bigger the organization, the more likely it is to have an Equal Employment Opportunities policy, which should help to reduce bias.

Bearing all this in mind, some applicants ask how much information to include in a CV. You may decide, for example, to omit your age, marital status or nationality. It's entirely your decision how much detail you want to convey in your own CV. It may be more difficult to avoid these topics if you have to fill in a standard application form, however.

Clearly, an organization may need to check on work permits if someone is not of EU nationality. There again, if the job is likely to involve extensive spells of foreign travel, it may not be ideal for someone who is in a long-term relationship or who has children at home. Often, therefore, there are good reasons for the employer asking for personal information.

▶ Should I include a photograph?

Our advice on this is a firm 'no' unless it is specifically asked for. Generally, it provides the employer with another criterion on which to unfairly judge an applicant before the interview stage. As we've seen above, people often form an opinion on someone based purely on outward appearance – on the colour or length of hair say, or how old they look. This is of course very unfair as there are very few jobs where appearance is of paramount importance. Not everyone looks like a model, or photographs like one. Research has shown that you're more likely to be shortlisted if you *don't* enclose a photograph.

Research has shown that you're more likely to get shortlisted if you **don't enclose a photograph.**

▶ Should I add my salary?

In general we do not recommend including your salary details in a CV as this may influence your chances of being selected for interview. If the advert specifies that you need to include this then it is best to put this at the end of your covering letter – that way it's less prominent as it's usually the CV that gets more attention (see also p. 209 for application forms and p. 279 for advice on salary negotiation at interview).

▶ Should I add names of referees?

There is mixed advice from recruiters on this topic. Our preference is to include referee contact details as the last item on your CV. The reason for saying this rather than 'Referees available on request' is that it makes it easier for the employer. They do not have to make an extra call to get names and addresses. We also wonder how many people who have put 'Referees available on request' have panicked when asked for them because they hadn't bothered to work out who the referees would be!

Who should I choose?

There are many cases of candidates who have unwittingly continued to use a referee who has written extremely negative things about them. On other occasions, it is clear that the candidate has failed to ask the permission of a referee in advance when comments such as 'Last time I had contact with him he was unemployed in Cardiff' are made. This brings us to our next golden rule: Always ensure that you know your referee well, and that they are happy to write or say something positive about you.

Top Tips Choosing referees

- Always ensure that you know your referees well, and that they're happy to write or say something positive about you.
- Phone them first to check their contact details and to confirm that haven't changed location. This will give you a chance to brief them on the sort of job you're applying for and to thank them for their help.
- Don't use the same referee for scores of different jobs, be selective.
- Choose referees preferably who have supervised you in recent jobs, especially the one you currently hold.
- Don't forget a courtesy call is always appreciated if you get the job.

Not only should you ask the referee's permission, you should also treat them with respect. That means you should inform them what sort of job you're applying for (you don't want a referee to express surprise on the phone). Don't abuse your referee by making them respond to hundreds of different employers that you have indiscriminately applied to. Also, don't forget to thank them for acting as your referee. And they will appreciate hearing from you later on, especially if you get the job. You may well want to use them again, so it always pays to stay on good terms.

The best referees are people who have supervised you in your recent jobs, especially the one you currently hold. Not only does this look more impressive, but it also tells the employer that you are not at loggerheads with your current supervisor. If this is not practical (because you are trying to maintain confidentiality), try using someone who has previously supervised you and has left the company or who now works in a different area. Whatever you decide, remember that it is important to choose as recent a referee as possible, since this is more likely to relate to the position you are applying for.

The best referees
are people who have supervised you in **your most recent jobs.**

If you cannot get a reference from a current or recent employer, or alternatively, if the job ad has asked for 'character references', you'll need to approach some other people. This is going to cause outrage among some readers, but there are some people who are more suitable than others. In general, people in 'professional' jobs are generally seen as 'good' referees:

- lawyers
- judges
- teachers
- lecturers

- police officers
- government councillors
- company directors (but the company needs to be respectable)
- senior managers.

Finally, here are a couple of golden 'don'ts':

- Don't invent your own reference.
- Don't use relatives or friends with different names as referees.

We have genuinely seen a CV where the candidate had included a statement from a referee, who was his best friend's mother, and that was dated more than 14 years before! And another where a candidate using a false name and address of a referee turned out to be himself using a fake Scottish accent! Unfortunately for him, the accent wore off as the reference progressed and he said some unbelievably good things about himself. Needless to say, neither of these applicants got the job!

So far in this part of the book, we've looked at what to include in your CV in terms of content so that you emerge as a top candidate. We've also in this chapter covered a few tricky issues that can sometimes pose a dilemma for applicants.

*   *   *

But content is not everything – nowadays presentation is all-important too; you don't want a poorly designed CV to scupper your chances of being selected for interview. The next chapter offers guidance on how to lay out your CV, what fonts and headings to use, and examines the topic of wacky CVs and whether they really do help you to stand out from the crowd.

Chapter eight

Presenting
your
cv

◗ Layout

The first thing to say about the layout of your CV is do not put the words 'Résumé' or 'Curriculum Vitae' on the top of your CV. Quite apart from insulting the reader – what else could the document be? – it's a waste of valuable space.

At the top of the first page of your CV, put your full name (or the name you wish to be known by). It should be in bold type, at a size of 18–20 points, centred on the page. Leave plenty of white space below this heading, before you list your personal contact details.

Aligned on the left side of your page, give your home address. Use the right-hand side on the same lines to give your telephone and mobile phone numbers, fax (if applicable) and email address.

The remainder of your CV appears in the following order:

- date of birth and nationality (if you decide to include these; see p. 160)
- education/training details
- professional associations
- work history
- interests and extra-curricular activities
- names of referees come last (see Chapter 7).

◗ Headings

Headings have to be consistent in appearance. They must all be the same font (e.g. Times New Roman or Arial) and size. In the example given on page 177, there are three different levels of headings. If you follow this example, you may decide to put your name in caps, bold, in 18 or 20 points. Then the major headings ('Education' and 'Work history') could be 14 points, bold. You may opt for 12 points italic for the subheadings.

Making the same type of headings look the same is another example of the Gestalt law of similarity. The reader finds it easy to see the separate sections.

IAN GREGORY CHAPPELL

360 Edgecliff Avenue	Telephone: 01924 523124 (H)
Wakefield	01924 523421 (W)
West Yorkshire	07803 644644 (M)
WF4 2NO	Fax: 01924 523422
	Email: igchappell@hotmail.com

Education
1979–1985   St Mark of the Blessed Taylor High School, Leeds
1985–1989   Electrical Engineering, Salford University
                       First Class Honours

Work history
1989-1994   Optus   Leeds
An international telecommunications company.

Communications Engineer
I was responsible...

Senior Communications Manager
I did...

1994 – Present   Telstra   Wakefield

Operations Manager
I am currently responsible for...

▶ White space and grouping

You must leave plenty of white space on your CV; see above for an example of a well laid-out CV. If you put too much writing on a page, your CV will be hard to read and look cluttered. You should also allow a generous margin of at least 2.5 centimetres on all sides.

Leave plenty of
white space on your CV.

White space can be used to apply the Gestalt principle of proximity (that things close to each other belong together). In the example, there is plenty of space between the person's contact details and their education. There are smaller gaps between their school and university, and then there is a larger gap again between education and the work history. The size of the gaps tells the reader that the things close together are all related. The larger gap indicates to the reader they are moving on to some different type of information.

▶ Font

Use the same font throughout. Here are some good and bad examples:

The fast cat jumped over the lazy dog. (Arial)

The fast cat jumped over the lazy dog. (Times New Roman)

The fast cat jumped over the lazy dog. (Courier)

The fast cat jumped over the lazy dog. (Bookman)

The fast cat jumped over the lazy dog. (Comic Sans MS)

The fast cat jumped over the lazy dog. (Impact)

The first two are both acceptable fonts; the second two are less acceptable, but still OK; the last two are definitely not suitable.

▶ Bullet points or continuous prose?

We did some research to see if recruiters had a preference for work histories presented as bullet points or as continuous prose (that is, as a series of normal sentences). The results were not straightforward. Recruiters tended to prefer candidates to write complete sentences, but if the CV had been rewritten by a recruitment agency, they tended to prefer bullet points!

So what should you do?

Bullet points are quick and easy to read, and look attractive on the page, as long as there are not too many of them. The risk with bullet points is that people tend to be too brief and the bullet point becomes meaningless. For example:

'I have good working knowledge of Word and Excel and some experience of Lotus.'

Compare this with:

● Word, Excel, Lotus.

The first sentence provides more information than the bullet. If you're going to use bullet points, make sure they're meaningful.

Finally it's worth noting that writing complete sentences allows you to show off your communication skills if your spelling and grammar are good.

Top Tips **CV layout and presentation**

- Don't underline headings as it tends to look messy, and headings may also be misread by computer scanners.
- Don't use both sides of the paper. People may forget to photocopy or scan both sides.
- Don't use colour in your CV. It often looks tacky and cannot be photocopied easily.
- Don't put clip-art, cartoons or other illustrations on your CV.
- Do use high-quality paper that is white (other colours may not scan or copy well).
- Do get your CV laser-printed. Using old or cheaper printers is not acceptable now that high-quality laser printers are commonly available.

- If you are sending out photocopies, do ensure that the quality of the copy is excellent (a good copy is almost indistinguishable from an original).
- Don't fold your CV – buy an A4 envelope.

▶ Wacky CVs

You will hear stories of people getting interviews and jobs because they used gimmicky, 'way-out' CVs. There may have been the odd occasion when this approach paid off but these are exceptional cases and we would never recommend them. Don't be tempted, not even for a minute. Some of you might be saying, 'Well, what's wrong with that idea?' or possibly, 'But you haven't read my CV'. Let's look at a few memorable examples.

CV delivered by a bikini-clad woman

If you were going for a job as doorman in the Playboy Club circa 1975, this might just be a good move. Come on! Anyone using a semi-clad woman to advance their application will probably be written off as insensitive and coarse at best, and mysogynist and chauvinist at worst. Think carefully about targeting the particular requirements of the position.

Bank manager's CV set out like a cheque book

When has being a raging individualist been a prerequisite for working in a bank? A recruiter might ask themself why a bank manager needed to use gimmicks: what are they hiding? (And how would I get it in the photocopier?)

Architect's 3-D CV in the form of a house

This is a bit more understandable, but again, the candidate is risking appearing a bit twee or lightweight. And, of course, there are practical problems for recruiters receiving these sorts of CVs. How do they file or copy them easily?

Advertising candidate CV with condom attached

... Please!

Using coloured paper or unusual fonts

In a study we conducted with recruiters, all of them hated the unusual CV we showed them – it was on coloured paper and printed with a strange font. When we presented the same CV on white paper in a standard font, all the recruiters were impressed.

Wacky CVs?
Don't be tempted,
not even for a minute!

▶ Taste test

So, why do recruiters dislike 'wacky' CVs? The answers could fill another book, but there are some examples in life that reinforce this view. Firstly, there is good old taste. A painting by Picasso may be a great work of art to one person, and worse than a child's scribble to another. People's tastes differ. Many people tend to like things that are familiar. They also find them more memorable. It's sobering to recall that in a survey conducted in the UK recently, the most common response to the request to name an artist was 'Rolf Harris'!

Secondly, people's opinions differ. Just think about politics and sport. In most countries there are two or three parties that have widespread support and then lots of 'minority interest' parties. Think about the arguments that rage about the selection of sportsmen and women to national teams. How does all this relate to CVs? All we are saying here is that things that are unusual will attract attention – like a Picasso painting or an unusual decision by a selector – and in return will elicit a reaction, positive or negative. If you don't know how the reader will react, why run the risk of rejection unnecessarily?

In the next chaper, we'll examine briefly the topic of covering letters – what to include and how to structure them.

Chapter nine

Covering
letters

Y ou should write a short covering letter, whether you're posting off a CV or a job application form. In the past it was common practice for employers to ask for a *handwritten* covering letter, but this practice is fast disappearing.

Why a handwritten letter, you may ask? Well, for one thing, it's a good way for the employer to assess the applicant's spelling ability (without the aid of an electronic spellchecker). Also, some employers believe it can reveal the applicant's personality, a science known as graphology (see Chapter 18 for the web address of British Institute of Graphologists). For example, if the person doesn't dot the i's or cross the t's, then this might indicate a sloppy approach to work generally. No doubt many people are relieved that email has restored a level playing field in this respect!

▶ Why is a covering letter necessary?

The cover letter serves several purposes:

● it lets administrative staff know quickly what the correspondence is about
● it's often the first thing an employer reads
● it allows you to say why you are applying
● it sets the tone for the CV.

Many authors suggest you should produce a fairly standard 'one-size-fits-all' CV and direct your efforts into tailoring the cover letter. We don't think this is the best approach – we believe you should tailor the CV for each job. Usually it is the CV that gets more attention, and generally it is the CV that is used as the basis of questions asked in employment interviews (not the covering letter).

Having said that, we wouldn't want to downplay the importance of the covering letter. The cover letter deserves to be given equal attention to the CV. Think of it as a 'sales pitch' to highlight that special quality that makes you stand out from the other applicants. The covering letter should make the employer reach straight for your CV and invite you to the next stage – the interview.

▶ Application letter rules

Here are the basic guidelines for writing a letter of application for a job:

- you must write a new one for each application
- the addressee must be correct – do not cut and paste letters
- the date must be correct
- they should never be more than one page long
- they should be as well laid out as your CV
- unless a handwritten response is specifically asked for, you should type your letters.

Your letter should include the following information:

- your (typed) name, home address, phone and mobile numbers, and email address
- the name of the person to whom you are writing (get this from the job advertisement, or phone the company and ask whom you should address the letter to)
- their job title
- their address
- the initial greeting (for example, 'Dear Ms Smith' or 'Dear Sir')
- in the first sentence:
  - the job you are applying for
  - reference number
  - where you saw the post advertised
- one or two concise sentences summing up relevant experience (e.g. 'I have two years' experience as a call centre operator and enjoy dealing with the public and helping to resolve their problems')

- a couple of sentences outlining why this job is right for you
- your salary, if you are asked to provide this
- your willingness to meet and discuss the opportunity
- your signature and your name typed below it.

The following example will give you a guide.

---

25 Newberry Gardens
Newton Mearns
Glasgow G78 1PG

12 July 2003

Mr Stephen Jones
Sales Director
Jones and Sons Engineering
45 Sunny Street
Glasgow G89 2PL

Dear Mr Brown

Re: Business Development Manager – the *Herald*, 11 July 2003

Your advertisement in the *Herald* on 11 July 2003 was of great interest to me and I believe that my skills and previous experience would make a real contribution to the future plans of your organisation.

The prime focus of my career within business development has included five years as sales manager at Brown and Smith Engineering. I have been responsible for the development of various successful sales strategies on an international level and, heading a team of six, was responsible for achieving at least 250% of budget over the past two consecutive years.

I am particularly interested in this position and would value the opportunity to meet and discuss this application in more detail.

Yours sincerely

[your signature]

John Smith

Enc

Top tips   Covering letters

Always make sure that your covering letter expresses:

- your interest in the project
- your enthusiasm for the job/field/organization
- your knowledge of the subject
- your willingness to meet informally to discuss opportunities that may arise
- your belief that you've got something to offer

. . . and that it glosses over:

- your lack of relevant experience or contacts
- the fact that this would represent a career change for you
- your desperation to get into this field.

Let's now turn our attention to the best way to deliver your CV and the issue of scanned electronic CVs, which demand a slightly different approach.

10

Delivering

your

cv

◗ Posting your CV

A job advertisement will often ask applicants to send in a CV, and will specify whether they wish you to post it to them, along with a covering letter, using the ordinary post office service, or email it.

The popularity of email lies of course in its speed of transmission, and it is undoubtedly the best option if there is an imminent closing date by which applications have to be received.

Always take a photocopy or printout of your complete CV and covering letter before you post them off. You should keep these handy in case you get an unexpected telephone interview (see p. 239). If you've been applying for a number of jobs, it's all too easy to forget the name of the person or company you've written to (or worse still, to get them mixed up) when you receive that all-important phone call, and that could prove a disaster. Also, if you're asked to attend an interview, you should take a copy of your CV and covering letter to jog your memory as to what precisely you highlighted in your application. This is particularly important if you're tailoring each CV to the individual job, as we have suggested.

Always take a copy of your CV
and covering letter
before posting them off.

If you decide to post your CV, it's a good idea to go along to the Post Office and ask to send it Recorded Delivery. It should cost you less than a pound extra (depending on weight), on top of the cost of the first or second class stamp, and gives you peace of mind that someone has to sign for it at the other end. Don't bother registering your application, as this costs a lot more and is only for sending valuables such as money, jewellery, etc. when you can claim monetary compensation. When you use Recorded Delivery, they will give you a Proof of Posting receipt which which has a tracking number printed on it. You can then go to the Royal Mail website (*www.royalmail.com*), to the Track & Trace page where you can key in the reference number and check that it's been delivered. As you've put all that effort into the application, it's well worth the extra money. It will also emphasize to the person who receives it at the other end your keenness for the job and general efficiency.

◗ Electronic CVs

Most recruitment agencies (especially online ones) now ask you to post your CV to them electronically, while some provide a standard online application form with various fields for you to complete, and will give you the option of attaching your own CV to this (see Chapter 11, p. 212 on 'Electronic application forms').

One advantage of this approach for the recruitment agencies is that they can electronically scan CVs, in order to do all the screening automatically. This is a labour-saving innovation which speeds up the process. It is now possible that only a computer will read your CV!

It's now possible that **only a computer** will read your CV!

Tips for CVs that will be scanned

All scanners work on the same principles. They are looking for key words or phrases that have been programmed into the computer. The words that companies scan for are often nouns and proper nouns, for instance, 'Excel' or 'Word' or 'automatic payroll systems'.

If you think it likely that your CV will be scanned electronically, this may be the time to use jargon or specialist language – provided that it is meaningful to people in your own industry. For instance, you might use terms like:

- AI (artificial intelligence)
- HTML (a computer programming language)
- ROI (return on investment)
- WYSIWYG (what you see is what you get).

Top Tip **Electronic CVs**

Use lots of nouns and keywords in your CV to increase the chances that scanners will pick up on them: see p. 193 for suggestions.

Format is also important for scanned CVs. Layout should be clear and easy for a scanner to read. The use of headings can assist here – remember, where you might otherwise refrain from using a heading for fear of insulting your reader's intelligence, computers do not have feelings, so spell everything out for them!

Headings such as the following may be useful:

- Experience
- Education
- Qualifications
- Work history
- Positions held
- Affiliations
- References.

The computer programs used to read your CV are becoming increasingly sophisticated, and therefore it is a canny idea to use some keywords to describe your personal qualities here too. Refer back to the job ad for the particular qualities they're looking for. You might also consider using some of the following:

- commitment
- communicator
- dynamic
- energetic
- experienced
- initiative
- innovative
- intelligent
- leader or leadership
- logical
- motivated
- outgoing
- persuasive
- reliable
- self-starter
- skilled
- sociable
- team player

Unusual fonts are never a good idea, as we discussed in the previous chapters, especially when the CV might be scanned. The 'safest' in terms of computer compatibility are Times New Roman and Arial. The font size should be in the normal letter range of 10 to 14 point. Although earlier we suggested that an 18–20 point font for your name, err on the side of caution if you think the CV is going to be scanned and use a smaller font.

When you write your telephone and mobile numbers, list each one on a separate line, as a scanner may read numbers on the same line as one number. This will cause difficulties for people who subsequently look you up on a computer database when they want to contact you. Underlining can make scanning more difficult, and doesn't look appealing generally, so avoid it.

The layout also affects the number of characters per line. In general, keep to no more than 70 to 80 characters per line, or scanning programs may reproduce the CV with some lines wrapped around onto the next line, causing the formatting to be messed up.

Avoid using columns like a newspaper. Start each new piece of information on a new line, fully aligned to the left. Look back at the Chapter 8 for some more tips on layout.

Don't put lines, pictures or graphics on your CV, as these will confuse the scanner.

Finally, if you are 'snail mailing' your CV to the employer via ordinary post, avoid folding it to fit the envelope. Put the CV in an appropriately sized envelope, and preferably one that has a reinforced cardboard back, to help prevent creasing.

▶ Emailing CVs

As an alternative to mailing your CV, some employers are now happy to receive them electronically via email. This can speed up the recruitment process and can save money too. If you are applying for a job that requires some IT knowledge, then sending your CV by email will demonstrate that you are familiar with this type of technology.

There are a few pointers to take into consideration. First, as with scanned CVs, you should keep to a maximum of 70 to 80 characters per line. Any more and you risk losing the formatting.

You should send the CV as an attachment. Don't be tempted to copy and paste it into the body of the email – you will lose most of the formatting. Remember, even though you may have a fancy email program that allows you to include formatting and graphics in the message body, the majority of email programs do not allow this, and all you will do is send an unintelligible mess to your prospective employer.

Always send your CV as an attachment to an email – **never cut and paste it in,** or you'll lose most of the formatting.

If you do decide to attach the CV as a file, you need to consider carefully what word processing program you're going to use to generate the CV and, just as importantly, what version of the program you are going to use. Many large-scale commercial companies hold back from buying the very latest version of a piece of software because of cost, and to ensure that the new version is bug-free.

Often the job ad will specify which programs are acceptable and which are not. If there are no guidelines, phone the company and ask. If this is not possible, the safest bet is to send a PC compatible file (not a Mac file), using Microsoft Word, Version 6 for Windows 95. It is a slightly older version, which means most people should be able to read it. Another safe bet is to save and send the file as 'Text only', but you will lose all your formatting by doing this, and you have to ask whether you are losing more than you are gaining by sending your CV by email.

CVs sent electronically may not be as secure as those sent by conventional mail. If your application is very sensitive, this point needs considering. Many companies now routinely monitor their employees' email and Net usage, making this a less confidential medium. One solution is to get your own email account. Many companies are now offering these free of charge. Alternatively, you could visit one of the internet cafés and booths that are springing up in shopping centres, airports and high streets around the world. They will often provide a suitable service and may be able to assist you if you are unsure how the email process works.

Email is an easy and quick way to send things off. Resist the temptation to compose your CV and mail it off immediately. Many of us have had that sinking feeling just after we have hit the send button that we have sent the wrong version, sent it to the wrong person, or have included a glaring error. Always print off a copy of your CV and have someone else read it for errors before mailing or emailing it.

Always print off a copy of your CV and **have someone else read it** for typos before mailing or emailing it.

▶ Web page CVs

Another innovation is the web page as a CV. These fall into two categories: (a) individuals who build a personal web page and bring it to the employer's attention; and (b) companies that allow you to enter your details either into their standard CV proforma or by cutting and pasting your file onto their site. The CV is then indexed and stored on their site, for future employers to search through.

Personal web pages demonstrate the remarkable things that people will reveal about themselves that they'd never dream of including in a professional document!

Employers are generally not interested in 'meeting the babies', 'looking at my boat', or 'sitting in my front room'. If you intend to set up your web page as a substitute CV, then you must apply the same levels of professionalism as you would to a conventional CV. The key difference with a web page CV is that you can include far more information, provided it is appropriately indexed and the site is easily navigable. However, the initial key pages of the site should convey all the critical information of a conventional CV. Use the extra potential of a website for additional optional information in links that employers can choose to follow.

Website CVs become public documents, which potentially can be accessed by anyone, including your current boss! Do you really want all your personal details laid out for everyone to see?

Before we move on to the next stage of the recruitment process – the interview – let's just take a look at how to fill in an application form if this is sent to you electronically or by mail.

> The closest to perfection
> a person ever comes is when
> he fills out a
> job application form.
>
> **Stanley J. Randall**

11

Application

forms

▶ Why do employers use them?

If you have prepared a good CV then you should have no trouble applying the same principles to an application form. Application forms are tailored in response to employers' specific requirements with the overall aim of easily identifying relevant information and suitable candidates. Employers want to be able to extract the same information from an application form as they would from a good CV, namely:

- skills
- achievements
- relevance.

As many as 95 percent of CVs received by employers in response to a vacancy advertisement will contain irrelevant information – imagine how long it would take to screen 100 of these CVs searching for the information that is important? For this reason many employers choose to use application forms to make the process of selecting candidates for interview a more structured and focused exercise, allowing every candidate to be screened on the same level and in direct comparison with each other. Application forms will also allow the employer to ask for information not normally included on a CV, as well as attracting only candidates who are seriously interested in the job due to the time it takes to complete a good application.

Application forms **allow every candidate** to be screen on the same level and in **direct comparison** with each other.

While the application form process is designed to make candidate selection easier for employers, it's not so user-friendly towards potential employees. It requires time and effort to complete an application form to the best of your ability and the process is as demanding each and every time you complete one.

Before you start completing the form, take the time to carefully read through any instructions, for example:

- Use black ink and complete in block capitals.
- Take a photocopy of the original to use as your draft copy.
- Ensure you have a copy of the original job advertisement, your CV and any additional information available on the organization such as website information, company brochure etc.
- Answer every question. If the question does not apply to you, then write n/a (not applicable) in the box or section to show that you have not accidentally omitted answering the question.

Remember to think about the presentation of your application form, do a dummy run on a photocopy of a blank form so you can see how to fill the space provided. Rule faint pencil lines to ensure you write in a neat straight line. It is up to you whether you write in sentences or bullet points but in general, if you are pushed for space, stick to bullet points.

Let's take a look at a sample application form and discuss the key sections.

Glasgow City Council

PLEASE COMPLETE ALL DETAILS IN BLOCK CAPITALS USING BLACK INK

SECTION 1 – DETAILS OF VACANCY

Job title _____	Department _____

Reference number	Closing date
From what source did you learn of vacancy? If job centre, please state which:	Please give details of any dates during next six weeks when you would not be available for interview.

SECTION 2 – PERSONAL DETAILS

Surname _____ Forename(s) _____

Address _____

_____

Postcode _____

Home tel _____ Mobile _____ Work tel _____

Driving licence   Yes/No

Leisure interests

_____

_____

_____

_____

_____

_____

_____

_____

_____

SECTION 3 – EQUAL OPPORTUNITIES

The following information is required in order that equal opportunity policies can be monitored effectively. The aim of the policy is to ensure that no job applicant receives less favourable treatment on the grounds of race, disability, sex or age.

Date of birth _____ Age _____ Sex _____ Male/Female _____

Are you disabled? _____ Are you registered? _____

If you answered Yes above, please give brief details _____

_____

_____

Please describe your racial or ethnic origin UK/European _____ Indian _____

Pakistan _____ African/Caribbean _____

Other (please specify) _____

SECTION 4 – EDUCATION DETAILS

Dates (from/to)	School/College/University	Qualifications gained	Grade

SECTION 5 – TRAINING COURSES

Attendance at training courses relevant to your employment

Organising body	Course title	Duration	Date

SECTION 6 – MEMBERSHIP OF PROFESSIONAL BODIES

Body	Grade of membership	Whether by exam	Date

SECTION 7 EMPLOYMENT HISTORY

(starting with most recent)

Dates (from/to)	Employer's name and address	Job title and brief description of duties

Salary on leaving £ _____   Notice period _____

Reason for leaving _____

Previous employment

Dates (from/to)	Employer's name and address	Job title and brief description of duties

Salary on leaving £ _____   Notice period _____

Reason for leaving _____

Dates (from/to)	Employer's name and address	Job title and brief description of duties

Salary on leaving £ _____ Notice period _____

Reason for leaving _____

SECTION 8 – RELEVANT INFORMATION

Other relevant information and experience

The information you provide in this section is important in assessing your application. Please use this space to state your reasons for applying for the post, relating your skills, experience and personal qualities to the requirements of the job. You may include relevant details of the following: gaps in paid employment, unpaid work experience, voluntary activities, leisure interests and positions of responsibility held.

If you require more space please attach a separate sheet.

SECTION 9 – REFERENCES

Give the names of two persons to whom reference may be made in respect of your application. The first should be your last employer (or head teacher if school leaver). Referees are only contacted if candidates are to be interviewed, but if you do not wish a referee to be contacted until after a provisional offer of employment is made, please indicate in the appropriate box.

Reference 1 – present employer

Name	
Address	
Position	
Telephone number	
Contact prior to offer	Yes/No (please circle)

Reference 2 – previous employer

Name	
Address	
Position	
Telephone number	
Contact prior to offer	Yes/No (please circle)

SECTION 10 – DECLARATION

I declare that the information given in this application is true and that I have not withheld any information that might reasonably affect my suitability for employment with Glasgow City Council.

Signed _____   Date _____

▶ Key sections

Details of vacancy

Almost every application form will contain details of the vacancy some-where near to the beginning of the form. Local government, hospitals, civil service positions will usually use application forms in their recruitment process. They are likely to conduct ongoing recruitment over a wide variety of departments and for this reason the primary recruiter (usually an HR professional) needs to determine quickly which post you're applying for. If you are unsure exactly what to include, relate back to the original job advertisement, which should contain the details you're seeking.

Personal details

The personal details section normally contains exactly the same informa-tion you would expect to find in a CV: your name, your address and how to contact you. It may also ask for your date of birth, although anti-age dis-crimination laws are due to be introduced in 2006 to comply with a European Union directive.

If asked driving questions in this section, state your current situation. If, for example, you are currently learning to drive or have a test date booked, then say so. If you are asked if you have a clean licence, be honest or it may come back to haunt you later.

Equal opportunities

Many employers monitor their recruitment and selection process to ensure that they are operating a fair equal opportunities programme. The infor-mation supplied in this section will not be used as part of the selection process and is designed to protect you against discrimination.

Education details

Unless specifically asked for, only supply details that relate to your education from secondary school onwards.

Training courses

This section is a good way to make you stand out during the application process. If you have been fortunate enough to undertake training courses with your present and previous employers then include details in this section.

Membership of professional bodies

This section is designed for professional membership bodies relating to your employment history, e.g. IPD, ACCA, SIMA etc. This isn't the place to mention that you belong to the local Bridge club!

Employment history

The employment history section, as in a CV, is designed to indicate to an employer whether you can do the job. Before completing this section, take some time out to read the job advertisement again and relate your experience to the job description. Remember to highlight the experience that is relevant to the post you're applying for. Use recognizable job titles and ensure that your dates follow in a chronological manner; be sure to look out for any gaps in your employment history and include them in the form, e.g. May 82 – August 90: career break to look after children.

Salary on leaving

While we do not recommend including your salary details in a CV, there is little you can do to avoid the question when included in an application form. If you choose to omit the information, it will be very apparent to an employer and it could be the difference between getting an interview or not.

If you received any additional emoluments on top of your basic pay (e.g. commission, annual bonus, share options, company car, membership of a company healthcare insurance scheme), then don't forget to mention this here too. These may prove to be useful bargaining chips if you are later offered the job and want to negotiate your salary package (see Chapter 19).

Reason for leaving

No matter what your reason for leaving a previous position, always try to reflect your decision-making process in a positive manner. You might, for example, have left a previous organization because you 'felt under-appreciated', but rather than include this as the reason, it would read so much better if you stated your reasons as something like 'to obtain better prospects with more responsibility'.

Relevant information

This section is the most important part of the application form. It's where you get the opportunity to highlight your skills and achievements to an employer and make them relevant to the position you are applying for, as well as personalizing the section to you. In the same way you use your CV as a sales brochure to highlight your abilities, this whole section is your chance to sell your skills and achievements to an employer.

Reasons for applying

Always the most difficult question! What are your reasons for looking for another job? Perhaps you want more responsibility and feel that this position could offer you the career progression that you are seeking. In that case you could open your narrative with the statement:

> 'Having worked in a secretarial role for the past six years, I am now seeking a position that can offer me career progression to the next level within a large organization. I feel that the position of Senior Secretary within the

Planning Department of Glasgow City Council offers the key characteristics I seek, namely (a) career progression, (b) more responsibility and (c) the ability to work closely within a small team.'

Examine your reasons for wanting to leave your current position as they will provide the pointers as to why you feel this position is right for you.

It is likely that you will rewrite this section several times on a draft piece of paper before you are happy with the final result. Aim to fill at least three-quarters of the page and ensure that your handwriting is clear and legible. Use a ruler if you feel you have the tendency to slant off in a particular direction. Check your spelling.

Referees

See Chapter 7, p. 172, for advice on choosing the right referee.

▶ What else should I send off with the application form?

- **Don't** include your CV unless you are specifically asked to do so (you may be asked to attach a CV to an electronic application form; see below). If you feel you need more space to sell your abilities, then attach a separate sheet of paper, clearly marking at the top of the page your name, address, telephone number, email address and position applied for.

- **Don't** include a photo of yourself (Chapter 7, p. 171 gives the reasons why this is a bad idea).

- **Do** include a covering letter with your application form (see Chapter 9).

Keep a copy of the application form to help you prepare for interview and post the original off to the employer in an A4 envelope at least three days prior to the closing date. If you are unsure whether the application will arrive in time, then consider delivering by hand or using a guaranteed next-day delivery service (see p. 191).

▶ Electronic application forms

The guidelines given above on the best way to complete an application form apply generally, whether you are sent a paper application form to complete or whether you obtain the application form online. Some recruitment agencies give you the option to download a proforma, print it off, before completing it in pen and mailing it back to them; alternatively you may prefer to complete it electronically and email it back. Either way, make sure to print off copies for your own reference in case you're invited for an interview.

You may find that you have a little less space and flexibility with an online electronic application form than with a paper one, so make sure to be as precise as possible to highlight your greatest strengths. You may choose to use bullet points rather than full sentences in an online application form, as this should give you more room to include relevant information.

You may have **less space with** an online application form, so be as precise as possible to highlight **your greatest strengths.**

You may also be asked to attach your own CV to the email/online application form. This will give you the opportunity to fill in some more details if space has been very restricted. See Chapter 10, p. 194, for further information on emailing CVs.

The advice on not attaching a photo of yourself (see Chapter 7, p. 171) applies particularly to electronic job applications. In addition to the possibility of the photo being used in a discriminatory fashion, it could also hit a firewall installed by the receiving company and be instantly deleted.

▶ On your marks, get set … go!

So now you've presented your strengths, skills, abilities and experience via a CV and/or application form. You've tailored it to the specific application, along with the covering letter, so as to highlight the closeness of the fit between you and the job. You've taken a copy before sending it off well before the closing date for applications, maybe by email or by Recorded Delivery.

And now you just have to wait for the response. Don't expect that you'll be lucky with the very first application, sometimes it can take a while without getting any positive responses. Sometimes it's like buses – you wait for ages and then two or three come along together!

> Success is that old ABC –
> Ability, Breaks and Courage
>
> **Charles Luckman**

Part **three**

Proving
yourself

Chapter twelve

Interviews

Well done! The interviewer started out with a pile of applications which have been sifted through and slimmed down to the people whom they are inviting for interview – including you.

The interviewer isn't going to invite anyone whom they don't reckon can do the job, so the list of interviewees will be made up entirely of well-qualified people. Once again, you should be encouraged by this. You have arrived at the interview stage because of the time and effort you have successfully put into the job-hunting process so far.

But the interviewer has a problem. They are spoilt for choice. They have a list of maybe half a dozen or a dozen applicants, all of whom they think ought to be able to do the job. So whom do they offer it to? They need more information before they can decide, and that's what the interviews are for.

The interviewer has to decide which of the candidates is going to be most suited to the job. They aren't trying to measure you against each other, but against the standards for the job itself. One of you may be far more experienced than another, but experience may not be the most important thing. Perhaps fitting in with the team will matter more, or skill using a particular piece of software.

Even so, it's going to be a hard choice. All the candidates will have strong and weak points, and the interviewer will have to balance these the one against the other. Do they want someone who has long experience, or would they rather go for someone with shorter but more relevant experience? What if the person with the least appropriate qualifications looks as if they'll fit in best with the company culture? Should they opt for the person who looks reliable and solid, or the more creative candidate who seems less reliable?

It's tough being an interviewer. And it's tough for you too, because you know less about what they're looking for than they do. However, even if you don't know what their priorities are, you know broadly what they're after. And if you know where your strengths and weaknesses are, you can prepare to promote your strong points and find ways of making your weak spots look less like weaknesses.

▶ Preparing responses for the interview

If you simply walk into the interview and answer each question as it's asked, without having done any preparation, you'll probably put on a fairly decent show. But if you really want this job, that's not enough. You have no idea how tough the competition is. If it's fairly weak, an unprepared interview might still get you the job. But what if it's strong? A missed opportunity – something you might have said but forgot to mention – might tip the balance against you.

Top Tip for interviews

Before you get to the interview, prepare a mental list of all the most important points you want to make – all the things that will convince the interviewer that you are the best person for the job.

You've already assessed yourself to establish what your key strengths are. You're going to want to drive these home. If your strengths can be objectively measured – qualifications, skill at using particular equipment, that sort of thing – simply telling the interviewer that you possess them will be sufficient. But some strengths – such as experience or diplomacy skills, for example – will need to be illustrated with examples. So think of examples in advance of the interview.

Suppose you consider diplomacy to be one of your key skills. And your objective tells you that it is one of the things you have to persuade your interviewer that you are good at. When they ask you about it (and they will if it's one of their key requirements for the job), it's not enough simply to assure them that it's something you're good at. Even if it was important in your last job, that doesn't prove you were good at that part of the job.

No, you need to give them strong examples of your key strengths during the interview. Tell them about the time an angry customer stormed into the store throwing tomatoes at all the staff, and you calmed them down. Or about the time the entire team of delivery drivers was about to stage a walk-out, until you talked to them. Tell them about both if you get the chance.

Give them **strong examples of your key strengths** during the interview.

You may be able to think of an example to illustrate your strengths on the spot when you're asked. But if you prepare in advance, you won't just come up with *any* example, you'll come up with the best, and the most relevant to the job you're applying for.

So that's your basic list of strengths. You will also need to go through the job description in much the same way, finding examples to demonstrate that you have experience in all the key areas of responsibility. If you don't have a copy of the job description (which would normally be sent out with the application form), phone the interviewer's office and ask them to send you one. It's standard practice, so they won't mind being asked.

▶ Preparing a portfolio

Your interviewer might be interested to see some evidence to back up any strengths and experience that you tell them about. While they are unlikely to expect to see anything other than perhaps proof of qualifications, they may well be impressed by anything else you can offer them such as:

- testimonials from satisfied customers, suppliers or employers
- copies of key reports you've written
- examples of past work

- press cuttings you've generated
- press articles about events you've organized.

So find anything you can which will help to persuade them that you really *are* as good as you look, and take it along. Clearly it's not a good idea to turn up at the interview pushing a wheelbarrow of stuff in front of you. Take what's portable, and will fit into a neat folder – or a portfolio if it involves a lot of design or artwork. Then let the interviewer know what else you could send them – or bring to a second interview – if they want to see it.

Choose examples that will convey the broad range of your work – particularly if you work in a creative field such as advertising. This will demonstrate your flexibility and responsiveness to different client needs. The Gestalt Principle of Proximity that we discussed in relation to CVs works here too (see p. 164). For example, you may have worked as one member of a large creative team on an advertising campaign, but that shouldn't stop you bringing along a copy of the final product.

Be ready to explain the background to your portfolio. To return to the advertising example, this might be involve highlighting the main requirements voiced by the client (in terms of product, slogan, target market, type of media carrying the advert, budget, etc.). Then how the finished advert fulfilled these requirements, and how sucessful the campaign was (make sure you pick a success story). Of course, you'll also need to explain your own contribution to the success.

▶ Be prepared

You know what you want to say at the interview now and what you are intending to take along. Whatever questions the interviewer puts to you, there are certain key points that you want to get across and which you have prepared. But how long have you got to say them? Have you got to cram your key selling points into 15 minutes, or have you got an hour to bring them out slowly, one by one?

The only way you can find out the answer to this is by asking. So you need to contact your interviewer's office (preferably at the same time as any other requests you have to make) and simply ask, 'Please could you tell me how much time has been allocated to my interview?' Again, it's a totally reasonable question, and one they should be happy to answer.

You now have all the advance information you need, and all your preparation is in place. The final step is to be ready for the interview on the day itself. And you can start by being on time. It doesn't matter how early you arrive – you can always find the building and then go for a walk, for lunch or for a browse in the local shops so you don't arrive at reception too soon. But being as little as two or three minutes late may matter a lot – especially if your interviewer turns out to be a stickler for good time-keeping.

Of course, you can imagine scenarios where no amount of forward planning could have got you to the interview on time. But unless the reason is highly dramatic, you interviewer doesn't want to hear excuses. They just want you to be there on time. Leave plenty of time to get there.

Top Tips Interview checklist

- Find out how long the journey should take beforehand and add on at least another half-hour as a safety margin. You can't afford to be even a few minutes late.

- Take with you the letter inviting you to the interview, with the time on it, and any directions you've been sent.

- Don't forget a foldaway umbrella if the weather looks threatening.

- Enquire about parking if you're travelling by car and think it could be a problem.

- Take a mobile phone, or money for phone calls, in case you need to ring for directions. Then if you do still run late, despite all your precautions, at least you can phone ahead and let them know what's happening.

- Take your portfolio materials if relevant and a notepad and pen for jotting down notes during the interview.
- Take the list of questions you have prepared for the interviewer.
- Fit everything you're carrying into a smart briefcase; don't arrive with plastic bags as it leaves a poor impression. If you want to do shopping, leave it until after the interview.

▶ First impressions

Your interviewer will form a frighteningly large part of their opinion of you on the basis of a very small proportion of the time they spend with you. In fact, the first few moments will tell them a great deal about you, whether you like it or not. Your best defence against this, of course, is to make sure you send out the right messages.

From the way you dress to the way you say hello, you can prepare yourself to give the best possible first impression. In fact, why not start before you even get to the day of the interview? You can influence your interviewer's opinion:

- before the interview
- in the way you dress
- by the way you greet them.

When surveyed, interviewers cited the following among the key factors that impress them about a candidate:

- strong handshake
- being smartly and appropriately dressed.

Factors that impress them least included:

- lateness
- sloppy appearance
- poor grooming
- too much perfume or aftershave.

▶ What are you going to wear?

Knowing how to dress for an interview isn't that easy. Time was, you put on your best suit and tie, or your smartest tailored dress or skirt suit, and you knew you looked the part. Things aren't so simple any more. A smart, formal outfit just won't look right in an organization where the workforce all wear jeans and T-shirts. The interviewer will think, 'Very smart. They'll never fit in here.'

According to research, as much as 70 percent of employee turnover is due to staff not fitting in with the corporate culture, rather than an inability to do the job in terms of skills or experience. So your interviewer wants to see that you will fit in if they offer you the job. The way you dress is only a part of this, of course, but it is a large part of the interviewer's first impression of whether or not you're 'one of us'.

As much as **70 percent of employee** turnover is due to staff **not fitting in with** the corporate culture.

So you need to know what the dress code is at the organization you're applying to. That way you can pick an appropriate outfit. You may well have a pretty clear idea of what the dress code is likely to be; it is often fairly consistent across whole industries. Design and media companies tend to dress casually, accountancy firms are likely to dress smarter. If you're changing jobs within your own industry, the odds are you'll be pretty clear about the usual style.

But what if this is an industry you're not so sure about? There are several options:

- If you're lucky enough to know someone who works for the organization – or simply knows them as a supplier or a customer perhaps – you can ask their advice.

- If the organization is based nearby, turn up at lunchtime or going home time and watch people leaving the building to see what they are all wearing.
- Look through sales brochures and annual reports for photos of management and staff.

But failing all that, the answer is the same as usual: ask. When you're phoning your contact – the interviewer, their assistant or their secretary – ask them what the company dress code is. As always, they won't mind being asked, they'll be impressed at your initiative.

So what to wear, then? Just because you've found out what the regular employees wear, doesn't mean you're going to wear the same thing yourself. Sorry – it's not quite that simple. After all, you're not a regular employee (yet); you're an interviewee who needs to look as if they're making an extra effort. So dress a notch or two above the employees – look like they would if they were making an effort.

So for men:

If they wear ...	You wear ...
Casual	Smart casual
Smart casual	Casual suit
Casual suit (e.g. shirtsleeves, or no tie)	Casual suit with a jacket and tie
Smart suit	Smart suit

And for women:

If they wear ...	You wear...
Casual	Smart casual (e.g. trousers, but not jeans)
Smart casual	Smart
Smart	Smart

That makes it look a little simpler for women. In a sense it is, because there's more of a sliding scale. For men, either it's OK to remove your jacket, for example, or it isn't. But the point is the same: dress a notch or two above the people you'll be passing in the corridor when you go to the interview, unless they're already formally dressed, in which case you need only match them (rather than turning up in full evening dress).

Whatever you do, don't go out and buy a new outfit for your interview, unless you have plenty of time to break it in first. You need to be comfortable and relaxed, concentrating on the conversation, not on the zip that you've just discovered sticks into you painfully, or the waistband which felt fine when you tried the thing on in the shop, but turns out to be much too tight when you sit down. Pick clothes that are clean and smart, and relatively new, but ones that you know are comfortable and problem-free.

When it comes to the specifics of the outfit you choose to wear, here are a few more pointers you may find useful:

Top Tips **How to dress for interviews**

- Don't let your appearance overpower your personality. It's you applying for this job, not your clothes.
- Avoid any extremes of fashion.
- Choose an outfit that won't crease unduly.
- Avoid strong perfume or aftershave.
- Don't wear too much jewellery, or jewellery that is too large.
- Avoid large patterns in bright colours, unless restricted to a small area such as a tie or scarf.
- Dark colours will lend you more authority than pale ones.

When you arrive for the interview – a few minutes early – ask the receptionist to direct you to somewhere where you can freshen up. Tidy your hair and check your clothes, and double check your:

- teeth (especially if you've been eating)
- nose
- jewellery (especially earrings for women)
- zips and buttons (especially flies for men)
- shirt or blouse (make sure they are tucked in)
- make-up.

If you're a woman, it may be worth taking a spare pair of tights in case they ladder. If you're a man, it's worth bringing along a spare tie in case you spill food or drink down the first one. Alternatively, don't put your tie on until you reach the building.

▶ Interview behaviour

As well as the way you look, the way you greet the interviewer will be an important part of the first impression you create. So be ready to exude warmth and confidence as soon as you see them.

Top Tips **Making your entrance**

- Smile.
- Make eye contact with the interviewer.
- Offer a hand to shake as soon as they introduce themselves.
- Say 'Hello', 'Pleased to meet you', or whatever phrase you feel easy with.
- Shake hands firmly (you can practise your handshake with a friend) – with all the interviewers if there is more than one.
- Wait to be invited before sitting down.

The interviewer will generally chat for a minute or two at the start to put you at your ease. Be responsive, but remember that neither of you is here to chat. So when they ask, for example, how your journey was, they don't want a blow-by-blow account of it. A friendly but brief response will do fine. And if by any chance it was horrendous, express the fact (if you mention it at all) with humour rather than sounding like a whinger.

Many interviewers want an informal second opinion on candidates from one or more members of their team (after all, they'll have to work with whoever gets the job). So they may ask a team member to greet you at reception, give you a cup of coffee, or conduct you from reception to the interview room – and back again afterwards. In other words, you need to make as good a first impression as you can on everyone you meet – including the receptionist – because you don't know which of them may have an input into the final selection.

You need to make a **good first impression on** everyone you meet – including the receptionist.

A couple of words of words of warning. It never helps your image to smoke in an interview, and it often harms it. Even if your interviewer is a smoker and offers you a cigarette, decline it. Smoking can give you an air of being too informal, laid back and relaxed. Alternatively, a cigarette may make you appear nervous and neurotic; again, this is not an image you want to create.

Similarly, don't be tempted to have a quick drink prior to an interview to 'calm your neves'. Even one drink can be detectable on your breath and could set alarm bells ringing in the mind of the interviewer.

◗ Essential qualities

There are a few essential qualities you need to project, which we'll look at now.

Be responsive

Make an effort to give full (but not rambling) answers to your interviewer's questions, and to volunteer relevant information. Don't give one-word answers – they sound sullen and unhelpful, even if that's not your intention. So if they say, 'I see you trained originally in marketing?' don't just say, 'Yes'. Answer, for example, 'Yes, I did. But in my first marketing job I did a lot of PR work, and particularly enjoyed the press side of it, so I decided to specialize in press relations.'

Don't give one-word answers – they sound **sullen and unhelpful.**

Be confident

You may be feeling anything but confident, but confidence is an attractive quality in an employee, so you need to show you have it. Research shows that interviewers just don't like giving jobs to people who put themselves down. Of course, this doesn't mean you should be pushy and arrogant, but don't apologize for yourself. If your interviewer says, 'So it's two years since you did any actual face-to-face selling', don't say, 'I'm afraid so'. Say something like, 'It is, but I always feel it's one of those skills that you never lose once you've learnt it.' If you don't give the impression of believing in yourself, then no one else will.

Be energetic

People who project life and energy come across as so much more positive, capable and even inspiring than those who seem flat and sluggish. So stay upbeat, sit up straight, speak clearly and make eye contact (with all your interviewers if there's more than one).

Be enthusiastic

This is closely related to being energetic, and goes alongside it. We've seen that enthusiasm towards the job and the company is important to interviewers (yes, I know it was number five on the list, but they were all important). The best way to transmit this enthusiasm is by seeming interested in what both you and the interviewer are saying. If you genuinely are interested, you shouldn't find this too difficult – just make sure you let it show.

Body language

The way you come across visually can be as important as the way you come across verbally. And in fact, your body language can affect your verbal communication too. Here's an interesting exercise for you.

Cause and effect exercise

- Sit on a chair and fold your arms.
- Cross your legs.
- Slump in the chair.
- Now imagine you're at an interview and the interviewer is sitting in front of you. Don't look at them – stare at the floor instead.
- Don't allow yourself to use any facial expressions.
- Now answer out loud the question 'What do you enjoy most about your present job?'

That was Part 1 of the Exercise. Now for Part 2;

- Relax with your hands in your lap.
- Put both feet on the floor.

- Don't slump but lean forward slightly.
- Look straight at your imaginary interviewer.
- Smile.
- Now answer out loud the quesiton 'What do you enjoy the most about your present job?'

You should find that there is a marked difference in your tone as you answer the question using these two, very different physical approaches. When you adopt positive, upbeat body language (Part 2, as I'm sure you realize) your whole tone lifts, and sounds more confident, energetic and enthusiastic – all the qualities you'll need to project.

You'll find that the cause and effect can work both ways. If you are positive and upbeat, your body language will largely follow. Or start with the body language – get that right and you will *become* more positive and upbeat.

So it's worth knowing what the optimum body language signals are, but don't get hung up on them. If you're projecting the right qualities, and feeling the appropriate emotions, the body language will follow naturally. But if you sense that you are flagging, that you sound less positive than you would like to, you can monitor your body language and adapt it to lift your mood and your verbal tone.

So what are the essential points of body language to project during an interview? Look at our Top Tips:

Top Tips Watch your body language

- Make frequent eye contact with the interviewer. If there is more than one of them, make eye contact with them all but look chiefly at whichever one asked the question you are answering. This is the most important thing to remember.

- Don't perch on the edge of your chair. Sit well back in it – unless it's a very deep, upholstered chair in which case there's a danger of looking too relaxed if you get lost right in the back of it!
- Sit with both feet on the floor, leaning slightly towards the interviewer.
- Smile readily.
- Don't hide your face with your hands.
- Don't give off defensive signals by crossing your arms and your legs.
- Try to keep your hands still except when you're gesturing. Don't play with your hair or put your hands in your pockets.

Make frequent eye contact
with your interviewer.
If there is more than one interviewer,
make eye contact with
all of them.

▶ The interview

Let's recap on the format that the interview is likely to take:

1   After an initial brief chat, the interviewer will ask you questions from a general list that all candidates are being asked.

2   Then they will ask you questions arising from your own particular application. The questions, obviously, will form the bulk of the interview, and we'll be looking at them in more detail soon.

3   After this, the interviewer will probably tell you a bit more about the organization and the job.

4   Finally, they will ask for your questions.

Knowing what to expect is a big help. But you still need to know how to handle the interview professionally in general terms. So we'll take a look at the broad points of your interview style, the sort of questions to be ready for, and how to deal with different types of interview such as panel or telephone interviews. Finally, making a good exit is almost as important as making a good entrance, so we'll see how to wind up an interview cleanly and smartly.

▶ Interview style

Apart from answering the questions as positively as you can, there are a few other skills that will help to impress your interviewer (or avoid putting them off you). The *manner* in which you answer questions can be as important as the answers you give, so you need to deliver the whole package.

- Make sure you speak clearly, and answer questions without mumbling. Good body language and eye contact will help you to do this naturally.

- Don't interrupt the interviewer – even if they interrupt you.

- Apart from asking for clarification of a question if you need to, avoid asking more than a few brief questions during the interview. This is the interviewer's time to question *you* – you'll get a chance to ask them questions later on.

- Adopt a similar tone to that of the interviewer. If they are very formal, you need to follow suit. Be very wary of anything more than gentle humour unless your interviewer is injecting a lot of humour into the conversation (in which case, laugh politely at their jokes).

- Don't ask questions about salary at a first interview. It looks as though you're only interested in the money. If they offer you the job, there'll be plenty of time to discuss the salary later (negotiating your starting package is covered in Chapter 19).

Don't ask questions about salary **at a first interview.** It looks as though **you're only** interested in the money.

▶ Responding positively

We'll be dealing with specific interview questions in the next chapter but there are certain general guidelines for answering any question which you'll need to follow. All of these are aimed at giving the interviewer a positive view of you as someone who is confident, capable and honest.

- **Don't ramble.** Aim for all your answers to be no longer than 2 minutes, but many should be far shorter of course. At the other extreme – as we've already seen – try to avoid one-word answers unless your interviewer is clearly asking for clarification only (for example, 'So you're 18 now or 19?').

- **Use examples.** Give plenty of specific examples of your achievements, challenges and successes. Be prepared to back up every assertion, and demonstrate every skill or achievement, with a concrete example.

- **Remember the job description.** Keep your answers specific to the job in question. If your interviewer asks you, for example, what your greatest strength is, pick one that will be important in this job – and give an example of it.

- **Pause if you need to.** If you want to think for a moment before you start answering a question, that's fine. It shows you're considering it carefully.

- **Don't lie.** Be as honest as you can in your answers. You can – and should – put a positive spin on the truth, but don't change the facts. This includes admitting if you don't know the answer to a question, rather than floundering.

- **Don't criticize your present employer.** If you're new to the job market, don't denigrate your tutor or your college course. It can make you look negative and picky (the interviewer may wonder what the other side of the story is), and it will certainly make your interviewer question your loyalty.

You'll be interested to know what the experts consider the key 'dos and don'ts' of handling interviews. So here is a list of top points from a leading career management consultancy.

Top Tips Answering questions at interview

Dos:

- Answer the question that is asked and don't volunteer irrelevant information.
- Keep your answers concise and concentrate on the facts, not opinions.
- Speak clearly and confidently and don't allow yourself to be discouraged.
- Constantly remind yourself that you have something to sell and focus on how you can make a positive contribution in the role.
- Try to use examples to back up your answers.

Don'ts:

- Waffle.
- Try to be too clever.
- Lie, pretend or give evasive answers.
- Lose your temper, get flustered, panic.
- Criticize your former employers.

▶ Types of questions

As well as the specific and sometimes tricky questions covered in the next chapter, there are general types of questions you'll need to be prepared for. Here's a quick rundown:

- **Hypothetical questions.** These ask, 'If x happened, what would you do?' The thing to recognize is that there isn't necessarily a right answer. The interviewer may be more interested in how you go about addressing the problem than in your final outcome. It's fine to pause and think for a moment before you answer.

- **Technical questions.** If you are being interviewed for a technical post, be ready for questions that ask you to take the interviewer through a problem or process. This may be a hypothetical situation they set, or they may ask you to give an example from your own experience and take them through it in detail.

- **Stress questions.** Some interviewers will deliberately try to rile you or put you under pressure as a test. They want to see how you respond to this treatment, so don't rise to the bait, however hard it gets. Smile, keep your voice on an even level (a tell-tale sign of someone who is angry/stressed is that their voice rises) and don't be tempted to go on the counter-offensive. Many people feel this kind of interviewing technique is ethically dubious. But if you still want the job – and maybe the job you're applying for justifies this approach if it's customer-facing – you'd better make sure you remain calm and pleasant no matter what the pressure.

▶ Different types of interview

You will often find yourself in a one-to-one interview, very probably with the person who will be your line manager if you get the job. But of course, that's not the only type of interview there is. Almost all the guidelines in this chapter apply to any kind of interview, but there are a few extra pointers worth considering if you find yourself in one of the other types of interview.

Panel interview

You may find yourself interviewed by three or four people. This might include the line manager for the job, someone from personnel, perhaps a technical person if it's a technical post, maybe a union representative, perhaps even a psychologist.

Panel interviews are particularly popular in the public sector. So if you're applying for a public sector job, ask if you'll be interviewed by a panel. if the answer is yes, try to get their names and job titles in advance. Memorize them, so you can address them by name in the interview. Don't overdo this though as it can start to sound insincere.

Panel interviews tend, by their nature, to be more formal than some one-to-one interviews. This can make them more stressful, but there's no reason why they should be any harder to handle than any other interview. Look at our Top Tips for some guidance.

Top Tips Panel interview protocol

- Shake hands with everyone on the panel. If it happens to be a large panel – more than about half a dozen – your alternative is to make a spot decision as you walk in that you will shake hands only with the chairperson (the one who stands and greets you), unless the others offer you a hand.
- Make eye contact with everyone on the panel, and make sure they all feel included in your answers.
- Give the bulk of your attention to the person who asked the question you are answering.
- When you come to ask questions of your own, direct them primarily at the person who is chairing the interview (it'll be obvious who this is).

Sequential interview

This is more common in larger organizations. You may find yourself in a series of one-to-one interviews with different people – maybe the line manager for the job, a more senior manager, a personnel representative, perhaps a technical person. Apart from the danger of feeling you're running a mental marathon, this is quite a good system for you. You get to start each interview afresh, so even if you feel that you underperformed at the last one, you can still give a stunning performance at the next.

The interviewers, of course, are not operating in isolation. They will have discussed in advance what areas each will cover, and they will compare notes at the end before reaching a decision. They may also chat to each other between interviews. If this happens, you may find yourself being questioned about something you've already covered with the previous interviewer – very possibly they have asked the next person to probe the same area.

With sequential interviews, you need to bear in mind that each interviewer is looking at a different aspect of your application. There's no point in them all repeating the same exercise with you, after all.

Pairing up

See if you can match up the following questions with the person most likely to ask them, bearing in mind that different interviewers have different areas of interest and expertise.

A	*Personnel manager*	**1**	What do you consider your greatest strength?
B	*Line manager*	**2**	Where do you see yourself in five years' time?
C	*Technical manager*	**3**	What sort of team player are you?
D	*Senior manager*	**4**	How would you respond to a software failure on the SP21?

Answers: A3; B1; C4; D2

Of course, you may be asked these questions by a different interviewer than the one indicated above. But you need to be aware of what each interviewer is looking for, and give answers and examples that relate your ability to do the job to their particular discipline.

Telephone interview

Some interviewers use telephone interviews as a quick way of slimming down a lengthy list of applicants into a shortlist for interview. Others may use them if the job involves a lot of telephone work, so they can assess your telephone and communication skills. They are also often used as an initial interview for overseas jobs (see also 'Video interviews' in the next section). The interviewer may arrange an appointment for a telephone interview with you, or they may not. You won't necessarily get any warning that they are trying to contact you – the first you hear of it may be the phone call. So you need to be prepared.

Top Tips **Telephone interviews**

- Keep a copy of the CV and the application form by the phone, along with a pen and paper.
- Keep your diary near the phone – if they like the sound of you on the phone they may arrange an interview.
- If you may be out when they call, make provision for this. Give best times to contact you on your CV or covering letter, consider getting an answerphone if you don't already have one, and brief anyone else who may answer your phone to take clear messages with names, phone numbers and so on.
- Treat the telephone interview with the same importance you would a face-to-face interview. It may feel less formal, but it matters just as much.

- If you are not alone in the house, do your best to arrange to take the call in private. It's fine to ask the interviewer to hold on while you pick up another extension.

- Sit down during the interview if you can, remember to use the right body language (it will affect your tone of voice), and smile readily even though no one can see you.

- Make sure you write down the name of the interviewer and any other details they give you, such as their phone number, or directions on how to find them if they invite you for interview.

If you're offered a face-to-face interview at the end of a phone interview, take down the details. Then write confirming the interview arrangements. It all helps to give the interviewer a great impression of your efficiency and professionalism.

Video interview

These are much the same as a conventional one-to-one interview but the whole thing will be recorded on video. This may take place if the job is for an overseas organization recruiting within the UK. Often the interviews will be arranged and taped by an employment agency acting on behalf of an overseas client. They will then send the best of the videos to the client, who will choose a shortlist of candidates to attend a final interview abroad.

Some recruitment agencies use the same process for big UK clients or to allow other colleagues within their own organizations to see and judge competing candidates' performances.

What then should you do in particular to prepare for a video interview? There is no doubt that knowing that the whole thing is being recorded can add to the general anxiety felt by the applicant. Try not to let it: you only have one shot to make a good impression.

All the guidelines already given for a normal interview apply here too. Prepare yourself mentally for the questions you may have to face (typical questions are given in the next chapter), and decide on the main points about yourself that you want to highlight in your responses. Dress smartly (see p. 225 on what to wear); make a good entrance and exit (see p. 227 and below); in particular, watch your body language (see Tops Tips on p. 231). Try to remain as calm as possible, sit in an upright but relaxed position and remember to smile and make lots of eye contact with the interviewer. It's best not to look directly at the camera, although this will probably be positioned somewhere behind the interviewer and so will be pointing in your direction. All the other Top Tips on answering questions (i.e. not interrupting, giving concise answers, etc. – see p. 235) apply equally here too.

▶ Prepare your questions

A good interview should be rounded off with you asking a few well-thought-out questions about the company or the position. If you have conducted your research on the company and on the job, you should have thought of some key questions that would be particularly important to you during the decision-making process. The ultimate aim of asking questions at the end of an interview is to indicate to the employer that you are genuinely interested in the position and to give you the opportunity to find out if the organization is right for you. Prepare your questions while you are conducting your research on the company and take them along with you to the interview. Only ask questions that directly relate to the role or the company. You should ask questions that show a real interest in the organization and forward thinking on your behalf.

▶ Making an exit

The interviewer will signal when the interview is over. And just like any good salesperson, you may not expect to clinch a deal on the spot, but you will at least want to agree the next step. So ask what happens next, and when. You want to know whether there'll be a second round of interviews, whether you'll hear by phone or by letter, when they'll be in touch, and so on.

Apart from that, when the interview ends, stand up, collect your things and leave promptly. Before you go, shake hands with the interviewer again if they offer you a hand. Thank them for seeing you, smile warmly (however you feel inside) and make a clean exit.

If the interviewer accompanies you to reception or to the main exit, chatting as you go, remember that you are still on show. Don't be lulled by the official end to the interview into making any unguarded comments.

▶ After the interview

You will probably feel a strong sense of relief once the interview is over. But just because the interview is over, it doesn't mean there's nothing more you can do. So as soon as you get back home from the interview, you'll need to do two things:

1 Write a letter of thanks to the interviewer.
2 Make notes.

Saying thank you

I know this sounds depressingly like that endless round of 'thank-you' letters parents make small children write after Christmas and birthdays. But you need to write and thank the interviewer as soon as possible, since you want your letter to arrive before they make their decision. In order to make sure you're in time, you can always email it, especially if you know they're going to make their decision quickly. Your thank-you letter has two purposes:

- It reminds the interviewer who you are, in much the same way an advertisement does.

- It gives you a chance to mention (briefly) anything important you missed saying at the interview itself.

Since you will almost certainly be the only candidate who writes following the interview, it will do a lot to bring your name to the interviewer's attention, even if you had slipped down the list. It can make the difference, for example, between whether or not you get shortlisted for final interview. It shows you are keen on the job, committed and courteous with it.

A thank-you letter can make **the difference between whether or** not you get shortlisted for final interview.

So what's the letter going to say? It should say something along the lines of: 'Thank you for seeing me this morning. I very much enjoyed meeting you and I would like to confirm that I am still very interested in the post. I look forward to hearing from you.'

You may also want to add a brief note along the lines of: 'By the way, we discussed the possibility of working overseas, and I forgot to mention that I have previously taken evening language courses in both French and Spanish.' There's no need to add this kind of information unless there's something important you feel you omitted to say, and a single sentence will do fine. This is no place to launch into a long, defensive ramble because you think the interviewer had some reservation about your suitability and you feel like repeating what you've already said at the interview.

As with your application, your letter or email needs to look as professional as possible. The standards for email layout are fairly simple, but if you write a letter make sure it looks smart and professional, or its positive effects will be seriously diluted.

Making notes

Now, there's one more thing you'll need to do while you're waiting to hear: make notes about the interview while it's still fresh in your mind. Any general points you note about how it went will help with other interviews – do you feel you were well prepared, were you confident enough, did you ramble too much, were you too flippant, did you answer questions fluently? These are useful points to note for yourself so you can handle your next interview even better.

Make notes about the interview while it's still **fresh in your mind.**

There's another reason for making notes. You may get a second interview. In case this happens you need to note:

- the names of your interviewer and anyone else you met
- any questions you feel you could have dealt with better (so you can prepare for next time)
- any reservations you suspect the interviewer may have been left with
- anything you wish you'd said but didn't
- anything which seemed to impress them and will therefore be worth reinforcing next time.

In the next chapter we focus on the typical questions that you might be asked during interviews – including some of the toughest ones to answer – so you'll be well prepared.

13

Typical

interview

questions

There are some questions you can expect to be asked at most interviews, so these are the ones you really need to prepare for. Generally they come in the first half of the interview.

We'll be examining below some of the most popular interview questions, so you can see the best kind of answer to give to each one. But of course, there are general guidelines which apply to every answer you give. Look back to the box 'Top Tips on Answering Questions' to refresh your memory on this (p. 235). Treat this as a framework for all your individual responses.

It's worth stressing again the most important 'Don't' when it comes to interview questions. When asked what impresses them *least* in a candidate, most professional interviewers cited 'not listening to the question'. This includes answering the question the candidate *wants* to answer, rather than the one they were actually asked. So be careful to avoid this pitfall.

Asked **what impresses them least** in a candidate, most interviewers cited **'not listening to the question'.**

So let's look now at the questions you can expect to be asked. Some aren't too difficult, but don't let this lull you into a false sense of security, because there are also some really tough ones included here too. We'll be listing other really tough interview questions in the next section of this chapter.

The answers recommended here are not a script; the idea is to let you know the kind of answer that will impress the interviewer. You'll need to put it in your own words, and find your own examples to give.

Before the interview proper, why not enlist the assistance of a friend or family member in the role of interviewer so you can practise your responses? Try to make the interview situation as realistic as possible, come into the room, shake hands, sit down, etc. Ask them to make notes as you're answering, as this is common practice but can be quite off-putting if you're not used to it. Then ask them for feedback once the 'interview' is over and you've made your exit. Ask them to comment on your body language and style as well as the content of the responses you give. You're asking them for honest, constructive comments, so be prepared for this and don't get upset if you don't like everything they say. Reversing roles can be a revealing exercise too, with you taking the part of the interviewer.

So on now to those all-important questions …

▶ The most popular interview questions

'Tell me about yourself'

This one invariably crops up early on in the interview in one guise or another and is sometimes launched as a 'warming-up question'. 'Tell me about yourself' is not an invitation to relate your whole life history. In fact, you really need the interviewer to be more specific before you can give the answer they want. So ask them, 'What aspect of myself in particular would you like me to tell you about?' They are most likely to ask you to talk about what you're like at work.

You should aim to describe the kind of person you are in a couple of minutes at most. Concentrate on positive qualities, and link them to the key responsibilities of the job you're applying for. For example: 'I'm a people person – I enjoy working with people and being part of a team' or 'I'm the sort of person who likes to get stuck into a project, and I really enjoy seeing a project right through from initial planning to the final stages.'

If they ask what you're like away from work, what you like doing in your spare time, you still want to highlight how well you 'fit' the job on offer. So again, if you want to show you're a good team player, you might tell them, 'I'm very social; I have lots of friends and I spend a lot of time with them. I play a lot of sports such as ice hockey.'

There's no need to lie. You've got plenty of time to think about this question before you get to the interview and be ready with suitable and honest answers about your personal or business life.

If you're a graduate applying for your first job, your interviewer will want to know about your university career, and how it has helped prepare you for this job. Expect questions on the following topics:

● Why you chose your particular course.

● How your studies relate to this job.

● What project work you've done.

● What extra-curricular activities you got involved in.

'What do you enjoy most in your current job?'

This can be a kind of trick question. The interviewer is tempting you to divulge what it is that you *don't* like about your current job. And if you do that, then it may show that you'll dislike things about the job on offer too – which isn't very encouraging. So the only answer you can really give is to say that you enjoy everything about your job. But then be prepared for the next question, which will probably be: 'So why are you looking for another job?' (see p. 249 for some helpful advice on answering this one).

Alternatively, you can pick out one or two favourite parts of your current job – making sure that they'll be important elements of the job on offer too. So you might say, 'I'm lucky, really. I can't think of anything I don't enjoy about my job. But I suppose the thing I enjoy most is dealing directly with customers. That's why I've applied for this job; because I'd like the opportunity to spend even more of my time doing it.'

With all these problem questions, the main thing to remember is to accentuate the positive, eliminate the negative. And that applies to answering questions about you as a person (you are selling yourself, after all), any previous jobs and really all aspects of your life.

Accentuate the positive,
eliminate the negative.

'What is the biggest challenge you've faced at work?'

So long as you're prepared, this is a great question. You need to have an answer ready for it in order to get the best from it. The idea is that you not only describe the challenge, but also how you coped with it. So you need to pick an example that leaves you looking good.

There is something else behind this question too: the interviewer is also finding out what you consider a challenge. So think hard about the example you want to pick. Will it be a tough decision? A difficult situation? A system that needed overhauling to improve results? You get to choose, so pick something that will be relevant to this job, as always.

Just one rule of thumb to follow: it's dangerous to pick an example that involves problems with other people. It can give the impression that you find getting on with others is a big challenge.

'Why do you want to leave your present job?'

It doesn't matter if the real reason is that you can't stand working with your boss any longer, or the company pays pathetically low salaries. Keep that to yourself. The interviewer is looking for a positive reason for moving forward, not a negative aim to avoid a job you're not happy in.

The only really good answer to this question is, 'Because I want to broaden my experience and I think I can do that better in a new organization' (or words to that effect). If it's relevant to the job, you can expand on this briefly. For example, if the job entails giving a lot of presentations, you might say, 'In particular, I enjoy presenting and it's something I've become very good at. Unfortunately, there aren't that many opportunities for me to develop my skills further where I am now.'

'What is your present (or most recent) boss like?'

Never criticize any of your bosses – current, recent or otherwise. The interviewer may be your future boss, and wants to hear you being loyal to other bosses even behind their backs. So always be positive – even if your boss is a first rate sh**. Just say something like, 'I'm lucky to have a boss who is very good at her job', and leave it there.

Never criticize
any of your past bosses.

The point is not only that your interviewer wants to see that you are loyal, but also that your interviewer is aware they don't know the other side of the story. So you may know your complaints are justified, but to your interviewer they may just make you sound like a carping whinger who is likely to talk about them in the same terms if they employ you.

Here's a handy piece of advice from Phil Boyle, MD of Ramsey Hall (an executive recruitment company): 'Rephrase the question as the early part of the answer. This will give the interviewer the opportunity of correcting the question if you have misunderstood it.'

'What do you think is the role of a ... (your current/future position)?'

Clearly, we can't tell you the answer to this one, as it depends entirely on the individual position. But remember to answer in terms of the big picture:

● the overall objective of the job
● key responsibilities.

If they're asking about the job on offer, you can pick up big clues from the job description as advertised. If you're applying for a job in your usual line of work, you'll want to draw on your own experience.

This question is sometimes given as a test; if this happens the interviewer will interrupt to disagree with you. Their aim is to see whether you can defend your case calmly and convincingly, so don't be thrown by their interruption. Ask them politely to justify their assertion that your description of the role is wrong ('What makes you say that?'). Then show that you can argue your case well and without becoming defensive.

> **Top Tip** **Preparing responses**
>
> Although you need to prepare your answers in advance, it's not a good idea to learn them by rote. You'll sound as if you're giving a stilted recitation and this may damage your credibility as a candidate. Just prepare the main points you'll want to make.

'What do you know about our company?'

This is a great opportunity to demonstrate that you've done your homework. Keep to the relevant points – size, turnover, nature of the business, growth and business ethos (for example, 'I know you're a young, growing organization with a reputation for developing people'). Keep it brief, but add one or two things that suggest you've gone deeper than merely reading the annual report. For example: '... and I notice in the trade press that you've just signed a couple of very big deals in eastern Europe.' See p. 91 for Top Tips on researching companies.

'Why do you want this job?'

Try not to waffle about challenges and prospects. Talk in terms of benefits to them, and be specific about the kind of challenge you enjoy. For example: 'I'm a great organizer, and I'm looking for a post which gives me scope to plan and organize', or 'I get great satisfaction from working in a successful team, and this job seems to call for someone who can fit well into a tight, well-motivated team.'

This is also a good opportunity to show off the research you've done into the company – again keeping it brief and relevant. So you might say something like, 'I find growing companies have a more exciting, dynamic atmosphere to work in, and I know you've been growing by an average of 6 percent for the last four years.'

'What do you feel you can bring to this job?'

This is another question that gives you a chance to shine. You need to link your past experience or skills to the requirements of the job. So pick about three key strong points in your favour which are relevant to this job. For example: 'I'm very experienced at dealing with customers, including tricky ones. I get on easily with other people so I work well in a team. And I'm naturally organized and find it easy to handle paperwork and fit in with whatever systems I need to. As I understand it, these are all important skills for this job.'

'How long would you expect to stay with this company?'

The interviewer isn't going to employ someone who'll be off again before they've got their full value from them. So indicate that you'd like to stay a few years. 'I'd like to settle with this company and grow and develop within it. I see myself staying as long as I keep progressing here and making a contribution.'

'Where do you see yourself in five years' time?'

You want to be careful how you answer this because, if you give a specific goal and the interviewer knows they cannot fulfil it, they will be put off hiring you. So keep it open. But remember that they want to know you have drive and will keep increasing your value to them. Say something like, 'I'm certainly ambitious, and I like to keep moving and progressing. But you can't fit a job to a preset list of conditions. I find it's far more rewarding to let the job lead you forward.'

'What are your greatest strengths?'

Go for it. This is a perfect question – just focus your answers on the key responsibilities of the job to make sure your strengths are relevant to your interviewer. And make sure you don't waffle on for too long; pick one or two key strengths which are really important for this job.

Of course, you want to sell yourself but you want to avoid sounding arrogant. Prefacing the answer with something along the lines of 'My colleagues would say that ...' or 'I believe that ...' will help to modulate the self-congratulatory tone.

'What is your biggest weakness?'

Oooh, tricky. It invites you to say something negative about yourself. Resist. The best defence to use is one of the following:

● humour ('Double choc-chip ice cream')
● something personal, not work related ('I'm useless at getting round to household jobs – changing lightbulbs and fixing leaky taps')
● something from long ago, which you have now learnt from ('Fifteen years ago I'd have said paperwork, but I've learnt to set aside half an hour at the start of every day for it. Now I reckon I'm more on top of the paperwork than the rest of my colleagues')
● something which your interviewer will see as a strength ('I'm dreadful at stopping in the middle of something. I tend to stay at work until a task is done, even though my family often complain that I'm late home').

All of these questions should avoid giving away any real weaknesses (should you have any), and they also avoid making you come across as arrogant and too perfect – something which really gets up interviewers' noses.

Be prepared for the interviewer to ask you questions in a different form from the ones given here, or prepared in your mind. They may ask you, 'What experience do you have of dealing with difficult customers?' Equally, they may try to elicit the same information by asking, 'Tell me about a diffi-cult customer you've had to deal with. What did you do?' Or even, 'What do you think is the key to dealing with tricky or angry customers?' All of these are essentially different forms of the same question – you will need to be able to recognize them all as being a cue for the answer you've prepared.

'How would your colleagues describe you?'

This is an invitation to list your strong points, so grab it. Concentrate on your plus points as a colleague – supportive, a good team player, and so on. As with all these questions, it's unwise to make any outrageous claims. You could well come unstuck if your references are checked out or when you start the job, if you're offered it. But of course you'll put the best complex-ion on things. So if you're a bit of a loner but get on with everyone, you might give an answer like, 'They'd say I was one of the quieter members of the team, popular and can be relied on to pull with the team when it's facing any kind of challenge.'

'How would your friends describe you?'

'What friends?' is the wrong answer to this question. In fact, it runs along much the same lines as 'How would your colleagues describe you?' Don't be unrealistic about yourself, but pick out the strongest points which will be relevant. It's always worth mentioning loyalty and supportiveness.

The interviewer is simply trying to get a more rounded picture of the kind of person you are, to help them assess whether you'll fit in with the people you'll be working with.

'What outside interests do you have?'

Your interviewer is trying to find out more about you. Your interests will tell them whether you are sporty, competitive, enjoy dangerous hobbies, like solo or group activities, and so on. Don't invent hobbies. You don't want your interviewer to say, 'Bungee jumping? Me too! Maybe we could go for a jump together sometime?' Do though select those hobbies or interests which show you as the kind of person your interviewer is looking for.

Don't invent hobbies. You don't want your interviewer to say, 'Bungee jumping? Me too! Maybe we could go for a jump together sometime?'

'What have you read and enjoyed lately?'

Don't make up some fashionable answer here, or name a leading business book you haven't actually read. You may be caught out by follow-up questions if you're unlucky enough to pick a title the interviewer *has* read. You don't have to mention the most recent book you've read, so pick one you've genuinely enjoyed which is slightly offbeat – you're not one of the crowd. You might want to choose an unusual classic, an avant-garde title or a biography – pick something which will show a side of you you'd like the interviewer to see.

▶ Check you're ready

Here's a list of all the questions in this chapter. When you have prepared an answer to each one, jot down a note of it in the middle column. In the right-hand column, make a note of the best example you can give to back up your answer. Make sure you are ready to answer any of the questions in this chapter.

Question	Answer	Example
Tell me about yourself.		
What do you enjoy most in your current job?		
What is the biggest challenge you've faced at work?		
Why do you want to leave your present job?		
What is your present (or most recent) boss like?		
What do you think is the role of a ... (whatever your current job is)?		
What do you know about our company?		
Why do you want this job?		
What do you feel you can bring to this job?		
How long would you expect to stay with this company?		
What are your greatest strengths?		
What is your biggest weakness?		
Where do you see yourself in five years' time?		
How would your colleagues describe you?		
How would your friends describe you?		
What outside interests do you have?		
What have you read and enjoyed lately?		

▶ Difficult interview questions

It's fair to say that almost any question can seem tough. But compared with 'How long have you been in your current job?', the questions that follow really *are* tough. They're not necessarily intended to make you wriggle (though some are); they may simply be the interviewer's best way of finding out what they need to know.

As far as the interviewer is concerned, this isn't a competition. You're both on the same side, so there should be no element of trying to get the better of you, or knock you down a peg or two; certainly not if your interviewer is professional. Tough questions are generally tough simply because you're not sure how to answer them.

But the point is that, whatever the interviewer's intent, any question can make you feel uncomfortable if you're not prepared for it. Well, that's OK – you soon will be.

Any question can make you feel uncomfortable if you're **not prepared for it.**

According to professional interviewers, they don't ask deliberately tough questions without a good reason. So what is a good reason? Chiefly:

- to see how you react under pressure.
- to confirm that you're telling the truth (if they doubt it).

Interviewers will be particularly keen to see how you respond to questioning under pressure if they have some indication – for example, from psychometric tests – that you don't handle pressure as well as you might. In your responses, you need to stick to the three principal ground rules:

- Stay calm.
- Don't get defensive.
- Pause for a moment before you answer if you wish.

Whatever the temptation, don't argue with your interviewer. If they see you as difficult and argumentative, it will put them off employing you. They may even be testing you to see how you respond to their belligerent questioning. So if you tell them you run a team of three people and they say, 'That's hardly managing, is it? This job entails running a team of ten', don't get defensive. Say something like, 'I can see that it looks very different on the surface, but I'd say the same principles apply whether you manage one person or a hundred.'

The following questions are divided into broad categories to help you find your way around them:

1   Questions about you
2   Questions about your career
3   Questions about this job
4   Questions inviting you to criticize yourself
5   Questions inviting you to be negative
6   Questions about your salary
7   Unexpected questions
8   Very personal questions.

▶ Questions about you

Not all the questions in this section will necessarily apply to you. If you're applying for a job that doesn't involve working as part of a team, you're not likely to be asked about your teamwork skills. If you're not applying for a management job, you won't be asked about your management style. But whatever job you are being interviewed for, you'll find that some of the questions here will apply to you and you'll need to be ready with your answers.

What will you be asked?

Have a look at the questions in this list, and think about which ones you're likely to be asked for each of the jobs listed. Tick those you think are most likely to be asked for each job.

	Production manager	Sales assistant	Accounts clerk	Project supervisor
1 Are you a natural leader?				
2 What motivates you?				
3 How do you work in a team?				
4 How do you operate under stress?				
5 What do you dislike most at work?				
6 How well do you take direction?				
7 Do you enjoy routine tasks?				

Answers: there is no guarantee of what anyone will or won't be asked, but your answers should look something like this.
Production manager: 1, 2, 3, 5
Sales assistant: 2, 3, 4, 5, 6
Accounts clerk: 2, 5, 6, 7
Project supervisor: 1, 2, 3, 4, 5

'What motivates you?'

You need to give an answer, as always, that also benefits your potential employer and links into the key responsibilities of the job. So don't say, 'My pay packet'. Give an answer such as, 'I'm happiest when I can see a project through from start to finish', or 'I get a real kick out of running a team that is happy and knows it's successful.'

'How well do you take direction?'

Keep in mind the fact that your interviewer may well become your boss if this interview goes according to plan, so it's *their* direction you'll need to take. The answer, obviously, has to be that you take direction well. You can add credibility to your answer by expanding it to add something like, 'I don't see how a team can function effectively unless its members are happy to take direction from the team leader.'

'How do you handle criticism?'

Again, your interviewer may anticipate being your boss, and inevitably having to criticize you from time to time. They want to know whether the task will be easy for them, or whether you'll make it unpleasant.

So give an answer along the lines of: 'I'm happy to be given constructive criticism. In fact, I think being prepared to take constructive criticism on board is the only way I can hope to learn from mistakes and improve my performance.'

'Do you enjoy routine tasks?'

You're not likely to be asked this question unless you're applying for a job that will entail routine tasks. So clearly your answer should be, 'Yes'. However, one-word answers aren't advisable, because your reply will carry more weight if you elaborate briefly to show that you have understood the question and have thought out your response. So you could add, 'Yes, I have an orderly approach to work and I get satisfaction from carrying out routine work successfully.'

'What is your management style?'

There's no point in lying to questions like this, so give an honest answer. But again, make sure it's relevant. You don't need to give a 20-minute rant on the subject – just a couple of clear sentences will do: 'I prefer a carrot rather than a stick approach, and I have an open-door policy', or 'I believe a manager has to be firm with the team, and the team appreciate it so long as you are also scrupulously fair.' It always helps to back up your answers with a personal anecdote or example – a time there was a problem in your team which you resolved firmly but fairly.

> It always helps to **back up your answers** with a personal anecdote or example.

'Are you a good manager?'

This is a similar question to the one about your management style, but it's blunter. The answer clearly has to be 'Yes'; if you haven't already been asked about your style, you can describe it briefly as we saw in the answer above. Again, it is also a good idea to relate a brief anecdote illustrating your approach to managing people.

'Are you a natural leader?'

Since you're only going to be asked this if the job calls for a leader, the answer has to be in the affirmative. Follow your answer with one or two brief examples, bearing in mind that they don't have to come exclusively from work. You might point out that you were Head Boy or Prefect at school, or that you direct your local amateur theatrical society, as well as giving an example from your work background.

Natural leaders, after all, often start young. So if you've been leading groups of people since you were at school, it suggests your leadership skills really are natural, and that people follow you through choice.

'How do you work in a team?'

This is another question you need to answer honestly, but pick a relevant way to express your teamwork style. Give a brief answer, such as, 'I enjoy being part of a team, and I like the flexibility it demands. I get a real kick out of collective success.' Follow your remarks with an anecdote or example demonstrating what you mean. If teamwork is an important part of the job, you should certainly expect this question (or a variant of it) and have an anecdote ready.

'How do you approach a typical project?'

If you are applying for a project-based job, you should expect to be asked this question. You don't need to give a rambling answer, but show that you take into account the main components of effective project planning:

- Plan the schedule backwards from the completion/delivery date.
- Work out what you need to get the job done effectively and on time.
- Budget cost, time and resources.
- Allow a contingency.

'How do you operate under stress?'

Again, a question you'll only be asked if it applies to the job. A full answer will sell you better than a brief one. So say that you work well under pressure – say you enjoy it if that's true – and give an example of a time you've handled a situation well under pressure.

Best of three

It's a good idea to think of the three personal characteristics you most want to demonstrate to the interviewer. Any more than three, and your message will become diluted. So pick three characteristics (out of your numerous strong points) which:

● are genuinely strong traits of yours

● are important characteristics for the job you're applying for.

Once you have identified the three characteristics you want to promote, prepare examples and anecdotes which emphasize them, as well as making whatever other point you want to illustrate. And when asked questions such as, 'What would your boss say about you?', bring these characteristics directly into play.

Here is a list to give you an idea of the characteristics you could choose from (you may come up with others that aren't on this list):

● Honesty	● Enthusiasm	● Dedication
● Drive	● Attention to detail	● Integrity
● Energy	● Reliability	● Creativity
● Flexibility	● Initiative	● Authority
● Patience	● Leadership	● Diplomacy
● Confidence	● Focus on objectives	● Determination
● Good communication	● Good interpersonal skills	● Calmness under pressure

You might also want to add that you practice good time management to make sure that you minimize the stress you have to operate under (but, as always, don't say this if it isn't true).

Never mention at interview any job that wasn't included in your CV.

'How creative are you?'

Again, a question for people who need to be creative. So, presumably, you have examples you can give; be ready with them. If you have to do a lot of creative thinking, outline one or two key creative techniques you use, too, to show that you take your creativity seriously.

'How do you get the best from people?'

If you're a manager, this is a question you may well be asked. The kind of skills that interviewers want to hear about include:

● good communication
● teamwork skills
● recognizing each person as an individual
● setting a sound example
● praising good performances.

'How do you resolve conflict in your team?'

You need to answer this question honestly, as always. And find an example of conflict in your team that you can use to demonstrate your skills at resolving it. The kind of techniques you need to demonstrate include:

● fairness
● addressing problems with individuals privately
● making sure you get to the root of the problem
● finding a solution that the people involved are willing to buy into.

Assuming it's true, you would also do well to point out, 'I find if a team is run fairly and the team members are well motivated, conflict very rarely arises.'

'What would your boss say about you?'

Your interviewer may well be your prospective boss, so be careful! They want to know that you're an effective worker, but they don't want you stepping on their toes. You may be highly ambitious but don't want to come across as too much of a threat. So describe yourself as any boss would want to see you. For example, 'My boss would describe me as hard working, easy to motivate and loyal. She'd say that I work well on my own initiative, and I'm a supportive member of the team.' Resist the temptation to say 'I think my boss would say ....'. Be positive and certain in your answer, but if you've put your boss's name down as a reference, be careful that he or she would back up your answer.

'What do you dislike most at work?'

You love work, remember? This interviewer can safely hire you, knowing that you will be well motivated every minute of your working life. So if asked, you can't think of anything you dislike. The only possible exception is if this job is very different from your last, in which case you might say something like, 'I really enjoy my work. But occasionally I get a little frustrated in a small company that I don't get to meet customers as often as I'd like. That's one of the reasons why this job appeals to me so much.'

Top Tip How to handle an incompetent interviewer

What do you do if you're faced with an incompetent interviewer? Well, the biggest mistake incompetent interviewers make is that they don't encourage you to answer questions fully. They ask closed questions (requiring one-word answers), or they never ask you for examples or experiences to back up your claims.

The trick is to do their job for them. Volunteer full answers even if the questions don't demand them. Give examples without being asked. And if you have one of those interviewers who keeps wandering off the point, or stopping the interview to deal with interruptions, impress them by always being able to answer accurately when they ask, 'Where were we?'

▶ Questions about your career

Your interviewer needs to know if you're at the right point on the career ladder for them. But they also need to know where you think you're going. Are you planning to move up the organization much faster or slower than they expect in this job? So the questions in this section are all designed to tell the interviewer how this job would fit into the broader picture for you in the long term.

This is one of those areas where it's important to be honest. It's not just that interviews can only work on the principle that everyone is honest, quite apart from the ethical approach to being honest. It's also the fact that if you mislead the interviewer, you could end up being offered a job that's detrimental to your career. The interviewer knows far better than you whether this job suits your long-term aims – but only if you tell them straight what those aims are.

If you mislead the interviewer, you could end up being offered a job that's detrimental to your career.

At the same time, you want this job, so you will – always – put your answers in the best possible light. But you'll do it without misleading the interviewer.

'Why have you been so long with your present employer?'

The answer to avoid is one that implies you were getting stale and should have moved earlier. Any answer that contradicts this unspoken worry on the interviewer's part is fine. For example, 'I've been there for several years, but in a variety of different roles', or 'The job was growing constantly, so it felt as though I was undergoing frequent changes without actually changing employer.'

'Why have you been such a short time with your present employer?'

Your interviewer doesn't want to take on someone who is going to leave in 6 months' time. So convince them that you're not really a job-hopper, whatever your CV may appear to show. 'I'd like to settle in one company for several years, but I've found up until now that I've had to move in order to widen my experience and avoid getting stale in the job.'

'You look like a job-hopper to me'

This is the previous question but worse. If it is not only your current or most recent employer that you've spent a short time with, but previous employers too, your interviewer will quite understandably be concerned that you'll leave them within a few months too. Nowadays people typically change jobs roughly every two to five years, but much more frequently than this looks worrying to a potential employer. And some industries expect their people to stay with them longer than that.

If your CV gives the impression that you barely sit down at your desk before you're off again, you can expect this question. So how do you reassure the interviewer that this time, you're here to stay? The last thing you want to do is launch into a lengthy, defensive justification for each job move in turn. Far better to give a catch-all reason for moving so frequently.

So adopt this kind of approach: 'I'd like to find a company I can settle down in and really make a mark. Until now I've found that I've had to change jobs in order to keep finding challenge in my work. For example ...' Then you can briefly explain just one of your career moves, and why it made so much sense. Finish by saying, 'What I'm looking for is a company dynamic enough for me to find fresh challenges without having to move to another organization.'

Top Tip ... and what NOT to mention

Never mention anything at the interview that isn't on your CV. You may have managed to 'lose' on your CV those 4 months you spent stacking supermarket shelves. But if you make reference to it at the interview, it will call into question the credibility of your whole CV. So either put it on the CV, or make sure you don't refer to it at the interview.

'Why haven't you found a new job yet?'

The implication behind this question is that you can't be much good if no one wants to give you a job. So you need to indicate that it has been your choice to spend some time job hunting. You need to give a reply such as, 'It's important that I only accept a job that seems really right for me, and where I can see that I can make a contribution to the company.'

If you have turned down any offers, then say so: 'I have had job offers, but I didn't feel the positions were right for me, or that I was right for the companies concerned.'

'What were your most significant achievements in your current (or most recent) job?'

It's unlikely that this job will require exactly the same achievements as the last – although it's great if you can find a clear parallel. So what the interviewer really wants to know about is the qualities you must have exhibited in order to score the achievement. Be ready with something that is:

● recent (otherwise it implies you've achieved little of note since)
● difficult to achieve
● as relevant as possible to the job you're applying for.

'If you could start again, what career decisions would you make differently?'

You're on a hiding to nothing if you start trying to think of hypothetical improvements to your past career. Anything you say will suggest that you're not happy with the way things are – and why would anyone want to hire someone who doesn't really want to be where they are?

So the only reasonable answer is that you wouldn't change anything; you're happy with things as they are now. You might add something like, 'I'm not the kind of person to look back with regrets. I like to invest my energy in looking forward.'

'Do you consider your career so far has been successful?'

Clearly it's better to be a success than a failure, so unless you've spent long periods out of work and stuck in dead-end jobs, the answer to this question is 'Yes'. To expand on this answer (as you always should on a one-word answer), you can go on to redefine success in your own terms. This is particularly sensible if your career on paper may look less than outstanding, even if it's respectable.

Perhaps you haven't moved up the career ladder as fast as you might. So you might say, 'What matters to me – more than money or status – is to have a job that's interesting and challenging, and I've been lucky in that respect. So my career so far has been very successful.'

If your career on paper is less than outstanding, **then redefine success in** your own terms.

And what if your career has had its low points, and perhaps not brought you as far as it might? There's no point in pretending your CV glitters if it clearly doesn't – so show you're positive and forward-looking: 'I've had one or two career problems in the past, but those are firmly behind me. From now on I intend to build on the good breaks I've had and enjoy a very successful career.'

'When would you expect promotion?'

Don't give a firm timescale here. The answer is, you should expect promotion when you deserve it. 'I would hope to be promoted once I have demonstrated my value to the company, and shown that I'm worth it.'

And show how this job suits your long-term aims: 'That's why I want to join a company that is growing; so that the promotion opportunities will be there when I'm ready to move up', or 'That's why I want to join a large organization so there are plenty of opportunities when I've gained the skills and experience.'

▶ Questions about this job

Your interviewer is well aware that there are thousands of jobs being advertised every day. So why have you applied for this particular one? They are looking for evidence that the job really suits you – that it fits in with your general aptitudes, suits your long-term goals, and involves doing things you enjoy.

This is why they will use these questions to delve deeper into how strongly you feel about this job, how enthusiastic you really are about it, and whether you would enjoy it and be able to contribute to the organization.

Top Tip Don't drop your guard

Never drop your guard at an interview. Trained interviewers are very skilled at catching you off-guard to see how you react. They may be friendly and relaxed and then suddenly fire a tough question at you. Or they may follow a series of easy questions with a trick one, having lulled you into a false sense of security.

So treat every question as a fresh start, and never assume that this is turning out to be an easy interview.

'How can you attend this interview while you're employed elsewhere?'

The hidden pitfall here is that you must avoid coming across as being dishonest in any way. So if you told your boss you had to stay home for the washing machine engineer to call, or that you had a doctor's appointment, keep quiet about it. Otherwise your interviewer knows that if they offer you the job, they'll be wondering what's going on every time you ask for time off to visit the doctor.

Ideally, your boss knows you're looking for work and is aware you're at an interview. However, often this isn't the case. Assuming your boss actually has no idea where you are, the only valid justification for taking time off to come here is that you were owed holiday or time off and you took it in order to be at this interview.

'How does this job fit into your career plan?'

It's dangerous to commit yourself too precisely to a career plan. So you might say something like, 'Business changes so rapidly these days, it's hard to plan precisely. But I know I want to get ahead in this industry/in marketing/in management and I think the opportunities to do that in this company are excellent.'

'What appeals to you least about this job?'

Careful here. Naming almost anything will give the interviewer the impression that you are less than 100 percent enthusiastic about this job. So either tell them that it all appeals to you or, if you feel too glib giving this kind of answer, come up with a part of the job which is:

- a small part of it
- of no major importance
- universally unpopular.

One of the best examples of this is filing, or paperwork in a job where the paperwork isn't a significant part of the job (but absolutely not if it's important to the job). But you should still express it in positive terms: 'I can't say I find paperwork terribly inspiring. But it's important to make sure it gets done. And actually, it can be quite therapeutic.'

'Are you talking to other organizations as well as us?'

You want to show your interviewer that you're in demand. It makes you a more attractive prospect, and if you're offered the job it can help to push up the salary you manage to negotiate. At the same time, if you tell them you've had three other offers already, they may be put off you if they still have a long way to go – another round of interviews, for example. So indicate that you are talking to others without suggesting you're on the verge of taking another job. If it's not a downright lie, let them know if you're doing well. For example, 'I've reached the final round of interviews with three other organizations.'

You want to show your interviewer **that you're in demand.** It makes you a **more attractive prospect.**

'What other types of job or organization are you applying to?'

There's no need to divulge exactly who you've applied to. Occasionally you may be asked directly where else you've applied, but you can avoid answering by saying that the companies concerned haven't advertised and you don't feel you should divulge the information. That lets you off the hook and shows you can keep a confidence.

But the interviewer can get round it with this question – asking not for names of companies but merely types of job and company. The important thing here is to show that you want this job. If it becomes plain that you're applying for all sorts of different jobs in different industries, it may cast doubt on your commitment to this post. So indicate that you're applying for similar jobs within the same field.

'How long would it take you to make a useful contribution to this company?'

You might be thinking that you can't answer this question without more information. Quite right. So ask for the information you need:

● What would my key objectives be for the first 6 months?
● Are there any specific projects you would need me to start work on straightaway?

You can use the answers to these enquiries to help with your answer. But broadly speaking, you should indicate that (unless there is an urgent project) you would expect to spend the first week or two settling in and learning the ropes. After that you'd expect to be making a useful contribution within the first few weeks, and to show significant successes within 4 to 6 months.

'Do you think you may be overqualified for this job?'

The worry the interviewer is revealing here is that if they offer the job, you'll quickly become bored and leave. You may have reservations on this front yourself, but at this stage you should still be doing your best to get offered the job. If you're going to turn it down, do so later when you've had a better chance to think about it – don't write it off half-way through the interview.

So for the moment, you're going to give the best answer you can. Say that strong, dynamic companies can always use whatever talents they have to hand. You want to stay with the company for a while and, if your experience and skills are strong enough, you're sure they will find a way to keep you challenged and making a full contribution.

'What do you think are the key trends in this industry?'

This question isn't difficult so long as you've done your research – which is what the interviewer wants to establish. This question is really the advanced version of, 'What do you know about our company?' So the important thing here is to make sure you do your homework, and identify the key industry trends, ready to impress your interviewer. (See our earlier Top Tips on researching a company, p. 91).

Even if you're applying for a job in the industry you already work in, you should still prepare an answer to this question. It won't necessarily come to you, clearly and succinctly, in the heat of the moment.

Top Tip Handling multiple quesions

One of the ways in which interviewers can test you is by asking you more than one question at a time. For example: 'How would you approach a typical project, what is the biggest project you have handled in the past, and what were the major difficulties you encountered?'

Unskilled interviewers may do this unintentionally, but skilled interviewers are more likely to do it as a test of your intelligence. The more questions you answer (and you have to hold each one in your head while you answer the others), the brighter they will assume you to be. If you repeat the question back to them as soon as they ask it, this will help you to fix it in your mind.

▶ Questions inviting you to criticize yourself

Uh-oh. These are tricky questions, and ones you want to be careful with. You have a bit of a dilemma here: you don't want to admit to any faults or errors but, on the other hand, arrogance is one of the factors most interviewers cite as being particularly irritating. So how can you avoid conceding mistakes without appearing cocky and just too perfect?

A classic question in this category is 'What is your biggest weakness?', which we dealt with earlier (p. 253). And the recommended type of answer we looked at then applies for all these questions too. Here are the four techniques for criticizing yourself without admitting to anything damaging:

- Use humour – but be careful. This isn't the best approach if you sense that your interviewer has no sense of humour. But if they seem ready for a laugh, and it suits your personality to do it, you can use humour. If you do it every time, however, it starts to look like a cop-out (which it is, of course).

- Give an example from your personal rather than your work life, where the question allows. For example, 'I used to find getting up in the mornings a real challenge, but since I started walking the dog before breakfast I find I really enjoy getting up.'

- Pick something from a long time ago, which you can demonstrate that you've learnt from. For example, 'Decisions without a deadline used to be a problem for me – I never got round to making them. Then I discovered the trick of imposing a deadline on myself just so the decision would get made. Now I never delay decisions unnecessarily.'

- Give an answer which you claim is a fault or a weakness, but your interviewer will see as a strength. For example, 'I can be a bit of a perfectionist. I just can't bring myself to turn out work that I feel isn't as good as it could be.'

'Describe a difficult situation which, with hindsight, you could have handled better'

Again, the trick here is to be ready with something from a long time ago. And try to prepare an example where it really wasn't your fault you handled it as you did. For example, 'With hindsight, I can see that it would have been quicker to evacuate everyone straight down the main staircase rather than use the fire escape, but because the phones were down I had no way of knowing that the main staircase was safe.'

'What sort of decisions do you find difficult?'

You've never found a decision difficult in your life, of course. But the danger with some of these questions is that if you come across as being too implausibly perfect, you risk sounding glib and arrogant. So you have to admit to some minor failings, but make sure they have been overcome or are irrelevant to the job you're applying for – or else make you sound human. So you could say, 'The kind of decisions I dislike most are the ones that people won't like. They aren't actually difficult, but I don't like making a decision to sack someone, for example.' If you've never had to sack anyone, find another example of something others don't like.

With intelligent handling of the questions, and following the guidelines here, you should be able to perform excellently at interview without any need to lie.

'Describe a situation in which your work was criticized'

If you pick an instance where the criticism was clearly unfair and you were in the right, you risk looking as if you are simply taking an opportunity to air an old grievance – maybe you're someone who bears grudges (the interviewer will think). So you need to go for the 'distant past' option.

Interviewers may well ask you this question – or a variation on it – if they want to see how you cope with tough questioning. So make sure you have an answer ready in case you need it. You should answer in two stages:

1 Briefly describe the task and the criticism you received for it.

2 Explain how you learnt from it and you haven't repeated such mistakes since.

Not only does this make you sound human, and as though you haven't been criticized for a long time, but it also shows that you can take constructive criticism on board and learn from it.

Top Tip **Avoid lying at interview**

Honesty is the best policy for a number of reasons:

● A skilled interviewer may well be able to tell if you're lying.

● Any dishonesty may show up when your interviewer checks references or qualifications.

● If you successfully get the job by being dishonest, your new boss will notice as soon as you fail to live up to the working style or standards you 'promised' at interview. You may have got the job, but once you're in it you'll be off to a pretty poor start.

▶ Questions inviting you to be negative

These questions are intended to find out if you are naturally negative or even bitchy when given the opportunity, or whether your natural instinct is to be positive. So whatever you do, don't take the bait. Refuse to be critical or negative about other people or organizations.

Refuse to be critical or negative about other people or organizations.

'What is your present boss's greatest weakness?'

'Where do I start?' is not the right response to this question. Earlier (p. 250) we looked at the popular question, 'What is your present (or most recent) boss like?' This is the tough version of the same question – it really invites you to land yourself in it. So don't fall for it, no matter how long a list of complaints you may privately have about your boss. Remember, this interviewer may one day be your boss. So tell them what they would like to hear about themselves.

Say something along the lines of: 'To be honest, I'm lucky to have a very supportive boss who is good at her job and very easy to work with.' Then look as if you're really trying to think of a weakness and add, 'I can't think of anything – if I did, it could only be something so picky it wouldn't be worth mentioning.'

'How do you evaluate your present company?'

It's a great company which has taught you a lot and given you lots of excellent opportunities. I don't care what you tell your mates, as far as the interviewer is concerned, that's your answer and you're sticking with it.

This reply may understandably be followed with the question, 'Then why do you want to leave your job?' We've already looked at how to answer this (p. 249).

'What sort of people do you find it difficult to work with?'

As always, you need to resist criticizing other people. Don't be drawn into bitching about the PA in your department who's always trying to boss people around, or the programmer who is always moaning about their workload. Start by saying that you generally find most people are easy to work with, but if you had to pick a type you found difficult it would be people who don't pull their weight, and don't seem to care about the standard of their work.

Preparation exercises

You're bound to be asked some pretty tough questions during your interview. We all have areas we might prefer not to be asked about, or topics we find tricky. Or maybe we just get nervous when we're put on the spot. So here are a few ideas to help you prepare for the trickiest questions.

1   Sit down and think up the five or six questions you'd *least* like to be asked. Maybe you spent a long time in one job without promotion, and you don't want to come across as a low achiever. Or perhaps you find some people tricky to deal with and you don't want to answer too many questions about how you handle difficult people. Write down your list of 'hate' questions, and then work out answers to all of them.
2   Enlist the help of a couple of friends or colleagues. Maybe you could ask them to call you out of the blue once or twice in the next few days, and fire tough questions at you.
3   Ask a few friends and colleagues to tell you the toughest questions they've ever been asked at interview, and then work out how you'd answer them.

▶ Questions about your salary

The general rule when it comes to questions about salary is to get *them* to name a figure rather than allow them to put the ball into your court. If you name a salary, you can bet you'll never get more than the figure you've named. So unless – or until – you have a very clear idea of exactly what they're expecting to pay you, don't commit yourself to a specific figure.

When it comes to salary,
get *them* to name a figure rather
than allow them to put
the ball into your court.

The following questions are intended to get you to name your price. The recommended answers are intended to sidestep the issue without causing offence or appearing unreasonable. Once you are offered the job, then you can negotiate – following the guidelines set out in Chapter 19. You may wish to read this before attending an interview. You never know, they may offer you the job on the spot – although this is very unlikely.

'What is your present salary?'

You don't want to answer this. If you're offered the job, they'll try to get away with paying you as close as they can to your existing salary – at best it will hold the negotiating level down.

Say something such as, 'I think salaries can be misleading, as it's really the whole remuneration package that counts. Of course, that's harder to quantify.' Then ask if you can return to the question later, once you get to a point where you need to talk about it in more detail (i.e. when they offer you the job).

'What salary are you expecting?'

You don't want to answer this one either, because there's no chance of getting any more than you say now, and a good chance of scaring them off if you ask too much. So answer a question with a question: 'What salary would you expect to pay for this post?' or ask what salary range has been allocated. If they refuse to answer at this stage, you can reasonably do so too.

If they quote a salary and ask for your response, let them know you were thinking of something a little higher, but not out of their reach (assuming you'd agree to that yourself). If they suggest a range, quote them back a range which is higher but overlaps. So if they say £20–25,000 you might say you were thinking of £24–28,000. You're edging them up, but you're not putting them off.

'How much do you think you're worth?'

All these salary questions are good news, essentially. Why would they bother to ask unless they were thinking of offering you the job? This partic-ular question is really the previous one again with a nasty twist to it. It's just a matter of justifying what you're asking for – once you've played the previous game of making them go first.

You should already have an idea of the going rate for the job in the indus-try or the organization (especially if it's an internal job), so ask for a little more and explain that you've studied salary surveys and so on and, since your experience and skills are above average for the job, you believe you're worth above the average pay. By the way, you can expect the interviewer to respond by saying that the figure you name is too high – that's just part of the negotiating tactic. Don't let it dent your confidence.

Expect the interviewer to say that the salary figure you name **is too high –** that's just part of **the negotiating tactic.**

▶ Unexpected questions

Some interviewers like to catch you off-guard, and many of these questions are intended for just that purpose. They're not just trying to be unpleasant for the sake of it. They either have a good reason for wanting to know the answer, or they want to know how you cope with the pressure of an unexpected question. The key rules here are:

● Pause before you answer if you need to (interviewers rather like this as they can see you're really thinking about your answer).

● If you're unsure what the interviewer means by the question, ask for clarification.

● Stay cool and unflustered, and don't argue with the interviewer.

'Sell me this pen'

Some interviewers like asking this kind of question even if you're not applying for a sales post. The aim is to see that you focus not on features ('It's solid silver') but on the benefits to them ('It will impress people'). So give them four or five benefits of the pen (or notepad, or paperclip or whatever they've asked you to sell them), and then finish, half-jokingly, with a standard closing technique: 'Shall I put you down for two dozen?' or 'Would you prefer it in black or red?'

'Tell me a story'

This is a semi-trick question. You're supposed to demonstrate whether you have a sufficiently logical mental approach to ask for the question to be more specific before you answer it. So ask the interviewer, 'What kind of story?' They will probably ask for a story about you, and are likely to specify whether they want a work-related or a personal story. Then just relate some anecdote which shows you in a good light (so have one ready).

'What do you think about privatization/global warming/the Balkans (or whatever)?'

The interviewer is trying to find out how much of an interest you take in the world in general, and also to get an idea of your values and attitude to life. Whatever the topic, you need to demonstrate in your answer that you can see both sides of an argument, that you don't view things in an over-simplistic way, that you can discuss a subject fluently, and that you are capable of making judgements.

So don't rant on about your particular views (if you hold strong views) without acknowledging the other side of the debate. You are most likely to be asked these kinds of questions by companies to whom they are relevant. Pharmaceutical companies may ask your views on supplying cost-price drugs to developing countries; banks might ask your views on interest rates. So take into account their likely view on the subject.

▶ Very personal questions

There is another category of question that you shouldn't be asked, but it's as well to be prepared. Certain questions are technically illegal, or can be if there isn't a sound, relevant reason for asking them. These include questions relating to your race, religion or sex, questions about your medical history, or about your future plans for a family, and that sort of thing. But what do you do if you're asked? You can obviously answer if you wish to, but what if you'd rather not?

Certain questions are technically illegal, or can be if there **isn't a relevant reason** for asking them.

While you're perfectly entitled to get defensive and demand that your interviewer retract the question, such behaviour may not help you get this job. Your best bet is to say politely, 'Can I ask why you need to know that?' Unless there's a legitimate reason, this will almost certainly lead to a retraction. If they persist in asking you something totally unreasonable, you will have to choose between refusing firmly or answering anyway (whether truthfully or not).

* * *

Hopefully, you'll now be feeling much more confident about what to expect at interview and any tough questions that might be fired at you. But what if you're asked to give a presentation?

If you're not used to giving presentations, this can be a nerve-wracking experience, but preparation is everything. In the next chapter we'll guide you through the process of picking a suitable topic, structuring the presentation, organizing your material, using prompt notes and controlling your voice and nerves. Think of it as another opportunity to shine and sell yourself.

In the modern world of business,
it is useless to be a
creative, original thinker
unless you can also
sell what you create.

David Ogilvy

Chapter fourteen

Presentations

Usually it will be at second or even third interview stage that you may be asked to prepare a presentation, and you'll be given advance notice. Presentations are time-consuming for the audience as well as the person preparing them, so it's common to keep this stage of the recruitment process to the final few candidates. Of course, if your job is one where you work mainly by yourself, then you may escape the presentation stage altogether. However, for a lot of jobs, especially in large organizations, giving presentations is an integral part of the role and they'll want to see how you perform.

Recruiters will take different approaches to asking you to give a presentation. They will almost always give you a warning that you will have to do this, but the topic upon which you present may be either chosen by you or it may be something selected for candidates by employers. If the topic is notified in advance, this may be as far ahead as being part of your letter of invitation, or it may be just 20–30 minutes beforehand, as a further test of your ability to organize information under pressure. At senior management level, it is likely that a topic will be chosen for you and that you will be given a more complex range of information to work on.

If you have to choose a topic, you'll be able to pick a subject that interests you and that you'll enjoy speaking about. On the other hand, if you are allocated a set topic, then you don't face the agonizing decision of whether you have selected something appropriate – and you know that other candidates have been allocated the same subject and that you're all in the same boat. We'll be looking soon at some examples of topics that were set for presentations for graduate level recruitment (see p. 293).

▶ Why include presentations in the recruitment process?

Consider how many real work situations require this skill and you can see why it's a much used test. Teaching a class of students, presenting a new product or service idea to a sales team, running a staff training session for new recruits, presenting annual turnover figures to a board of directors, giving evidence to a parliamentary committee, prosecuting or defending a case in court, giving information to a group of holiday-makers about their resort and the facilities on offer – the list is endless.

Remember that this exercise is not designed to humiliate you and make you jump through unnecessary hoops. It's designed to test a skill that will be needed for the position you're applying for, and to provide the interviewer with some idea of how you cope in a potentially stressful situation.

▶ Presentation fundamentals

You may be quite familiar with either giving presentations yourself or of sitting through those given by others. You may already have a good idea of what works and what doesn't. You know what keeps your attention and what causes surreptitious glances at your watch; what inspires you or what leaves you thinking about the pile of work in your in-tray that you had to abandon to attend this event. However, you should still prepare carefully before every presentation.

Whatever the subject you are talking on, the length of time you have been allocated to speak, the time you have been given to prepare, or the level of career entry or career development at which you are participating, there are some fundamental guidelines that will always apply.

You need to prepare **not just** the content of the presentation, **but also the delivery.**

The main stages are as follows:

1 Structure your information

2 Organize your material

3 Control your voice

4 Use prompt notes

5 Use visual aids

6 Watch the time.

Let's look at each of these in more depth.

1 Structure your information

If you're still in education, or have recently left college, school or university, you'll be well aware that any essay, project or other assignment has to have a structure. Any project needs an opening that sets the scene, some interesting content that follows a logical pathway, and a conclusion that is related to what has gone before. The same applies to any presentation. Whether it lasts for 5 minutes or 30 minutes, and whatever the subject, your presentation must have a clear structure and include a short introduction and a concluding summary. Don't forget to thank your audience for listening at the end.

Whatever the subject, **your presentation must have** a clear structure and include **a short introduction and** a concluding summary

2 Organize your material

Organize yourself by working out the main points that you want to get across. Don't go for too many of these – between three and six is probably enough. Don't be like one much-quoted Oxford don who was overheard turning to a somewhat weary-looking colleague and saying 'And eleventh ...'. Our concentration spans and capacity to retain new information are limited, even though this varies from one individual to another.

3 Control your voice

In the public arena, when you are speaking to a group, mastering your breathing is essential – not just for the preparation, but for the delivery too.

Actors, singers and those who play wind instruments learn a great deal about how to use their breathing both to improve the quality of their voices (or sound of their instruments) and to control nerves and anxiety. Many businesses that offer their staff presenting skills training will include a mini version of such breath training as part of that course. However, you can practise much of it without ever attending a course.

Breathing exercise

Lie down on the floor in some private place. Begin breathing deeply and place one hand on your lower abdomen. You should be able to feel your abdomen pushing against your hand as you breathe in and then sinking as you breathe out. The point of this exercise is that most of us don't use the total capacity of our lungs. On average we use only about one-third of our lung capacity and this tends to be the top third, which inevitably makes our voices sound more nasal and less resonant. As a bonus, this kind of deep abdominal breathing really does help you to feel in control.

Speaking exercise

Think also about making your voice sound interesting. Modulate it rather than speaking in a monotone – put some feeling into what you're saying. There is a very good exercise to help develop this, which you can do with a friend. Ask them to sit down with their back to you, so that they can't see your facial expressions. Pick a list of neutral words, perhaps the numbers one to ten, or nothing that is likely to provoke humour. Say those neutral words in a very soft voice, no more than a whisper, but try to put some feeling like enthusiasm, concern or delight into those words. Note beforehand which words you are going to use to convey which emotions and then get your partner to write down their responses and see how well they coincide with yours.

Correct breathing will also help you to speak more loudly without shouting. It's very easy – especially when you are nervous – to speak softly, but if your audience can't hear what you're saying, then you've lost them immediately. Always check that everybody can hear you – ask them once you have given some very brief introduction such as 'Good morning, today I am going to talk about our latest product launch ...'. Checking that your audience can hear you not only serves a practical purpose but immediately lets them know this is a two-way event – you are interested in their experience, as well as wanting to put across your own points.

If your audience can't hear **what you're saying,** then you've **lost them immediately.**

One actor who runs training courses says that if you think of the volume of your voice as being on a scale of 1 to 6, when you are speaking to a group you should always aim to have the volume dial at 4. You may often feel that this is too loud – if you are the speaker – but for your audience clarity is paramount. It also conveys the notion that you are confident about what you are saying – and that you feel it is worth hearing.

4 Use prompt notes

Don't read from a script – it sounds boring, it stops you making eye contact with your audience, and in fact it really stops you engaging with them at all. However, it's fine, indeed wise, to have prompt notes. These are most easily handled if they are a written on small cards – index cards or blank postcards are ideal. You should number these, so that in the unlikely event of you dropping them all, you can easily put them back in order without your presentation falling apart.

Don't read from a script –
it sounds boring and
stops you making eye contact
with your audience.

Top Tip **Public speaking**

There is a tendency to speak far too quickly when you are giving a presentation. This may be because you're anxious or feel that you must cover everything – or simply because you can't wait to get it over with! Make a conscious effort to slow down – your audience will find it easier to absorb what you are saying, easier to ask questions (if you have invited them to) and you will appear much more confident. If you feel ill at ease, then so will your audience.

5 Use visual aids

Your options to use visual aids will vary, but in many situations, especially at management development level, you may have a full range of equipment available to you, including PowerPoint, OHP, flip-charts and white boards.

There's no rule that says that because everything is available, you have to use it all. It is, however, reasonable to assume that if visual aids equipment has been made available to you, then you should use some of it. Bear in mind that different members of an audience respond differently – some people really like visual information, others concentrate more on what you're saying. By offering both words and visual aids, you have the chance of winning the attention of most of your audience.

6 Watch the time

Keep an eye on the time. When planning your presentation, make sure that you deliver it at a moderate pace in the time allowed, with a few minutes to spare. In this way, if there are any questions or interruptions, you can take this in your stride without having to miss out sections of what you had planned to say.

Rehearse at home prior to the interview, preferably in front of an audience of friends or family and check how long it's taken. They should also be able to provide useful feedback on the content and tone. Rehearsing it in front of a live audience should also help you to get over your nerves if this your first presentation.

It's not a bad idea to have one optional section in your presentation, which you can either miss out or include, according to how time is going. Remember that where presentations are being given as part of a selection process, the time-keeping tends to be very strict – you may even be cut off in mid-sentence.

Top Tip **If things do go wrong ...**

Try not to get flustered if things do go wrong – coping in adverse circumstances can gain you marks. Losing your thread, showing the wrong slide or dropping your prompt cards doesn't mean you have failed – bursting into tears or running out of the room probably does. Using humour can help – 'This is designed to show you how NOT to give a presentation!' will usually raise a smile.

▶ Topics for presentations

Here are some examples of topics that have been set as subjects for presentations at graduate selection level:

- The achievement of which I am most proud.
- How I set about planning an assignment.
- This interests me – I hope it interests you too.
- Getting people to work well together.
- The customer is always right.
- Good reasons to become a ... [whatever the position applied for].
- Business studies [or any other subject that you have been studying] is a really useful subject.
- Staying one step ahead of your competitors.
- Taking a year off to travel puts you behind on the career ladder.
- How university education should be funded.
- How I would solve London's transport problems.
- The impact of email on business communications.

Unless you are specifically asked to speak about your course, it's a good idea to think of something different – for example, talk about a decision, an achievement or an interest. The chances are that other candidates will also be tempted to resort to talking about their studies as a good, safe option, so even though you may present it incredibly well, if yours is the tenth talk on the same subject, even the most fair-minded and scrupulous assessor may be affected by the boredom factor.

If yours is the tenth talk on **the same subject, even** the most fair-minded assessor may be **affected by the boredom factor.**

Employers will not ask you to speak on overtly political topics, but they may ask you to speak on more general current issues: how you see Britain's role in Europe, factors to consider in a good environmental policy, the impact of global markets on a particular sphere of employment, etc.

As well as the general topics listed above, you may be asked to give a presentation that relates directly to your job. For example, someone applying for a job as a trainee teacher might be asked to talk about what makes an interesting lesson, a trainee lawyer might be asked to talk about the Human Rights Act, etc.

When someone is asked to give a presentation at middle and senior management level, the topics are far more likely to relate directly to the business concerned. They are also more likely to be based on reading material beforehand and presenting a report on what they've just read.

In addition to being asked to give a presentation at the interview, there's a whole range of other tests you may be expected to sit. These can be broadly divided into four categories: verbal, numerical, diagrammatic and psychometric (personality) tests. In the next chapter we'll offer guidance on how to prepare for these mentally and intellectually, and pass on some important tips for what to remember on the day.

15

Selection

tests

mployers use selection tests as part of their recuitment efforts for a variety of reasons:

- to verify applicants' claims (information supplied on CV and at interview may not be true)
- to sift the best candidates from the rest
- to eradicate subjectivity (interviewer bias)
- to make the right choice.

Preparation is one of the four big Ps of test-taking – Preparation, Practice, Performance and Positive thinking. There are many steps you can take to ensure that you perform at the optimum of your ability on the day you take the test. Preparation falls into three categories: psychological preparation, intellectual preparation and what we might choose to call commonsense or practical preparation.

Preparation is one of the four big Ps of test-taking– **Preparation, Practice, Performance** and **Positive thinking.**

Before we look at the various types of test you may be asked to sit, there are some general guidelines on how to prepare yourself psychologically. Most people experience nerves to some extent about being tested and such fears can often increase as the day of the test approaches. It's important not to let these negative feelings mar your performance on the day. Let's look at some ways to help you conquer your nerves.

▶ Psychological preparation

Relaxation

Feeling relaxed and confident about taking any sort of test is a very good way to improve performance. Much of this relaxation and confidence comes directly from doing the intellectual preparation mentioned above. It's far easier to feel confident if you know you are well prepared for the sorts of tasks you might face.

As with any other situations in life, not all candidates will feel equally worried about taking selection tests. I have talked to some people, both undergraduates and more experienced professional and managerial staff, who really do relish the challenge of some of these 'tests' and who prefer them to interviews. If, however, you are not in this group – and large numbers of people certainly are not – then being able to keep calm in potentially anxious situations is useful.

There are all sorts of relaxation tapes and advice guides on the market. Whether you want to use a product like this is very much a matter of personal choice, but some people do find that being talked through a relaxation exercise is beneficial. Try also some of the deep-breathing exercises outlined in Chapter 14 on giving presentations (p. 289). These are designed to help you sound confident and project your voice more effectively, but they have an added benefit of steadying your whole body.

Another good relaxation exercise is to lie on the floor, on a mat or a carpet, and progressively tense and relax different parts of your body. Begin with your toes, scrunching them up as tightly as you can, and then gradually move up your feet, legs, etc., finishing with the muscle groups in your neck and face.

Some people already have a chosen exercise regime that helps – this may be yoga, Pilates, going to the gym, or training for a marathon. It really doesn't matter what you choose – so long as it suits you.

Visualizing a positive outcome

Many hypnotherapists and counsellors dealing with stress management also teach their clients to visualize the stressful situation as having a positive outcome. There is nothing strange or mysterious about this – it is a very common technique to help you feel more positive about coping with any situation, whether it is sitting a written test, giving a presentation or attending an interview.

Visualize the stressful situation **having a positive outcome.**

Picture yourself turning up for the test, feeling calm and confident – arriving in good time, but not with so much time to spare that you have time on your hands. Picture the test room with its desks and chairs and decide whether you would like to sit near the front, at the end of a row, or close to a window if there is one. You are one of the first, though not the first, to arrive, so you can choose the spot that suits you best. Picture yourself feeling comfortable, breathing deeply and feeling quite eager to get started.

Follow this process through in your mind, making sure to picture the questions being not too difficult, your time management being good, and coming out at the end of the test session feeling that you have put in a good performance – the best you possibly could.

Although imagining that the questions are easy will not actually make them easy, having a positive and confident attitude will help. Sportsmen and women, musicians and actors will often apply techniques like this to aid their performances.

Banish negative thoughts

It is easy to impede your chances of success by allowing negative thoughts to crowd out positive ones. Things like 'I never do well at tests', 'I was hopeless at maths when I was at school', 'my memory isn't what it was', 'I hate doing things in timed situations', 'it's a long time since I have had to take any sort of test, I'll probably make a mess of it', all hinder good performance. If you feel that any of these really are true, e.g. 'I was never any good at maths at school', then make sure this is an area where you put in some extra preparation well before the test.

▶ Commonsense preparation

If you're going for an interview with a company, then as we discussed earlier in Chapter 4 you need to find out as much about it as you can beforehand. This process is exactly the same for tests – the more you know about them, the better.

Make sure that you know when and where to turn up and that you have read all the instructions. Do you need to bring anything with you (e.g. calculator or laptop)?

Often, the employer will send you some practice material with answers, so that you can familiarize yourself with what the questions will look like. Use this wisely – if you cannot immediately get the answers right, read any advice given with the practice material and try to work out the process to achieve the right answer. Be just as scrupulous if you do get answers right – unpick the steps you went through to achieve this, so that you can use the same mental process on other similar questions in the real test.

If the tests are part of a graduate selection programme, the whole process could involve social events too, so ensure that you have the appropriate clothes with you.

If you have a disability or some other special concern about the tests, contact the employer or the testing organization as soon as you are invited to a test. There may be special arrangements that they can and should make on your behalf, but they will not be able to do this without due warning.

Top Tips Preparing for tests

- Find out as much as you can about what sorts of test you'll be taking.

- Read the job description or any other information you have about the company – this will sometimes give you clues about what to expect. For example, if good numerical skills are stated as being essential, it might be reasonable to assume that these will be tested; if good presentation skills are important, you might be asked to give a presentation, etc. (See Chapter 14 for advice on preparing for presentations.)

- Look at books that help you prepare for specific tests. For example, there are books on specific areas like computer aptitudes and there are books with extensive examples of diagrammatic tests.

- Visit testing companies' and employers' websites.

- Seek appropriate coaching if you think you need it.

Find out as much as you can about what sorts of tests you'll be taking.

You may also find it useful to complete the skills questionnaire on the next page, which will give you an idea of where you already have strengths/skills/knowledge and so help you refine your preparation. Even before you add up your scores for each of the six sections, you will easily see where your strengths – and therefore your weaknesses – lie. In terms of aptitude tests, *Section 3 Communicating* relates to verbal reasoning, *6 Numerical* relates to numerical reasoning and *4 Problem-solving* relates most closely to diagrammatic reasoning. Although the questionnaire is not an objective measure, it may help you clarify your likely areas of difficulty in test sessions.

Skills questionnaire

Rate how good you are at the following:	Score 6 = high 1 = low
1 Creative	
Drawing, painting	
Performing music	
Writing creatively	
Using your imagination in work situations	
Being sensitive to aesthetic qualities	
2 Influencing	
Negotiating a deal or a successful outcome	
Persuading people around to your point of view	
Selling a product, a service or an idea	
Managing other people	
Organizing events, seminars, conferences, etc.	
Promoting ideas effectively	
3 Communicating	
Writing reports, summaries, proposals and letters	
Learning foreign languages	
Reporting on events	
Speaking in public	
Understanding complex written information	
4 Problem solving	
Analyzing information	
Using maps and other diagrammatic information	
Restoring equipment	
Detecting faults in a system	
5 Social	
Relating to a wide range of people	
Showing insight and understanding	
Explaining, teaching, training	
Offering support and advice	
Listening to others	
Building relationships and networks	

6 Numerical	
Interpreting graphs	
Interpreting statistical data	
Solving quantitative problems	
Producing accounts and budgets	
Interpreting financial information	

▶ Types of tests and how to prepare

There is a variety of tests that you may be asked to sit, and these can be broadly grouped under the following four headings:

1 verbal

2 numerical

3 diagrammatic

4 personality.

The kind of tests you have to sit will affect your preparation. If you are simply told that you will have to sit a range of tests, then you might reasonably assume that it is most likely to include a group of ability tests and the most common combination of these is verbal reasoning, numerical reasoning and diagrammatic reasoning.

To some extent the area of work you are applying for will dictate the tests you are most likely to encounter. Diagrammatic reasoning tests, for example, are used to select those who are most suitable to work in computing, especially software and systems development, whereas verbal reasoning tests are used across an extensive range of jobs in management, retail, leisure, customer services – in short, any job where you may be called upon to use your communication skills.

Employers should, if they are following best practice, notify you in advance that you will be required to sit tests. You should not turn up expecting only an interview and then find that you are going to sit a battery of tests and selection exercises.

Of course, if you follow the advice we gave earlier, you'll remember to phone up the organization prior to the interview to find out how long it's scheduled to last. If it's more than a half-hour, ask if you'll be expected to sit any tests and, if so, what sort of tests.

Phone up the organization prior to the interview and **ask how long it's scheduled to last** … and if you'll be expected to sit any tests.

Some people worry that if tests are measuring fixed abilities, then preparation will make little difference to their overall score. Before jumping to this conclusion remember that:

- being familiar with what to expect will help, especially if you've been out of the tests and examination system for some time
- the first time you take an aptitude test your score may be low because you're not used to doing them
- you may be tested for abilities that you haven't exercised for a long time, such as numerical ability, so practice can vastly improve your score.

So how different are these tests to other examination or testing procedures that you have experienced? Whatever the type of test, the answers are nearly always multiple choice, so if you've only recently left school, you'll be familiar with these. You'll see a question and this will be followed by three or four possible answers and you have to choose the correct one. Some typical test paper questions are included in Chapter 17, where the examples are laid out in the way they would be in many test papers. This chapter will show you some individual examples of different types of question and some particular ways of preparing for each kind of test.

▶ 1 Verbal tests

Verbal tests might be the ones that we anticipate giving us fewest problems. We speak and write all the time, and verbal communication and usage is absolutely a part of everyone's daily life. But even if we do not expect to have too hard a time with these tests, they can prove daunting.

This was brought home to me when working with university undergraduates and postgraduates who sometimes came to discuss their test results with me. Those who were studying predominantly word-based academic disciplines were always particularly surprised and upset if they found a verbal test difficult, or if they did not achieve a good score. Verbal tests, however, are not the same as actually using words, conversing, discussing, presenting or writing. They test very specific skills, as outlined below.

Spelling tests

These tests may take various forms. For example, two spellings of the same word are given and you are asked to choose the one that is correct.

Example 1

accommodation

accomodation

In this instance the first spelling is correct and you will be asked to tick it, put a circle round it or underline the incorrect word.

Sometimes you will be given a whole list of words where some are spelt correctly and some incorrectly and you have to pick out those that are wrong.

Example 2

collaborate	promolgate
discerning	controversy
advisery	developement
assimilate	improvement

Three of the above words are spelt incorrectly and should be underlined.

Answer

The correct spellings are advisory, promulgate and development.

It's a myth that employers don't care about spelling any more just because everyone now uses spell-checkers. The spell-checker offers you several options if you have spelt the word wrongly, but if you don't know what you are aiming for, you can still make a mistake. The spell-checker does not question the meaning of the words you have used. Fairly or unfairly, poor spelling is often equated with a generally sloppy or careless attitude and there may still be occasions when you are writing down something for a customer, a client or a colleague and do not have any electronic support available.

Commonly misspelt words

There are some words that are frequently spelt wrongly. Those below are the ones you are most likely to meet in either a test or a business context:

advisory affect analysis assessment businesses committee controversy correspondence development discerning effective efficient forecast fundamental improvement independent maintenance persistent separate syndicate

Learn to spot the difference too between *principle* (noun meaning fundamental rule) and *principal* (adjective meaning 'main', though as a noun it can also mean the head of a college). This one often crops up.

Testing your understanding of word meanings

You may be given a group of four words and asked to pick out the word that has a different meaning from the other three.

Example 3

(a) weary   (b) tired   (c) exhausted   (d) fatigued

Answer

The odd one out is 'exhausted' because this has another meaning: a supply or a resource can be exhausted, so the word is not only a description of feeling as if you need a rest. It is easy to pick 'weary' because this is an adjective and all the others are past tenses of a verb.

Example 4

(a) quick   (b) fast   (c) rapid   (d) running

Answer

In this example, the odd one out is the word 'running' which is the only verb. Again, there is a slight trick in the question because both the words 'rapid' and 'running' tend to make you think of water and lead you in the wrong direction.

In these tests you'll often find more than one answer that seem to be right, so you need to think carefully about the result and go through a logical and methodical process before making your final decision.

In another version of this type of question, you're given a word and then asked to choose a word with a similar meaning from a given list of four or five words.

Example 5

'Quarrelsome' means the same as:

(a) furious   b) aggressive   (c) argumentative   (d) irritable

Answer

The correct answer is 'argumentative' because while all four words are associated with bad-tempered behaviour, only 'argumentative' and 'quarrelsome' mean liable to disagree and take a contrary point of view.

Sometimes you'll be asked to find the opposite to a word by selecting from a given list.

Example 6

'Fertile' means the opposite of:

(a) desert   (b) barren   (c) arid   (d) fecund

Answer

The correct answer is 'barren'.

There are also tests that ask you to work out the relationship of one word to another.

Example 7

'Wardrobe' is to 'clothes' as 'dustbin' is to:

(a) dirt   (b) recycling centre   (c) rubbish   (d) waste bin

Answer

The correct answer is 'rubbish', because a dustbin contains rubbish in the way that a wardrobe contains clothes.

Top Tip Verbal tests

When you are dealing with questions about word meanings and word relationships, pay really close attention to the question. Note phrases like 'the same as' or 'the opposite of', because it is very easy to get into a rhythm of thinking that a series of questions that *look* similar are asking the same thing, when in fact there may be a variety of question types.

When you are taking tests like these, remember that there are certain standard ways in which words relate to one another:

- **same meanings**, e.g. prohibition and ban
- **opposite meanings**, e.g. lively and lethargic
- **signifying part to whole**, e.g. letter to word
- **sequences**, e.g. Tuesday, Wednesday, Thursday
- **same category groups**, e.g. colours, numbers, capital cities
- **dual meanings**, e.g. to cleave together, or to cleave, meaning to separate.

Grammatical usage tests

You'll encounter these tests for some clerical and administrative jobs, but occasionally at higher levels too, if a significant part of your work is going to involve producing good written material, reports, publicity brochures, press releases, etc.

Example 8

Which of the following sentences is grammatically correct?

(a) You can find a copy of our company's latest annual report on our website.

(b) You can find a copy of our companies latest annual report on our website.

(c) You can find a copy of our companies' latest annual report on our website.

(d) You can find copies of our five subsidiary companies' annual reports on our website.

Answer

The correct answers are (a) and (d).

People often make mistakes with apostrophes, but there is nothing mysterious about them. If something belongs to only one person or one object, e.g. a company, then the apostrophe comes *before* the 's'. If something belongs to a group of objects, e.g. five companies, then the apostrophe comes *after* the 's'. Unpick this by asking yourself whether it is one or many things that is being described.

Watch out though for the major exception of *it's*, which can only be used as a shortened form of 'it is' and not as a possessive. So use the apostrophe for 'It's a nice day' but not for 'the dog wagged its tail'.

In terms of preparation for aptitude tests, it's probably not worth attempting to revisit all the basic rules of English grammar in any great detail. But it is worth reminding yourself about differences between verbs (words of action), nouns (objects) and adjectives (words of description), because these will help when you're tackling any word-meaning exercises where you have to pick out similarities, differences and relationships.

Word placement tests

Yet another type of verbal test asks you to place words that either sound similar or have similar spellings in the correct place in pairs or groups of sentences.

Example 9

Look at the following two sentences and put the correct word (either 'there' or 'their') into the blank spaces:

- It had always been ... intention to develop a new range of fashion products.
- It was now at least six months since ... had been any significant development taking place.

Answer

'Their' should be placed in the first sentence and 'there' in the second.

Beware of tests like these: don't always assume that you have to use both words, but work out which has the appropriate meaning and place it carefully.

Verbal comprehension tests

One of the most common features of verbal ability tests is a series of verbal comprehension tests. These give you a short passage to read through, followed by a few statements based on information contained in the passage. It's a short job to work out whether these pieces of information are true or false, using what you have read.

Example 10

'Very large portions of two European languages, English and Italian, have evolved from the same root – Latin. In a real sense English and Italian are like dialects of each other. The fact that they do not look alike at first sight is partly because English has changed substantially over time and partly because English has two roots – Indo-Germanic and Latin. The double origin accounts for the fact that English is a very rich language and there are very often two words in English that mean essentially the same thing.'

(a) Italian has only one root.	True/False
(b) English and Italian share their Latin roots.	True/False
(c) Italian is not a rich language.	True/False
(d) English has two roots.	True/False
(e) In English there are often two words that mean the same thing.	True/False

Answers

(a) False (b) True (c) False (d) True (e) True

The most important technique here is to base your answers on what is actually written down – this is not a test of your general knowledge or a point for debate. For example, you cannot draw the conclusion that 'Italian is not a very rich language' from what you have read – you have been given a reason why English is a rich language, but you have not been told that Italian is not rich. Always go back and check your answers against the text that is there in front of you. Don't use any prior knowledge you have on the topic and don't make assumptions.

This type of test is extremely common, particularly in graduate selection tests.

Top Tips Improving your spelling

- If you don't own a dictionary, buy one. Don't leave it unopened on your bookshelf – always look up any word of which you don't know the spelling and/or the meaning.

- Buy a thesaurus – it will help you with word meanings and expand your vocabulary.

- Have a healthy suspicion of your spell-checker: words that look or sound roughly the same may have totally different meanings (e.g. principal/principle; affect/effect; their/there/they're; lose/loose).

- Be aware of different company policies on UK or US spelling for words such as organise/organize, colour/color, center/centre; analyse/analyze and programme/program.

- If you're not into reading, make an effort to read a little more. Choose something that interests you – quality newspapers, journals of interest in your academic or professional field and any fiction and non-fiction that you think you'll enjoy.

- Games like Scrabble can be useful, although this might develop your lateral thinking as much as your spelling – no prizes for spelling the word 'quiz', but it gets a tremendous Scrabble score!

- Design some of the word meaning tests described above for yourself – working through the process in reverse is very useful.

- Get a friend to do your word tests. If they have difficulty, then teach them the process you have already been through – explaining to someone how to do something is a great test of whether you really know how to do it yourself.

- Be aware of some of the most common mistakes in spelling (like 'its' – see box on p. 305).

▶ 2 Numerical tests

An ability to deal with numbers is a big requirement in so many businesses and professions. This does not mean that everyone has to be a top mathematician capable of dealing with complex formulae, algebra and trigonometry. It means an ability to interpret numbers for business purposes. It's likely that if you ask someone what jobs involve numbers, their answer will be 'accountant', 'actuary' or 'bank manager', but anyone looking at profit and loss in a shop, a restaurant or an IT company, or anyone responsible for their own department's budget, has to have a basic understanding of what numbers mean.

Basic arithmetic tests

Example 11

9 + 13

Answer

22

Additions are not normally as simple as this, though some arithmetic tests do start with simple questions and become gradually more difficult. Remember also that tests are timed and therefore with straightforward arithmetic you will be expected to cover a lot of ground in a short time.

Brush up on dealing with percentages. Statistical information forms a part of so many jobs and very often information is given as percentages.

Example 12

What is 13% of 127?

Answer

16.5

Example 13

If $59 = 25\%$, what equals 100%?

Answer

236

Problem-solving arithmetic questions

Example 14

Nineteen members of staff all wish to contribute to a retirement gift for the twentieth member of their department. They decide that they will all contribute a fixed amount, but this amount will be pro rata according to whether they work full-time or part-time.

Ten members of the department work full-time.
Four members of staff work three full days a week.
Five members of staff work for two and a half days a week.
The total amount collected is £149.00.

How much were those who worked for three days a week asked to contribute?

Answer

£6.00

Some questions include some basic algebra.

Example 15

If $3x + 3 = 15$, what is x?

Answer

4

Example 16

If $4x - 4 = 20$, what is x?

Answer

6

Data interpretation tests

Data interpretation tests form the basis of many numerical reasoning tests, since these present the sort of problems you'll meet in a work situation.

Example 17

Look at the following table with its questions and answers.

| | Percentage of adults over 18 using local leisure facilities | | | |
	Adults 1999	Adults 2001	Males 2001	Females 2001
Swimming	10.5	14.5	6	8.5
Squash courts	11	9	7	2
Yoga classes	21	25	7	18
Weights and circuit training	22	19	13	6
Exercise classes	12	16	6	10

Assume for the purposes of this exercise that everyone involved was taking part in only one activity.

(a) In which year were the greatest number of people taking part in some kind of exercise?

(b) Were a higher proportion of males or females taking part in leisure activities of some kind in 2001?

(c) What was the most popular activity overall over the two years in question?

(d) What percentage of men took part in leisure activities in 2001?

Answers

(a) 2001

(b) Females

(c) Yoga classes

(d) 39%

Top Tips **Some basic maths**

- Remember that a minus multiplied by a minus always equals a plus.

- A minus multiplied by a plus always equals a minus.

- Work the problem in both directions with questions like: 'What is 17% of 347?' and 'If 43% = 72, what is 100?'

- Remember, percentages, decimals and fractions all represent ways of breaking something into parts and are simply ways of quantifying proportions.

- Remind yourself of very basic statistical concepts – mean, median and mode: *Mean* is the calculated average; *median* is the midpoint; *mode* is the most common.

Example 18

If temperatures in the Mediterranean for ten days in May were as follows, what was the median temperature?

Day 1   14C

Day 2   17C

Day 3   16C

Day 4   15C

Day 5   18C

Day 6   20C

Day 7   19C

Day 8   21C

Day 9   21C

Day 10   22C

Answer

The median is 18C because it occurs halfway between the lowest and the highest points (14C and 22C).

Familiarize yourself with patterns of numbers:

- **basic tables**, e.g. 2, 4, 6, 8, 3, 6, 9, 12, etc.
- **squared numbers**, e.g. 2, 4, 16, 64, 5, 25, 125, 625, etc.
- **square roots**, e.g. square root of 9 is 3, of 36 is 6, etc.
- **prime numbers** (numbers only divisible by 1 or by themselves), e.g. 7, 11, 13, 17, etc.

Although you will not necessarily be tested on all of these, some forms of test ask you to look for patterns in groups of numbers, so reminding yourself of these gets you more used to number patterns.

Look at graphs and tables in textbooks, trade journals and the financial press. This information is usually given with a written explanation – and it may be exactly this kind of written explanation that you are asked to provide when presented with a graph or a chart as part of a numerical reasoning test.

Remind yourself what different charts look like in Figures 1, 2 and 3. If you have Excel on your computer, you should be familiar with how to quickly change the appearance of charts based on the same basic data.

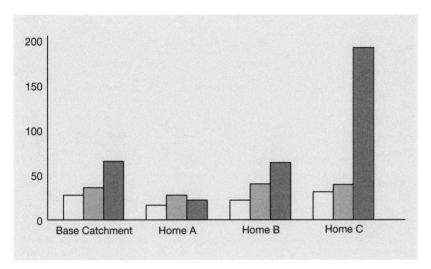

Figure 1 Bar chart

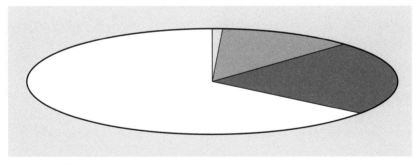

Figure 2 Pie chart

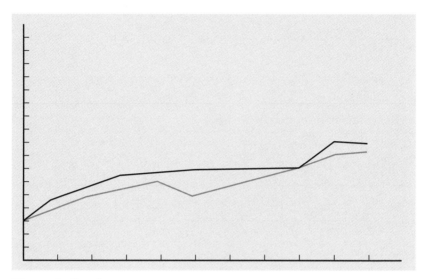

Figure 3 Graph

Top Tips Preparing for numerical tests

● Make sure you're familiar with the functions of a calculator – you're often allowed and required to use one in test sessions.

● Practise doing calculations in your head that you would usually do on a calculator. You could add up your shopping bill as you go round a supermarket, or add up what you have spent if you order something from a mail order catalogue. You can always double-check the figures with a calculator afterwards.

● Make yourself familiar with percentages – they occur frequently when you are interpreting statistics and they are not really difficult. Set yourself a few to work out and then check them with a calculator.

● Look at the financial and business press, which gives plenty of examples of financial data.

● Look at company annual reports.

- Do conversions of pounds sterling or euros into other currencies in your head.
- Explain basic mathematical processes to friends who are very good with numbers.
- Don't be afraid of numbers.

◗ 3 Diagrammatic reasoning tests

These tests are popular with employers for two reasons. First, they do not rely on the use of particular language skills for a successful performance. Second, they appear to be good predictors of success for working in such fields as computer programming. The tests provide a good measure of general intellectual reasoning because you're asked to find the underlying logical processes and solutions to a problem.

Finding patterns

Some tests ask you to find patterns or make links between different sets of information such as letters and numbers.

Example 19

What comes after A, B, D, G?

Answer

K: because A and B are one letter apart, B and D two letters apart, etc.

Example 20

If coffee is 3, 15, 6, 6, 5, 5, what is tea?

Answer

20, 5, 1: because numbers have been used to represent their respective places in the alphabet.

Example 21

What comes after red, blue, green?

(a) turquoise (b) pink (c) yellow (d) brown

Answer

Yellow: because the three previous colours have each lengthened by one letter.

This is an example where you can get thrown off the scent as you try to recall the order of the spectrum or look for something far more complicated than the straightforward logic required.

Example 22

Look at this diagram and decide how the sequence should continue.

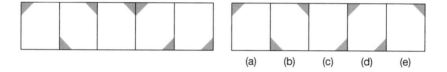

(a) (b) (c) (d) (e)

Answer

The correct answer is (b) because its diagonally opposite pair follows each single triangle. If you moved the single triangle one to the right, the only blank space would be the corner, which is diagonally opposite to it. These are the sorts of patterns that you have to seek out in diagrammatic tests.

Top Tips Diagrammatic reasoning tests

● Separate out the different elements that can be altered in these diagrams: shapes, orientation of shapes, number of lines or other elements involved, different colours, shaded or white areas. Once you start to identify these, the diagrams look far less daunting.

- Some magazine quiz books and even newspapers offer examples of these abstract brain teasers, so make use of them.
- When you have learned to solve these tests, explain them to someone who hasn't.

▶ 4 Personality tests

Remember the three questions at the back of every employer's mind when recruiting staff:

- Can they do the job?
- Will they do the job?
- Will they fit in?

Personality has a significant role to play in providing answers to all three questions and especially the second and third questions. Consider most working situations and remind yourself how the personality of your colleagues – those you manage and those who manage you – affects the day-to-day success of a business. If teams don't work well together or if a manager cannot motivate their staff, then productivity, sales targets, quality of service and customer care are all bound to suffer, along with staff turnover. This is something that employers really do want to get right.

Typical questions in personality questionnaires

Here are some examples of the types of question presented in personality questionnaires.

Example 23

I always enjoy meeting new people.

(a) True   (b) False

All you have to do is to tick or underline or cross out the appropriate response. The test booklet will make it clear, but you only have the two choices. Other questionnaires will give you a 'third way':

Example 24

'I am always methodical and organized when meeting a deadline.'

(a) True   (b) False   (c) Can't say

Others will give you a set of statements and you are asked to choose the one that best describes you:

Example 25

'If I go to a party I ...'

(a) Get into the spirit of things quickly and am often the centre of attention.

(b) Tend to look for any familiar faces first and start talking to someone I know.

(c) Stand in a quiet corner and observe things for a while.

(d) Approach someone who looks shy and start talking to them.

You may be asked to rate a statement according to whether you agree or disagree:

Example 26

'Other people always find it easy to talk to me.'

Strongly agree	Agree	Unsure	Disagree	Strongly disagree
1	2	3	4	5

Many candidates are more comfortable with tests like this because they prefer the degree of definition they feel it gives them.

Similarly you may be given descriptive words that you have to rate for agreement or disagreement. In this instance there would be instructions at the start of the test asking you to rate how strongly these words describe you.

Example 27

Calm

Lively

Conforming

Strongly agree	Agree	Unsure	Disagree	Strongly disagree
1	2	3	4	5

Preparing for and taking personality tests

Unlike aptitude and ability tests, there isn't a great deal of preparation that you can do or need to do if you are asked to complete a personality questionnaire. However, many candidates still feel very anxious about taking them. People tend to worry about what exactly is being tested and what might be revealed. Some people feel as though someone is prying into their business in a slightly underhand way. Of course, personality questionnaires are not that sinister – you are asked about all sorts of aspects of yourself during a selection interview and the reports that your referees complete may ask your referees questions about your work style, the way you relate to colleagues, customers, etc.

You should always be informed that you'll be required to take a personality test and should be told what will happen to the results and whether you'll be able to obtain any feedback. The 'test' session itself may be run in just as formal a setting as would be the case for any aptitude test, but the biggest difference is that there is unlikely to be a strict time limit. You will usually be given a recommended time – depending on the test concerned, this will be anything from 20 to 45 minutes, but you will not be penalized if you have not finished within this time and will normally be allowed to continue and complete the test. As with aptitude tests, you may be working with a booklet and answer sheet, a test booklet and computer, or increasingly you'll be asked to complete the whole questionnaire via a computer.

With a personality questionnaire – unlike aptitude tests – you do not need to rehearse and practise in advance, but do remember the following points:

Top Tips Personality questionnaires

- Listen carefully to any instructions the administrator gives you at the beginning of the session.

- Read any instructions contained in your booklet or on-screen.

- Don't waste time reading through the whole booklet and trying to second-guess what the questionnaire is seeking to find out – the test may not be timed, but doing this will not help you or affect your result.

- If the question offers you a 'not sure' or a '?' option, don't resort to this unless you really feel you cannot make a choice.

- Some questionnaires that have a longer rating scale – say 1 to 5, from strongly disagree to strongly agree, or something similar – may advise that you use the extreme ends of the scale only when you feel very strongly. This information will be contained in the written instructions at the beginning of the questionnaire and probably reiterated by the test administrator.

- Do take great care when entering your answers. It sounds obvious, but it's easy to get confused when you are rank ordering from 1 to 5 or ticking a series of either/or options. If you've read several statements that you think are true in your case, it is easy to get into the habit of just ticking the 'true' option.

- Read questions or statements carefully to ensure you understand them.

- Don't spend too long pondering a question and worrying about what to answer – with personality questionnaires it's usually best to go with your first response.

- Answer all the questions – leaving any out will affect your final profile.

- Respond as naturally as you can – don't try to guess which answer you think sounds best.
- Finally, try to enjoy it – you don't often get a quiet 45 minutes to think about nothing but you!

Don't be tempted to try to give the answers you think are the good ones. There is no such thing in these personality tests. Besides, a booklet containing anything from 100 to 200 questions will only be looking at four or five traits or 16 to 30 factors, so the same factor or trait is being measured by several different questions, all getting at the same point. It would be impossible as a candidate to unpick all this and there is really no point in trying. Many tests have an impression detector built into their design with questions put there deliberately to measure whether you are trying to convey a certain picture of yourself. Most important of all, you don't know what the 'right' answer is – because there isn't one – so don't waste time trying to guess what it is.

With personality tests,
don't waste time trying
to guess the right answer –
there isn't one!

Because you don't pass or fail – or even get a good or a poor score – on a personality questionnaire, giving back meaningful results of personality questionnaires is time consuming and therefore costly. This means at graduate or any other mass job-selection level, candidates are unlikely to be able to get hold of this information. However, if good practice is adhered to, applicants will be informed of what will happen to their results.

▶ Examples of the most common types of personality tests

There are many personality assessment tools on the market, but the three that we'll be examining below (The Myers-Briggs Type Indicator, the 16-Personality Factor Questionnaire and the Occupational Personality Questionnaire) are widely used. They also represent some of the different ways in which questions are asked and the range of factors and traits that are measured.

The Myers-Briggs Type Indicator

Based on the work of psychologist Carl Jung, the Myers-Briggs Type Indicator (MBTI) is widely used in occupational and other settings. It is a more popular tool for staff development and training than for selecting new recruits because it offers scope for examining someone's preferred ways of working, rather than offering the kind of assessments provided by some of the trait questionnaires. In this personality assessment you are measured along four independent dimensions:

- **Extroverted or introverted (E/I):** Extroverted people have a preference for dealing with the external world – with people, activity and objects. Introverted people are more concerned with the inner world of information and ideas. Extroverts like working with other people and seek variety in their work. Introverts like quiet, like to deal with one issue at a time, and are happiest working alone.

- **Sensing or intuitive (S/I):** Information gathered via the senses is the focus for the sensing person, who also likes to concentrate on the here and now. Those who are intuitive focus on the future, with possibilities and strategies. At work, the sensing person likes to solve practical problems and relies on experience rather than theory to tackle tasks. The intuitive person is far more concerned with the overview and enjoys coming up with new ways of doing things.

- **Thinking or feeling (T/F):** Thinking people are logical in the way they consider things and are less interested in social and personal consequences. Feeling people use subjective rather than objective information to reach decisions. Thinking people can be quite critical of others in the work setting and can appear insensitive. Feeling people enjoy working with others, pleasing people and helping others to feel included.

- **Judging or perceiving (J/P):** A judging person likes things to be structured and orderly and is very keen on things being properly planned. The perceiving person likes to be spontaneous. The judging person will focus determinedly on a task, sometimes to the exclusion of other things, while the perceiver is capable of being quite flexible. However, the perceiver can be hard to pin down to a particular course of action.

The MBTI questionnaire is designed to help people find out how they prefer to look at things and how they prefer to take decisions. The questionnaire comprises just over 80 questions and most of these are the type of question that gives you two options.

Example 28

Which of these two statements describes the way you more usually think or feel:

(a) You find it easy to keep a conversation going in almost any situation.

(b) You find it easy to keep a conversation going only with people that you know well.

Example 29

Do you usually get on well with people who are either:

(a) full of commonsense

or

(b) imaginative?

The questionnaire also contains a section that asks you to choose your preferred word from pairs of words such as 'concrete' or 'abstract', 'hard' or 'soft'.

The results of your questionnaire will be interpreted to produce a profile that places you on each of the four scales (E/I, S/I, T/F and J/P). You will be placed in one of 16 personality types represented by the letter on each scale to which your score is closest.

From reading the brief descriptions of the four scales above, it's easy to see that there is no right or wrong way to be. You can pick out desirable qualities for different work contexts and different working teams for any of the combinations, but you could also come up with some pretty unprepossessing combinations if you tried. The point about the MBTI – and this is true of many other questionnaires – is that they all suggest degrees of behaviour or likely ways of reacting, rather than absolutes.

When used in occupational settings, the MBTI indicates people's preferred working styles, but not their only possible working styles. So if you don't like to plan logically but prefer to let things take shape, this does not mean you *cannot* plan logically, rather it implies you are less comfortable working in this way. The MBTI is used often in career development counselling at work, or when companies are setting up mentoring and coaching programmes or going through periods of change. The MBTI is also widely applied in fields other than occupational testing – some people who have been through the process are so interested in their profiles that websites have sprung up where you can contact other people with a similar MBTI profile.

The 16-Personality Factor

Versions of the 16-Personality Factor (16PF) questionnaire have been in existence for more than 50 years. It's a very popular personality assessment that is used in selection and development at many different levels.

The 16PF is one of the questionnaires based on trait theories of personality. The standard version consists of around 185 questions exploring what sort of person you are. It asks about various subjects, such as your attitudes to other people, what you like doing and how you behave in particular situations. Most of the questions are of the type that give you three answer options: true/ can't say/ false.

Example 30

'I enjoy entertaining people and being the centre of attention.'

(a) True   (b) Can't say   (c) False

There are a few questions in the 16PF that look rather more like those you would expect to see in an aptitude test – asking you to pick out relationships between words, find patterns in letters and numbers – but these form only a small section of the test.

The factors that the 16PF measures are:

warmth	vigilance
intelligence	abstractedness
emotional stability	privateness
dominance	apprehension
liveliness	openness to change
rule consciousness	self reliance
social confidence	perfectionism
sensitivity	tension

▶ The Occupational Personality Questionnaire

This is another very popular personality tool, especially since it has been designed for use specifically in work settings. It is actually not one questionnaire but a whole group of them; employers can choose the version they think is most appropriate for their situation.

The most popular version of the Occupational Personality Questionnaire (OPQ) has 104 sets of four statements and for each of these you have to

state which one is the most like you and which the least. The personality scales on which it assesses candidates are:

persuasive	trusting	democratic
socially confident	achieving	conventional
data rational	independent	forward thinking
adaptable	modest	worrying
rule following	behavioural	affinitive
optimistic	innovative	caring
competitive	relaxed	variety seeking
controlling	emotionally confident	detail conscious
evaluative	decisive	tough minded
conceptual	outspoken	vigorous

The reports produced from scoring on these scales give a detailed profile of the kind of relationships you are likely to have with colleagues, the way you tackle problems, take decisions and plan assignments, and how competitive you are.

▶ So is there anything else you can do?

You've now run through a solid cross-section of different types of tests and prepared yourself intellectually for whatever challenge may be in store. You'll find a whole set of practice tests in Chapter 17 to hone your skills further. So is there anything else you can do to improve your chances?

Well, it's surprising how the most obvious things that can sometimes get overlooked, and how circumstances often seem to conspire to undermine your prospects, despite your best efforts. But don't let them! All it takes is a little planning, so you don't forget to set the alarm on the day of the test or end up rushing out of the flat with odd socks on or minus the test centre address. The next chapter will ensure you're prepared.

Chapter sixteen

16

What to do on the

day of

your test

▶ Before the test

Take care of yourself

This chapter focuses mainly on the day of your test, but it's worth giving a little thought to the day, or at least the evening, before. Too much alcohol or caffeine before facing any mentally taxing task is not a good idea, so try to think carefully about what you eat and drink on the evening prior to a test. Try to get a good night's sleep, too – don't stay up into the wee small hours working through mental arithmetic problems, reading the financial press or testing your knowledge of words.

On the day of your tests, make sure to eat breakfast. Many people skip breakfast if they are busy or anxious, but it's not wise to let your blood sugar plummet. You haven't eaten during all your hours of sleep, so give your system a bit of a boost. You'll know which foods make you feel good and which make you feel lethargic. If your tests are at a graduate selection centre or with a very large corporation, then your food is likely to be taken care of, so make sure you take full advantage of snacks and mealtimes whenever they are offered.

On the day of your tests, **make sure to eat breakfast.**

Check instructions

You should have done this before the day itself, but make sure that you have read any instructions carefully. Ensure that you know:

- what time to turn up
- where to turn up
- who you should report to

- what you should bring with you
- a contact number and name in case any problems arise.

Turn up for the test

This sounds too obvious to be true, but significant numbers of people do not turn up for test sessions to which they have been invited – so just being there increases your chances of being successful.

With the increasing impact of technology, you may find that some organizations ask you to do an initial test via a remote computer from home or at a careers centre. This would only be the case for an initial selection test, then, if you are successful at this stage, you would be invited to the more formal test sessions described here.

Turn up on time

This is true for any selection activity or appointment, but it is essential for test sessions. Plan your journey and, if you are driving, ensure that there'll be somewhere convenient for you to park. These tests are run under the same sorts of conditions as you would encounter in any formal examination, so if you're late, you'll not be able to sit the tests at all. In most instances you won't be offered an alternative date. This may be a little different if you are taking some tests set by an individual recruitment consultant or occupational psychologist on your own, but if you are taking part in any group test, this rule is pretty inflexible.

If something happens that really prevents you from turning up on time, it's worth letting the organization know, despite what has been said above. There may be a chance that you can be fitted in with another group of candidates and you have nothing to lose by asking – but you must have a very good reason.

Dress smartly

On many occasions you'll be taking tests as part of a wider recruitment process, perhaps involving interviews, discussions and role-plays. Even if this is not the case, it's much better to dress as smartly as you would for an interview – the other candidates probably will and you don't want to stand out as the person who didn't bother. You do need to be comfortable though – this is not the day to squeeze into the trousers that will only just do up or try out a new pair of shoes that might cause you discomfort. We looked at what to wear earlier in Chapter 12 on Interviews (p. 226) and the same rules apply here.

Dress as smartly as you would for an interview … you don't want to stand out as the candidate who didn't bother.

Time your arrival

Arrive with a little time to spare, but if you are very early, take a walk or go and have a cup of tea. Think about things other than the tests – these are not the sort of examinations where you should be going over information in your head at the last minute.

If you are early, you may get a chance to pick a seat that you like – near a window, a door, at the back, or whatever you prefer. Companies normally ensure that their test conditions are reasonably comfortable, so you won't have to fight for a desk or contend with demolition work going on in the room next door.

Check materials

The test instructions that you were sent in advance will have told you whether you will be working with pen/pencil and paper or whether – and this is increasingly the case – you will be working via a computer keyboard or a small hand-held computer. These factors themselves make no difference, but it's more reassuring if you know what to expect. In most instances all the test materials will be provided, so you don't have to bring your own pencils, calculators or anything else, but you may want to have some notepaper to hand to work things out before you commit your answers to the test paper itself.

The materials will either be a question book with appropriate spaces for you to fill in your answers, a test booklet and a computer to key in your answers, or a computer screen displaying the questions and showing you where and how to fill in your answers. If the test does come in pencil and paper form, it's most likely to be a test booklet with questions set out so that you either fill in answers in sections after each question, or you are given a separate answer sheet to complete as you work through the questions.

If you wear glasses or use a hearing aid, remember to take these items with you.

▶ During the test

Comply with instructions

You'll be told not to open your question book or work on your screen until the test administrator tells you to do so. Listen carefully to any other instructions they give verbally, such as what to do if you have a problem, reminders about where to enter your name, candidate number, etc.

Read any instructions carefully. You'll find clear information about how to fill in your answers, for example, putting a tick or a cross in a box, filling in a box, circling, underlining a letter or a number. These instructions will also tell you what to do if you realize you have answered something incorrectly and want to alter your answer. If you are doing a test via a computer, it's essential here too that you follow any instructions carefully.

Don't be tempted to race ahead and start reading questions until you know what to do. This will waste precious time, as you may have to back-track. Some tests get progressively more difficult as you work through, so if you start looking at some of the questions, you can make yourself panic unnecessarily and lose concentration on those questions that you *can* answer perfectly well.

Use sample questions to your advantage

Very often there are some sample questions at the beginning of the test, which the administrator will work through with the whole group. You are given an opportunity here to speak up if there is anything you don't understand – do take advantage of this. There is no mileage in impressing other candidates by appearing to know everything – they aren't employing you. You need to be sure that you really do understand what is required of you.

Read questions carefully

The fact that you're working quickly doesn't mean you should skim-read questions. The key to performing well on a verbal comprehension test is to read with care. With numerical tests, too, failing to read the question carefully can easily result in your choosing the wrong answer.

The key to performing well on
a verbal comprehension test is
to read with care.

Use time wisely

In general, tests such as spelling, arithmetic and data checking are run over a shorter time (10–15 minutes) and it's unlikely you'll have time to double-check any answers – testing your speed and accuracy is built into the test. Verbal, numerical and diagrammatic reasoning tests are usually run over a longer period (anything from 20 to 40 minutes) and contain a smaller number of more complex problems that require a different strategy from you.

If there is something you cannot answer, move on to the next question – you can always come back later. If you do end up tackling questions out of sequence, take great care not to get out of sequence with your answers – this can happen so easily, with serious consequences for your test score. With diagrammatic tests, it can sometimes help to move on to another question if you are really stuck – you may see things differently when you have worked through some other problems.

Continue to keep an eye on the clock – it's very easy to get engrossed in a particular question and lose track of time. Many candidates will not get right through all the questions, but the more correct answers you have the better, so move on rather than agonizing over a particular question.

Seek help

Once the test has officially started, the administrator won't be able to give you any help with questions that you don't understand (the only opportunity for that was when examples were worked through at the beginning). If this seems harsh, remember that it's exactly the same in any other examination situation, whether it's GCSEs, accountancy exams or driving test.

If you have any problems during the test session other than finding the questions difficult – for example, if you're having trouble with your computer screen, or your calculator won't work, or there seems to be something missing from your booklet, then do attract the attention of the administrator. Don't waste time trying to correct a technical problem yourself. Similarly if you feel unwell, don't hesitate to tell the administrator.

Work with intelligence

Studies have yielded different results on whether you should always go with your first answer. There is a tendency to believe that your intuition will have led you to the right answer first. There is no evidence for this; sometimes looking at something more carefully gives a better result. But don't take this approach to the extreme. Albert Einstein said that he often had to think through 99 different solutions to a problem and only the one-hundredth would be right – although you can stop short of this sort of intellectual rigour.

Don't just 'have a go' at answers unless you know this won't make things worse. Some tests are negatively scored, which means that as well as getting points for correct answers, you get points deducted for incorrect ones. Sometimes the administrator tells you about this, but sometimes the test booklet may just warn you not to guess answers. However, it is important not to let this approach stop you answering anything – you certainly won't score anything for handing back a blank answer sheet. If you're going to guess some of your answers, still try to work out what may be right – if there are several options, eliminate those which you're sure are incorrect, so reducing the amount of guessing you have to do.

This applies especially to numerical tests because the majority of them are designed so that you don't have to carry out detailed and lengthy calculations, but just have to spot a correct answer. For example, if you are asked to multiply 17.5 by 11.3, the correct answer is 197.75. Answers you are offered could include 1977, 519 and 75, as well as the correct answer. You need to be able to estimate quickly that 17 times 11 comes to something between 160 and 200 and not something as small as just under 20 or as large as nearly 2000.

Don't just 'have a go' at answers, unless you know they won't be scored negatively.

Look out for false trails

Similar looking numbers, similar sounding or looking words, and distractions in the question can all catch you out. Say you are given a series of numbers: 7, 14, 21, 28. You might assume that the answer to an anticipated question is 35, but the question might ask what is the sixth number in this sequence, the answer being 42. You might barely glance at the question because your brain has already seen the pattern and gone forging ahead. Look out for phrases like 'the next but one' or 'what letter comes before the list shown'. Tests do not contain trick questions, but they do demand that you stay on your toes and remain alert to exactly what is being asked.

Don't be distracted

Don't fall into the trap of convincing yourself that the candidate at the next desk is doing better than you because they seem to have worked further through the test booklet. You don't know anything about the quality of their answers, so just concentrate on your own performance. Don't worry about pausing from time to time to collect your thoughts, or to give your shoulders a stretch and take a few deep breaths – just don't make it a long pause.

The last few minutes

You may be warned a few minutes before the test time is up. If you are, make use of this to return to any questions you now feel you can answer, or to squeeze in a few more questions before the time is up – answering a few more questions can make a significant difference to your score.

Keep calm – stay confident

Even though examinations or tests of other kinds are familiar to you, some test material looks very strange. Don't be daunted if you haven't done questions quite like this before. Don't discourage yourself by believing you've got things wrong – just work steadily on through the questions.

Keeping a sense of balance is important. Just reading the advice above may have confused you – you may feel that you're being asked to work quickly yet to spend time working things out, to watch the clock yet to work steadily. The advice is not really conflicting – it's all aimed at having a calm, orderly and sensible approach to dealing with tests.

Self-confidence is not going to transform you instantly into a superb mathematician or a brilliant wordsmith, but it does help – if you feel confident and positive, you are far less likely to be put off. Tests can even be enjoyable – think of them as a mental exercise and the chance to do something different.

Top Tips Taking the test

- Learn what you can about the tests before you take them.
- Be well rested and make sure you've had something to eat and drink.
- Be on time.
- Follow written instructions precisely.
- Before the test starts, ask if there is anything you aren't sure about.
- Read all the questions carefully.
- Don't just 'have a go' at questions unless you know that a wrong answer won't be negatively scored.
- If you answer questions out of sequence, make sure you mark the right boxes.

- Keep an eye on the clock. It's very easy to get engrossed in an answer and lose track of time.
- Use your time wisely: some questions are more complex and demand that you spend more time on them.
- Seek help straightaway if you have a technical problem.
- If you don't know the answer to a particular question, move on to the next.
- Don't get distracted by how quickly the person next to you is working. Work at your own pace.
- Don't get discouraged if the questions are unfamiliar; stay confident.
- Use the last few minutes to revisit any questions you failed to answer initially.

▶ After the test

Your results

If you have taken a batch of aptitude tests – perhaps a verbal test, a numerical test and a diagrammatic test – as part of a graduate selection programme, and you are unsuccessful, it is not usual practice to give you your results. There is, however, no reason why you should not ask for these, though you are only likely to be given them over the telephone and not in a detailed feedback session. This can be frustrating and disappointing, but the alternative would be immensely costly to employers.

The employer may have various objectives in mind when setting the test, which you won't know about. For example, knowing that you got 50 questions right out of 60 would be of no significance unless you also know that most other people got more than 55, or less than 45. Without knowing what the target score is, simply being given your results is meaningless. It is also often the case, particularly with graduate recruiters, that they may have different scores in mind according to the different jobs in which you are going to be placed. For example, the diagrammatic reasoning score may be very important for someone who is going into IT development, the numerical test score may be the most significant for those going into financial management, and verbal reasoning may be of most significance for those going into human resource management or marketing. The employer may be working to a whole set of different targets aligned to these job functions.

As part of good test practice, you should be informed about how your results will be dealt with at the beginning of the test session, so you should know whether there is a possibility of getting any feedback, in what form this feedback will be and, if you're not going to find out the results, what is going to happen to them.

Even if the test material looked unusual to you, if you compare it to other problems you have solved or assignments you have completed, you will probably have some basic sense of how you've done. You'll know, for example, that you found numerical reasoning easier than diagrammatic, or that you found verbal reasoning easier than the other two tests. This sense of how you think you have done will help you to decide how to prepare for future tests.

There are circumstances that will adversely affect your test score. If you are feeling unwell for any reason or are short of sleep or have other things preying on your mind, it is quite likely that you will get a lower score than you would if you were at your best. There may be nothing you can do about this – you probably won't be able to organize an alternative test date – but it does mean that you shouldn't read too much into that one result. So if you don't pass, or you don't get through to the next round of the selection, don't assume your performance will be exactly the same on future occasions.

17

Practise

tests

▶ Verbal tests

Note that in these verbal tests there are no words that have different UK and US spellings, since this would add to the confusion. However, you do need to bear the differences in mind if you are taking an entrance test for a US college or business, or if you end up working for a company that has adopted US spelling.

Spelling

There are hundreds of thousands of words that could be put into a spelling test, but the samples below are words that you are more likely to use or encounter in work and business settings.

Verbal test 1

Look at the following two columns of words and underline any that you think are spelt incorrectly.

1	conglomerate	conglomorate
2	syndicate	syndecate
3	deliborate	deliberate
4	diligent	diligant
5	influenccial	influential
6	solusion	solution
7	accommodation	accomodation
8	contrervene	contravene
9	developement	development
10	disserning	discerning
11	maintenance	maintanance
12	improvment	improvement
13	constitutents	constituents
14	controvercy	controversy
15	serendipity	serrendipity

16 exclussive	exclusive
17 affluant	affluent
18 confidential	confidencial
19 concurring	concuring
20 alternative	alternitive
21 flambouyant	flamboyant
22 aquisitive	acquisitive
23 semantics	cemantics
24 discovery	descovery
25 acceptible	acceptable

Answers

Correct spellings are:

1	conglomerate	13	constituents
2	syndicate	14	controversy
3	deliberate	15	serendipity
5	diligent	16	exclusive
6	influential	17	affluent
6	solution	18	confidential
7	accommodation	19	concurring
8	contravene	20	alternative
9	development	21	flamboyant
10	discerning	22	acquisitive
11	maintenance	23	semantics
12	improvement	24	discovery
		25	acceptable

Verbal test 2

Underline any of the following words that are spelt incorrectly.

1	committee	11	warantee
2	legislation	12	legitimate
3	senario	13	foriegn
4	distributors	14	systematic
5	guarantee	15	stattutory
6	corrolory	16	credencials
7	eligible	17	contemporary
8	referrals	18	analisys
9	intigrated	19	competitors
10	fallacy	20	flagreant

Answers

The following are the correct spellings:

3   scenario
6   corollary
9   integrated
11 warrantee
13 foreign
15 statutory
16 credentials
18 analysis
20 flagrant

Word placement

Verbal test 3

1   Place the words 'here' and 'hear':
    Have you been waiting ... for long?
    When did you ... about this afternoon's meeting?

2 Place the words 'site', 'sight' and 'cite':

Have you visited the ... that we intend to develop?

We can ... several documents that indicate our intentions.

Well, the director wearing fancy dress will be an interesting ...

3 Place the words 'breaks' and 'brakes':

I am concerned about how many ... some staff seem to be taking before lunch.

Someone is going to have to put the ... on this before it gets out of hand.

4 Place the words 'stationary' and 'stationery':

How long is it since anyone tidied out the ... cupboard?

I think we are just going to have to remain ... for the time being.

5 Place the words 'fare' and 'fair':

We have to ensure that this new policy is ... to all staff.

I wasn't very impressed with the ... at the launch.

6 Place the words 'too' and 'two':

It is all ... easy to jump to conclusions here.

We need to finish the proposal within the next ... weeks.

7 Place the words 'wait' and 'weight':

We don't want customers to ... any longer than necessary.

It is very important that the correct ... is given on every occasion.

8 Place the words 'affect' and 'effect':

This could have quite a significant ... on staff morale.

This is likely to ... the way we develop the latest range of products.

9 Place the words 'principle' and 'principal':

The ... reason for developing the appraisal system is to implement better training policies.

I believe we should stick firmly to our basic ... here – the customer is always right.

10   Place the words 'its' and 'it's':

I wonder if ... always as difficult as this to raise extra income.

Well, the new model gets ... first showing at next month's exhibition.

Answers

1   Have you been waiting here for long?
When did you hear about this afternoon's meeting?

2   Have you visited the site that we intend to develop?
We can cite several documents that indicate our intentions.
Well, the director wearing fancy dress will be an interesting sight.

3   I am concerned about how many breaks some staff seem to be taking before lunch.
Someone is going to have to put the brakes on this before it gets out of hand.

4   How long is it since anyone tidied out the stationery cupboard?
I think we are just going to have to remain stationary for the time being.

5   We have to ensure that this new policy is fair to all staff.
I wasn't very impressed with the fare at the launch.

6   It is all too easy to jump to conclusions here.
We need to finish the proposal within the next two weeks.

7   We don't want customers to wait any longer than necessary.
It is very important that the correct weight is given on every occasion.

8   This could have quite a significant effect on staff morale.
This is likely to affect the way we develop the latest range of products.

9   The principal reason for developing the appraisal system is to develop better training policies.
I believe we should stick firmly to our basic principle here – the customer is always right.

10 I wonder if it's always as difficult as this to raise extra income.

Well, the new model gets its first showing at next month's exhibition.

Word relationships

Verbal test 4

1 Man is to boy as woman is to:
(a) daughter (b) female (c) girl (d) lady

2 Food is to eat as water is to:
(a) thirst (b) drink (c) bathe (d) swallow

3 Bird is to nest as man is to:
(a) house (b) home (c) garden (d) dwelling

4 Bicycle is to car as glider is to:
(a) aeroplane (b) sky (c) fly (d) parachute

5 Ship is to sea as train is to:
(a) platform (b) journey (c) rail (d) station

6 Wheel is to turn as flame is to:
(a) glow (b) hot (c) fire (d) burn

7 Water is to steam as ice is to:
(a) snow (b) water (c) vapour (d) cold

8 She is to hers as he is to:
(a) his (b) him (c) he's (d) their

9 Cotton is to thread as copper is to:
(a) insulation (b) link (c) electricity (d) wire

10 Tree is to forest as pebble is to:
(a) sand (b) beach (c) rock (d) flint

11 Bank is to money as library is to:
(a) reader (b) book (c) catalogue (d) reference

12 Black is to white as light is to:
(a) bulb (b) glow (c) dark (d) bright

13 Grass is to green as sky is to:
(a) clear (b) pleasant (c) blue (d) cloud

14 Touch is to feel as look is to:
(a) eye (b) sight (c) view (d) see

15 Circle is to sphere as square is to:
(a) oblong (b) box (c) cube (d) ellipse

Answers

1	c	9	d
2	b	10	b
3	a	11	b
4	a	12	c
5	c	13	c
6	d	14	d
7	b	15	c
8	a		

Synonyms

Synonyms are words with the same meaning. You need to find a word with a similar meaning from the options provided.

Verbal test 5

1 Lively means the same as:
(a) energetic (b) hurried (c) lethargic (d) speedy

2 Famous means the same as:
(a) notorious (b) celebrity (c) important (d) well known

3 Lucid means the same as:
(a) watery (b) clear (c) bright (d) luminous

4 Intrepid means the same as:
   (a) afraid (b) sensible (c) bold (d) determined

5 Calm means the same as:
   (a) restive (b) relaxed (c) slow (d) apathetic

6 Delve means the same as:
   (a) dig (b) deep (c) burrow (d) bury

7 Furtive means the same as:
   (a) quiet (b) secretive (c) whisper (d) deceptive

8 Concur means the same as:
   (a) dispute (b) concord (c) agree (d) comply

9 Saturnine means the same as:
   (a) silent (b) sensitive (c) serious (d) dejected

10 Passive means the same as:
    (a) tranquil (b) submissive (c) easy (d) gentle

Answers

1	a	6	a
2	d	7	b
3	b	8	c
4	c	9	d
5	b	10	b

Antonyms

Antonyms are words with opposite meanings.

Verbal test 6

1 Prompt is the opposite of:
   (a) swift (b) hurried (c) slow (d) early

2 Accept is the opposite of:
  (a) reject (b) comply (c) decide (d) receive

3 Above is the opposite of:
  (a) under (b) beneath (c) beside (d) nadir

4 Reveal is the opposite of:
  (a) expose (b) relieve (c) conceal (d) delete

5 Abbreviate is the opposite of:
  (a) extenuate (b) shorten (c) lengthen (d) précis

6 Blunt is the opposite of:
  (a) outspoken (b) flat (c) hard (d) sharp

7 Extravagant is the opposite of:
  (a) mean (b) frivolous (c) cautious (d) thrifty

8 Restrain is the opposite of:
  (a) liberate (b) constrain (c) control (d) reveal

9 Trivial is the opposite of:
  (a) crucial (b) decisive (c) important (d) inconsequential

10 Irritating is the opposite of:
  (a) soft (b) soothing (c) sensitive (d) sympathetic

Answers

1	c	6	d
2	a	7	d
3	b	8	a
4	c	9	c
5	c	10	b

When you are completing tests like the last two, you will often find a variety of types of question in the same test. Remember to remain alert to changes from same to opposite – beware of just slipping into a standard pattern to produce your answers.

▶ Logic tests

Logic test 1

1   Susan and Diane like pizza, but Geoff and Chris like pasta. Susan and Geoff both like pasta. Who likes pizza and pasta?

(a) Susan (b) Diane (c) Geoff (d) Chris

2   Joan and Rob earn more than Ian. Michael earns less than Ian. Andrew earns more than Ian. Who earns the least money?

(a) Joan (b) Rob (c) Ian (d) Michael (e) Andrew

3   John, Fred, Steve and Jo all have similar jobs, although Fred and John are the only ones who have full-time work. John and Steve travel to work by train, but the others are lucky enough to be able to walk to work. Only John and Jo have cars. Who owns a car, but travels to work by train?

(a) John (b) Fred (c) Steve (d) Jo

4   In the local tennis league a table shows how many games each member has won. Martin has won fewest games, followed in ascending order by Lisa, Karen and James, though Karen and James have won an equal number of games. Anne is one game ahead of Karen and James while Robert is two games ahead of Anne. Karen wins the next match. Who is now on the same level as Anne?

(a) Martin (b) Lisa (c) Karen (d) James (e) Robert

5   Caterers have been given a list of the special dietary requirements of some of the people attending a business lunch. Mr Reynolds and Ms Kelly eat fish and dairy products. Ms Wells and Mr Elcott eat vegetables and eggs. Mr Reynolds and Mr Elcott are the only ones who eat salad and fish. Which is the only food that Mr Elcott does not eat?

(a) fish (b) dairy produce (c) vegetables (d) eggs (e) salad

6   Mike, Barbara, Rachael, Jim and Colin all have PCs on their desks. Mike and Colin have printers on their desks. The other three have calculators. Mike and Jim have their desks in private offices, the other three work in an open-plan office. Who has a printer in a private office?

(a) Mike (b) Barbara (c) Rachael (d) Jim (e) Colin

Answers

1	a		4	c
2	d		5	b
3	a		6	a

▶ Numerical tests

This is just a quick mental warm-up for the David Singmaster tests that follow.

Numerical test 1

Find the next number in the series from one of the multiple choice answers of (a), (b), (c) or (d).

1	4	8	12	16		(a) 20	(b) 22	(c) 24	(d) 12
2	0.25	1	4	16		(a) 8	(b) 50	(c) 16	(d) 64
3	1	2	3	5		(a) 13	(b) 8	(c) 10	(d) 7
4	25	5	16	4	9	(a) 18	(b) 3	(c) 11	(d) 7
5	7	5	12	6	4	(a) 8	(b) 10	(c) 24	(d) 2
6	1	7	13	19	25	(a) 31	(b) 32	(c) 23	(d) 29
7	50	41	35	28	22	(a) 20	(b) 18	(c) 17	(d) 16
8	90	10	80	20	70	(a) 60	(b) 50	(c) 70	(d) 30
9	91	10	81	9	71	(a) 11	(b) 7	(c) 8	(d) 9
10	23	19	17	13		(a) 9	(b) 5	(c) 7	(d) 11

Answers

1	a		6	a
2	d		7	c
3	b		8	d
4	b		9	c
5	b		10	d

▶ David Singmaster problems

David Singmaster is a well-known mathematician and setter of perplexing problems. While you may not encounter questions exactly like these in aptitude tests, they provide an excellent intellectual work-out, since they demand logical thinking, lateral thinking and application of the knowledge you already possess. There are 14 problems below and the solutions follow on page 359.

Problem 1: Strange Relationships in Much Puzzling

The village of Much Puzzling has a baker, a brewer and a butcher, like most villages. The other day I was talking to the baker's wife and she remarked that these three jobs were held by a Mr Baker, a Mr Brewer and a Mr Butcher, but no man held the job corresponding to his surname.

'But everyone knows that, even a newcomer like myself!' I responded.

But she continued, 'I'll bet you don't know what Mrs Brewer told me just the other day. You see, each of the men married the sister of one of the other men. And no man married a girl of the same name as his occupation!'

'No, I didn't know that. That's quite remarkable.'

What was the butcher's wife's maiden name?

Problem 2: Home is the Hunter

Hiawatha, the mighty hunter, has wandered far in search of game. One morning he has breakfast at his camp. He gets up and heads north. After going 10 miles in a straight line, he stops for lunch. He eats hurriedly, then gets up and again heads north. After going 10 miles in a straight line, he finds himself back at his morning's camp – honest Injun! Where on Earth is he?

Problem 3: The Squashed Fly

Two locomotives are heading towards each other from 100 miles apart on a straight track. The first is going at 60 mph and the second is going at 40 mph. A fly starts at the front of the first locomotive and flies to the second and then back to the first, then back to the second, etc. Eventually there is a terrible crash and our fly is squashed. If the fly can fly at 50 mph, how far does he fly before the smash?

Problem 4: Share and Share Alike

Jessica and her friend Pud like to eat a big lunch. One day Jessica brought four sandwiches and Pud brought five. Samantha got mugged on her way to school, but the mugger ran off with her lunch, although he left her purse. So Jessica and Pud shared their sandwiches with Samantha.

After eating, Samantha said, 'Thanks a million. I've got to see Mr Grind, but here's some money to pay for the sandwiches'. She left £3 and ran off.

Jessica said, 'Let me see, I brought four and you brought five, so I get 4/9 of £3, which is 4/3 of a pound, which is £1.33, near enough'.

Pud said, 'Ummm, I'm not sure that's fair'. Why?

Problem 5: Time Flies

If I fly from London to New York at about 700 mph, then I keep up with the Earth's rotation and arrive at the same time that I left. If I go faster, say in Concorde, then I arrive in New York at an earlier hour than I departed from London.

Suppose we continue this all the way around the Earth. Then it seems that we arrive back in London before we start! What is wrong with this?

Problem 6: A Striking Problem

My village church clock strikes the hours and makes one stroke on the half-hours. The other night I had trouble sleeping. I woke up and lay there listening to the clock. What is the longest time I could have been awake before I knew what time it was? And what time(s) could it have been then?

Problem 7: Solid Dominoes

Consider a 3×3 chessboard and a supply of dominoes that covers two adjacent cells of the board. Clearly one cannot cover the nine cells of the board with dominoes, but it is easy to cover the board if we omit the middle cell. Now consider a $3 \times 3 \times 3$ array of cells and a supply of 'solid dominoes' or 'bicubes', i.e. blocks that cover two adjacent cubical cells of the array. Again we cannot expect to cover the 27 cells with solid dominoes, but can we do it if we omit the middle cell of the array?

Problem 8: Square Cutting

Take any square sheet of paper, perhaps a paper napkin. Using one straight cut with scissors, divide it into four equal squares. Once you've done that, work out how to divide a similar square of paper into four equal triangles.

Problem 9: She's a Square

Jessica's friend Katie says she will be x years old in the year x^2. How old was she in 2002?

Problem 10: A Shorter Century

Every reader of these problems already knows that the twenty-first century didn't start until 1 January 2001 because there wasn't a year 0. But do you know that the twenty-first century will be shorter than the twentieth century. Why?

Problem 11: A Grave Misunderstanding?

Salisbury Cathedral is one of the great glories of English architecture. While wandering through it, I came across a tomb slab in the North Choir Aisle with the following remarkable inscription:

> Here lies the body of Tho the sonn of Tho.
> Lambert gent who was borne May ye.13 ad. 1683 & dyed Feb 19 the same year.

How can this be?

Problem 12: Screwed Up

A cylindrical helix is just a spiral on a cylinder, like an ordinary spring or the thread on a bolt. There are two kinds – a right-handed helix and a left-handed helix. If I turn a left-handed helix over (i.e. end for end), does it become a right-handed helix? Give as simple an explanation as you can.

Problem 13: Want a Date?

Quickly now, what year was it 3000 years before 2002?

Problem 14: Sum Trouble

Jessica and her friend Hannah were looking at a puzzle book that asked how to put plus and minus signs into the sequence 123456789 in order to make it add up to 100. After a bit, they looked at the answer and found: $1 + 2 + 3 - 4 + 5 + 6 + 78 + 9 = 100$.

Hannah said, 'I bet there are more ways to do this'.

Jessica replied, 'Sure, but I don't like that minus sign, it's too complicated. I'd rather have only plus signs. I wonder if that's possible'.

'If it were possible, they'd have asked for it', replied Hannah.

'Possibly. Or perhaps it's too easy', mused Jessica.

Who is right?

Solution 1: Strange Relationships in Much Puzzling

There are several ways to approach this. The simplest is to observe that the baker's wife cannot be Mrs Brewer (unless she talks to herself). She also cannot be Mrs Baker, since the baker is not Mr Baker. Hence she must be Mrs Butcher.

Now the brewer cannot be Mr Brewer and we have just seen that he cannot be Mr Butcher, so he must be Mr Baker and the butcher must be Mr Brewer.

Mr Brewer, the butcher, didn't marry his sister, Miss Brewer, nor did he marry Miss Butcher, so he must have married Miss Baker.

More generally, you can form a tabular arrangement of the surnames, jobs and wives' maiden names. There are just two arrangements compatible with the baker's wife's information. The fact that the baker's wife is not Mrs Brewer determines one of these arrangements. Indeed, any such piece of information determines the entire arrangement.

If the baker's wife does talk to herself, then she is Mrs Brewer and the other arrangement holds, in which Mr Baker, the butcher, married Miss Brewer. This problem uses simple logic, but most people find it useful to make a table of the situation.

Solution 2: Home is the Hunter

This seems quite impossible, but is actually quite easy. Hiawatha is anywhere less than 10 miles from the North Pole, but not at the Pole. So when he heads north and goes 10 miles, he crosses over the Pole and continues a bit beyond. After lunch, he returns the way he came.

This problem requires you to extend your horizons. As stated, the problem seems impossible since you tend to think of any section of the Earth as being more or less flat and aligned with the four directions – north, east, south and west. You have to ask yourself where on earth does our normal conception break down. Once you make this 'aha' shift, the answer is easily found. Indeed the phrase 'where on Earth' has been included to help you to find the answer. Note that the problem also makes careful use of language. Hiawatha 'heads north and goes 10 miles' is carefully different than 'Hiawatha goes 10 miles north', but people often think incorrectly even when the correct phrase is repeated to them.

Solution 3: The Squashed Fly

If you answer 50 mph you're right in a way. The trains are approaching from 100 miles apart at a total speed of 100 mph, so they'll collide in just one hour, during which time our fly has flown 50 miles (no flies on him!).

But sadly, you're all wrong! Since the first train is going at 60 mph and the poor fly can only do 50 mph, he remains stuck fast on the front of the first locomotive, totally unable to do anything but stare at the oncoming disaster. Some people claim that the fly would be able to head away from the first locomotive at a total speed of 110 mph, but air resistance would keep him from getting more than a negligible distance.

The key idea is already expressed in the solution. This is a trick variation on a classic problem, dating back to about 1900. Many people know the problem when the fly can fly at 100 mph and hence leap into using the standard solution of that version, not noting the change of value of the fly's speed. Moral: don't solve your problem until you've read it very carefully!

Solution 4: Share and Share Alike

Since they shared the sandwiches, they each ate three sandwiches and so each sandwich is worth £1. So Jessica gave one sandwich to Samantha while Pud gave two, so Jessica should get £1 and Pud should get £2.

This is a classic, dating back to at least 1202, but people have trouble figuring out how to proceed. The key ideas are to examine the distribution of the sandwiches and to determine the value of a sandwich.

Solution 5: Time Flies

One actually can arrive back in New York at an earlier hour than one leaves, but it is on the next day. We cross the International Date Line.

Again, this initially seems to be an impossibility, but we soon realize there must be somewhere where the argument breaks down. For this question you do need a small amount of special knowledge, namely that there is an International Date Line. Incidentally, though the idea was developed around 1300, the Date Line was not adopted until 1884.

Solution 6: A Striking Problem

I could have been awake for an hour and a half and it could then be either 1.30 or 2.00. This can happen in two ways:

- I could have woken up as I heard one stroke. Not knowing whether it was part of an hour or not, it could be any time. After half an hour, I hear one stroke. Then I know it is either a half-hour or 1.00. After a second half-hour, I hear a single stroke again. Then I know it must be either 1.00 or 1.30, but I won't know which until I hear the clock after another half-hour – if I then hear a fourth consecutive single stroke, it is 1.30, while if I then hear two strokes, it is 2.00.

- Alternatively, I might have woken up just after the clock struck, without hearing it. After half an hour, I hear one stroke and the situation is the same as the above. However, in this case, I do not get to hear four consecutive single strokes and I have waited perhaps a second less than in the previous case.

This is probably best done by trial and error, using the observation that the answer must involve one o'clock in some way.

Solution 7: Solid Dominoes

No, it cannot be done. View the $3 \times 3 \times 3$ array as a three-dimensional chessboard, with the cells alternately coloured black and white. Suppose the corners are coloured black. Then the layers look like the following.

BWB	WBW	BWB
WBW	BWB	WBW
BWB	WBW	BWB

There are 5 + 4 + 5 = 14 black cells and 4 + 5 + 4 = 13 white cells. Now when we remove the middle cell, we are removing a white cell and leaving a pattern of 14 black and 12 white cells. Since a domino covers one black and one white cell, no matter where it is placed, no collection of dominoes can cover the board with the middle deleted.

Solution 8: Square Cutting

Fold the square along a diagonal. Fold the resulting triangle in half, along the bisector of its right angle, which is along the other diagonal of the original square. This yields another right-angled triangle having both the vertical and horizontal midlines of the square lying along the bisector of the right angle of the triangle. Hence a single cut along this bisector will produce four squares.

To divide into four triangles, fold the square in half to make the diagonals lie together, rather than the midlines. This is done by simply folding along one midline, then the other, to yield a square, and then cut along the diagonal that passes through the corner which was the original centre of the square.

Solution 9: She's a Square

The only square year in the near future is 2025 (45^2). Hence Katie was born in 1980 and she will be 22 years old in 2002.

Solution 10: A Shorter Century

The year 2000 was a leap year, but the year 2100 is not, so the twentieth century is a day longer. (The twenty-first century will be lengthened by a few 'leap seconds' to compensate for the fact that the Earth is running a bit slow, so it will be a bit less than a day shorter.) This uses a little specialized knowledge, but the fact should be fairly well known to everyone who has lived through the recent millennium muddles. Incidentally, Ruth Rendell's Inspector Wexford detected a literary forgery that claimed to be a diary, because it had the date 29 February 1900 in it.

Solution 11: A Grave Misunderstanding?

The explanation lies not in ourselves but in our stars – or rather in our calendars. From the early Middle Ages until the adoption of the Gregorian calendar in 1582, the new year began on 25 March. Hence dates up to 25 March were considered as part of the previous year. Because of religious differences, England did not adopt the Gregorian calendar until 1751, after the death of young Thomas Lambert.

Because of the difference between English and continental dates during 1582–1751, you must be cautious with English historical dates that occur on 1 January to 24 March in these years. Indeed, you sometimes see English dates of this period written as 1 Feb 1691/2, meaning that some people thought it was 1691 while others thought it was 1692. To confuse matters even more, Scotland changed to using 1 January as the beginning of the year in 1600, though it didn't adopt the Gregorian calendar.

Solution 12: Screwed Up

The handedness remains the same when it is turned over. You may be able to see this mentally, but otherwise consider putting a nut on a bolt. If the handedness of a helix changed in turning it over, then half the time we tried to put a nut on, it wouldn't fit and we would have to turn it over. But we know this isn't true – it doesn't matter which end of the nut is up.

The problem here is that very few people can visualize the process carefully, so you have to search for some other way to demonstrate the result. Here we have to resort to real-world instances of a mathematical concept, so the idea of a bolt was given in the problem.

Solution 13: Want a date?

In 2002 one year ago was 2001, two years ago was 2000, and 2002 years ago was 0, so 3000 years ago was 998, i.e. 998 BC. Unfortunately this is wrong — it was 999 BC because there wasn't a year 0! When Dionysius Exiguus set out the calendar in the sixth century, zero hadn't become known in Europe and so he omitted a year 0. Thus the year before AD 1 is 1 BC.

This is a trick problem dependent on special knowledge – but knowledge that most people have.

Solution 14: Sum Trouble

Hannah is right – there is no way to insert just plus signs into the sequence to make it add up to 100. You have to use the ancient technique of 'casting out nines', or the more modern equivalent of congruence (mod 9). For those who don't know or don't remember this, the idea is that any number is congruent to the sum of its digits and that the arithmetic operations +, – and × are preserved by this congruence. For example, 21 is congruent to (adds up to) 3 and 32 is congruent to (adds up to) 5. So 21 + 32 = 53 is congruent to 3 + 5 = 8.

If the sum of the digits is greater than 9, we can repeat the process. For example, 58 is congruent to (5 + 8 =) 13, which is congruent to (1 + 3 =) 4. We also have that 9 is congruent to 0. Now we also have 21 – 32 = –11 is congruent to (3 – 5 =) –2, which is congruent to 7. And 21 × 32 = 672 is congruent to 3 × 5 = 15, which is congruent to (1 + 5 =) 6.

Another way to form the sum of the digits is simply to 'cast out a nine' each time the sum exceeds 9. For example, if we consider 672 and say 6 + 7 is 13, casting out 9 leaves 4, 4 + 2 is 6.

How does this apply to Jessica's problem? Quite easily. No matter how we insert plus signs, the terms will contain all the digits 1, 2 ... 9 and the sum of the terms will hence be congruent to the sum of these digits (mod 9). But 1 + 2 + ... ±9 = 45, which is congruent to 9 or 0, while 100 is congruent to 1. So no sum with digits 1, 2 ... 9 can add up to 100, not even if we reorder them. Observe that the solution given had a –4 instead of a +4, which had the effect of subtracting 8 and so the sum of the numbers and the sum of the digits comes out 9 – 8 = 1 (mod 9) as required.

▶ Saville and Holdsworth tests

Ability tests are frequently used by employers as part of the selection process. You could be asked to complete one of a number of different types of ability test. The following verbal reasoning, numerical reasoning and diagrammatic reasoning tests have been developed by Saville and Holdsworth, a talent management company that provides assessment and development solutions to help companies make the most of their human resources. Items from several types of test are included to give you some practice in answering a variety of questions. The answers are provided from p. 376.

Verbal reasoning tests

This section consists of a series of passages, each of which is followed by several statements. Your task is to evaluate each statement in the light of the passage that precedes it, and to decide whether each statement is true, false, or you cannot say without further information. Time yourself and see how many exercises you can do in 8 minutes.

Passage 1

Many dual-career parents are concerned about arrangements for their children during the summer months when the children are at home. There are several ways that employers can cope with this problem: allowing the dual wife or husband to have a lighter load during these months; allowing the dual wife or husband to build up a backlog of working time during other months to relieve them during the summer months; providing facilities on site during the summer months for young children (perhaps using students training in the field of primary education), or some combination of all of these. However, building up a backlog of working time has generally proved difficult to achieve.

Statements

Mark each statement as true/false/cannot say without further information:

1   Increasingly, both parents of children are pursuing their own careers.

2   Students training in primary education can assist with the provision of arrangements for children during the summer holidays.

3   The best solution to the problem is to lighten the workload of one or both of the parents during the summer months.

4   Building up a backlog of working time is an easy-to-implement solution for coping with the problem of working parents' summer arrangements.

Passage 2

Computing technology undoubtedly makes it possible for more people to spend more time working at home. It is easier nowadays to obtain information at home and to communicate with the workplace. Telecommuting, where people work predominantly at or from home and stay in touch using the phone, personal computer, fax, email, internet or videoconferencing, is becoming increasingly common in some professions.

Statements

Mark each statement as true/false/cannot say without further information:

5   Telecommuting increases the efficiency of work.

6   The advance of technology has increased the possibility for sales representatives to spend time working away from the office.

7   Internet access is necessary for telecommuters to stay in touch.

8   People who do work from home can keep in touch with the workplace using phone, fax, email and videoconferencing.

Passage 3

Mensa was founded in 1946, after a chance meeting on a train between an Oxford postgraduate called Lancelot Ware and Roland Berrill, a 50-year-old Australian of private means. The two men discovered a mutual interest in IQ testing. When Ware tested Berrill and announced that he was in the top

1 percent of the population, the latter is said to have burst into tears. He was rejected by Oxford and this was the very first time he had ever been told that he was good at anything. From that day forward, the reassurance of the insecure has always been an inseparable part of Mensa's operations. However, that wasn't the aim of Mensa. It was intended to be a contact organization and research body – and there was always the notion that a useful chain reaction might occur with a critical mass of brainpower.

Statements

Mark each as true/false/cannot say without further information:

9 Lancelot Ware and Roland Berrill arranged to meet on the train in 1946.

10 Ware's IQ was in the top 1 percent.

11 One of Mensa's aims was to be a research body.

12 There was no IQ testing in Australia in 1946.

Passage 4

New technology can affect greatly the amount and nature of social interaction experienced by staff in an organization. Some of the ways this happens are easy to imagine. Well-established work groups may be broken up, redundancies may occur, communication may become less face-to-face and more computer-mediated, and the sheer amount of information conveyed by the new technology may replace the need for interpersonal communication of any kind.

Statements

Mark each as true/false/cannot say without further information:

13 The introduction of new technology is likely to reduce social interaction.

14 Social interaction among staff is important in the running of any organization.

15 Experienced staff need less social interaction.

16 Communication may become more impersonal with the introduction of new technology.

Numerical reasoning tests

You may be asked different types of numerical reasoning questions. These could consist of a table or chart displaying various facts and figures to which you need to refer. Alternatively, you may be presented with a series of number sequences, each of which has one number missing, which you have to replace from the options provided.

Numerical test type 1

This section consists of a number of statistical tables displaying various facts and figures, to which you will need to refer in order to answer the questions. For each question you are given five options to choose from. One and only one of the options is correct in each case. Your task is to decide which of these is the correct one.

You may wish to use rough paper and a calculator for this section. See how many questions you can answer in 15 minutes.

Table 1 Cement production, delivery and imports (thousands of tonnes)

Date	Quarter	Production	Deliveries	Imports
2002	Q1	2 786	2 781	307
	Q2	3 122	3 014	290
2001	Q1	3 016	2 976	357
	Q2	3 369	3 120	382
	Q3	3 242	3 097	349
	Q4	2 845	2 661	312
	Total	12 474	11 754	1 400
2000	Q1	2 918	2 814	228
	Q2	3 331	3 062	235
	Q3	3 364	3 108	278
	Q4	3 084	2 752	408
	Total	12 697	11 736	1 149

1 How many more tonnes of cement were produced than delivered in the first quarter of 2001 (in thousands of tonnes)?

(a) 5 (b) 40 (c) 104 (d) 249 (e) Cannot say

2 What percentage of the total imported cement in 2000 was imported in the third quarter?

(a) 19.8% (b) 20.4% (c) 24.2% (d) 35.5% (e) Cannot say

3 How does cement production in 2002 compare with that in 2001?

(a) Decrease by 47% (b) Decrease by 7.5% (c) Increase by 7.5% (d) Increase by 47% (e) Cannot say

Table 2 Participation in education and training of 16-year-olds

	1999	2000	2001
Full-time education (%)	69.4	69.8	71.2
Maintained schools (%)	*28.0*	*28.2*	*28.5*
Independent schools (%)	*6.4*	*6.3*	*6.2*
Further education (%)	*35.0*	*35.3*	*36.4*
Other education and training (%)	17.2	16.8	15.5
Not in any education or training (%)	14.2	14.2	14.0
Number of 16-year-olds (thousands)	610.0	600.4	609.1

4 In 2000, approximately how many 16-year-olds were not in any education or training?

(a) 45 250 (b) 50 550 (c) 62 000 (d) 85 250 (e) None of these

5 How many more 16-year-olds were there in full-time education in 2001, compared to 2000?

(a) 160 (b) 1 460 (c) 1 600 (d) 14 600 (e) 16 000

6 In 1999, approximately what proportion of 16-year-olds in full-time education were in independent schools?

(a) 6% (b) 9% (c) 11% (d) 14% (e) 19%

7 Which type(s) of full-time education showed a year-on-year decrease in the proportion of 16-year-old students between 1999 and 2001?

(a) Maintained schools (b) Independent schools (c) Further education (d) All of them (e) None of them

Table 3 Driving test applications and results (thousands of applicants)

	2000	2001
Applications received	1607.9	1631.4
Tests conducted	1482.9	1489.0
Tests passed	697.4	684.2

8 Approximately what percentage of applications received in 2000 resulted in tests being conducted?

(a) 84% (b) 87% (c) 92% (d) 95% (e) 97%

9 How many more tests were failed in 2001 than 2000?

(a) 1 930 (b) 2 010 (c) 15 700 (d) 19 300 (e) 20 100

10 By approximately what percentage did the number of applications received in 2001 increase from the previous year?

(a) 1.5% (b) 3.2% (c) 4.7% (d) 10.1% (e) 11.5%

11 If the pass rate falls by 1% per year between 2001 and 2005, how many passes will there be in 2005?

(a) 62 380 (b) 65 720 (c) 623 800 (d) 657 200 (e) Cannot say

Table 4 Emissions of carbon dioxide by source (figures in millions of tonnes)

	1995–97	1998–2000
Industrial combustion	111	108
Power stations	162	132
Transport	105	108
Domestic	72	69
Other sources	33	36

12 What was the total number of tonnes of carbon dioxide emitted by power stations between 1995 and 2000?

(a) 2 650 000 (b) 2 940 000 (c) 3 890 000 (d) 265 000 000 (e) 294 000 000

13 What was the approximate change in total carbon dioxide emissions between 1995–97 and 1998–2000?

(a) Decrease by 6% (b) Decrease by 5% (c) Decrease by 2%
(d) Increase by 4% (e) Increase by 5%

14 If the proportion of carbon dioxide emissions from domestic sources decreased to 10% in 2001–3, what would be the total number of tonnes emitted from domestic sources in 2001–3?

(a) 39 000 000 (b) 46 000 000 (c) 52 000 000 (d) 64 000 000
(e) Cannot say

15 In 1998–2000, approximately what proportion of carbon dioxide emissions were from industrial combustion and power stations combined?

(a) 48% (b) 53% (c) 57% (d) 67% (e) 80%

16 If emissions from power stations decrease by 10% in each of the next four three-year periods, what will they be in 2010–12?

(a) 71 800 000 (b) 79 200 000 (c) 86 600 000 (d) 94 000 000 (e) Cannot say

Numerical test type 2

This section consists of a series of number sequences, each of which has one number missing.

For each question you are given five options to choose from to replace the missing number. One and only one of the options is correct in each case. Your task is to decide which of these is the correct one.

1	3	?	17	24		(a) 4 (b) 5 (c) 7 (d) 9 (e) 10
2	5	6	9	14	?	(a) 17 (b) 18 (c) 21 (d) 24 (e) 25
3	40.6	36.4	?	28		(a) 30 (b) 30.2 (c) 31.6 (d) 32 (e) 32.2

Diagrammatic reasoning tests

You could be presented with several different types of diagrammatic reasoning questions. The items could consist of a series of diagrams for which you have to choose the next diagram in the series. Alternatively, you could be presented with figures, digits or letters that are then transformed by various commands. You have to decide either what transformations the commands are performing or what the outcome of transformations are.

Diagrammatic test type 1

Each problem in this section consists of a series of diagrams on the left of the page, which follow a logical sequence. You are to choose the next diagram in the series from the five options on the right. See how many you can complete in 4 minutes.

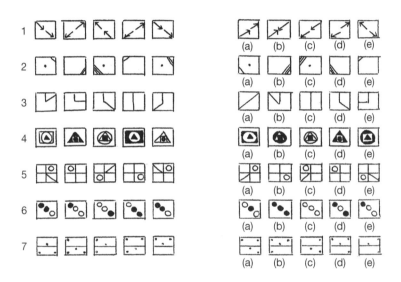

Diagrammatic test type 2

In this section, figures within boxes are presented in columns and are changed in some way by various commands contained in circles.

Each problem consists of several figures in a column. Work down the column, starting at the top and dealing with each command and adjacent figure in turn. You must choose from the five possible answers provided on the right-hand side of the page – the column that results from carrying out the given commands.

Key to commands:

⊗ invert figure

⬌ reverse figure

↻ rotate figure clockwise by 90°

↺ rotate figure anticlockwise by 90°

◎ omit figure

⇕ exchange contents of this box with contents of previous box

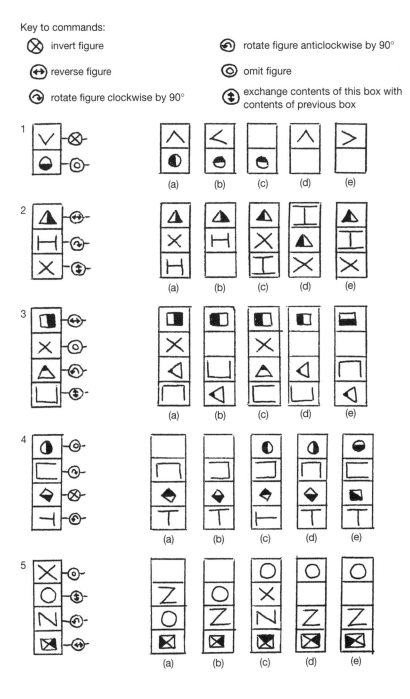

Diagrammatic test type 3

In this section there are a number of diagrams. Within each diagram, sequences of digits are altered in some ways by various commands. The commands are represented by symbols. For example:

In this example the command ⊙ replicates the first digit of the sequence. Your task is to work through a diagram, following paths that are indicated by sets of arrows, in order to determine the effect of the commands and then to answer the questions that follow each diagram. When tracing a path between two sequences, you must follow a path that includes only one colour of arrow.

Note that each symbol has a different meaning. If the same symbol occurs more than once in a diagram, it has the same meaning each time. However, the meanings of the symbols may differ from one diagram to the next.

See how many you can do in 12 minutes.

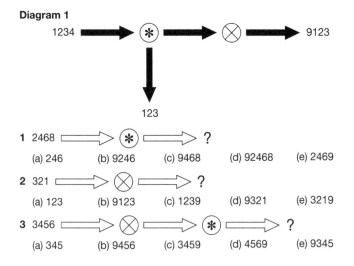

Diagram 1

1 2468

(a) 246 (b) 9246 (c) 9468 (d) 92468 (e) 2469

2 321

(a) 123 (b) 9123 (c) 1239 (d) 9321 (e) 3219

3 3456

(a) 345 (b) 9456 (c) 3459 (d) 4569 (e) 9345

Diagram 2

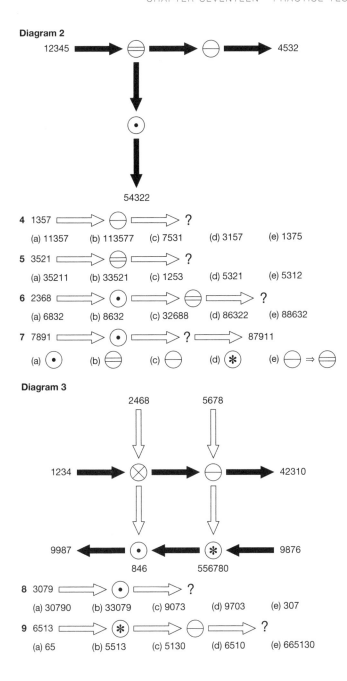

4 1357 ⟹ ⊖ ⟹ ?

   (a) 11357   (b) 113577   (c) 7531   (d) 3157   (e) 1375

5 3521 ⟹ ⊖ ⟹ ?

   (a) 35211   (b) 33521   (c) 1253   (d) 5321   (e) 5312

6 2368 ⟹ ⊙ ⟹ ⊖ ⟹ ?

   (a) 6832   (b) 8632   (c) 32688   (d) 86322   (e) 88632

7 7891 ⟹ ⊙ ⟹ ? ⟹ 87911

   (a) ⊙   (b) ⊖   (c) ⊖   (d) ✳   (e) ⊖ ⟹ ⊖

Diagram 3

8 3079 ⟹ ⊙ ⟹ ?

   (a) 30790   (b) 33079   (c) 9073   (d) 9703   (e) 307

9 6513 ⟹ ✳ ⟹ ⊖ ⟹ ?

   (a) 65   (b) 5513   (c) 5130   (d) 6510   (e) 665130

10 1927 ⟹ **?** ⟹ 71921

(a) ⊗   (b) ✳ ⇒ ⊗   (c) ⊗ ⇒ ⊗   (d) • ⇒ ✳ ⇒ •

(e) ⊗ ⇒ ✳ ⇒ ⊗

11 7319 ⟹ **?** ⟹ 137

(a) •   (b) ⊗ ⇒ •   (c) • ⇒ ⊗   (d) • ⇒ ⊗

(e) • ⇒ ⊗ ⇒ ⊗

Answers

Verbal:

1	Cannot say	9	False
2	True	10	Cannot say
3	Cannot say	11	True
4	False	12	Cannot say
5	Cannot say	13	True
6	Cannot say	14	Cannot say
7	False	15	Cannot say
8	True	16	True

Numerical

Numerical type 1:

1	b	9	d
2	c	10	a
3	e	11	e
4	d	12	e
5	d	13	a
6	b	14	e
7	b	15	b
8	c	16	c

Numerical type 2:

1 e   2 c   3 e

Diagrammatic

Diagrammatic type 1:

1	d	5	d
2	b	6	e
3	e	7	a
4	b		

Diagrammatic type 2:

1	d	4	a
2	c	5	e
3	b		

Diagrammatic type 3:

1	a	7	c
2	d	8	e
3	e	9	e
4	d	10	b
5	c	11	c
6	e		

Chapter eighteen

Useful test
websites and
other resources

▶ General information

British Institute of Graphologists (www.britishgraphology.org)

Provides information on all aspects of handwriting analysis. It offers advice to employers who are considering using graphology and also to anyone who wishes to obtain an analysis of their own handwriting to find out what sort of profile it produces.

British Psychological Society (www.bps.org.uk; www.psychtesting.org.uk)

The BPS Occupational Psychologists Division provides lots of useful information. It publishes annual directories, which include reviews of all the major personality tests and aptitude tests currently being used. These books are expensive, but may be available at some university libraries and good reference libraries. Online tests are now available at *www.psychtesting.org.uk*. The test reviews are helpful for employers who are considering using aptitude and personality tests in their selection processes.

The BPS also produces a booklet called *Psychological Testing: a Test Taker's Guide*. This includes information on testing in all settings, with sections on occupational testing, information about preparing for tests, obtaining results, and codes of practice for both test users and test takers.

Fulbright Commission (www.fulbright.co.uk)

The organization that administers the GMAT tests in the UK. Although these tests are designed for people who wish to study in the USA, the practice material may be of some interest. You can purchase practice books and CD-ROMs from the Fulbright Commission in London.

Prospects website (www.prospects.ac.uk)

The Prospects website contains a very useful psychometric testing subsection. This can be found by clicking on the 'Applications and Interviews' option. The psychometric testing section has information about the Saville and Holdsworth GAP series, the MBTI, the OPQ, the civil service selection test and some tests set by individual employers.

University careers services

Many university careers services run practice test sessions for current and recent graduates. Some may charge for this service, especially to past graduates, but this is not likely to be as expensive as having tests done privately. It is certainly worth following up if you are currently a student, or have graduated within the last two years.

▶ Test publishers

All have their own websites and these contain a range of valuable information, including advice for employers about which tests may suit which situations. Websites develop all the time, so check them all for information on helplines, advice to candidates and sample practice material. Some of the major test publishers in the UK are:

- Assessment for Selection and Employment (ASE) (*www.ase-solutions.co.uk*)
- The Morrisby Organisation (*www.morrisby.co.uk*)
- Oxford Psychologists Press Ltd (OPP) (*www.opp.co.uk*)
- The Psychological Corporation Ltd (*www.psychcorp.com*)
- Psytech International Ltd (*www.psytech.co.uk*)
- Saville and Holdsworth (*www.shlgroup.com*)
- The Test Agency Ltd (*www.testagency.co.uk*)

▶ Equal opportunities information

Commission for Racial Equality (www.cre.gov.uk)

Provides information and codes of practice for employers to help them avoid discrimination in their recruitment and selection processes. It can also provide advice to individuals who feel they may have been discriminated against.

Disability Rights Commission (www.drc-gb.org.uk)

Provides information on employment and the Disability Discrimination Act.

Dyslexia Institute (dyslexia-inst.org.uk)

Advises on any issue connected with dyslexia.

Equal Opportunities Commission (www.eoc.org.uk)

Provides guidance to employers on all aspects of gender equality in the workplace. It produces codes of practice and can also give advice to individuals who feel they may have been discriminated against.

Royal National Institute for the Blind (www.rnib.org.uk)

Can help employers to choose fair and appropriate selection methods and also works with some test developers and publishers to look at alternative ways of presenting test material.

Part **four**

Getting
an offer

Chapter nineteen

Negotiating a
salary
package

C ongratulations – you've been offered the job. If you want it, accept it happily – subject to negotiations, which we'll look at in a moment. If you know you don't want it – you hated the company or you've got a better offer – that's fine too. Turn the job down, but do it politely. You never know when you might encounter people again, maybe in a different organization within the same sector.

▶ Bad timing

The problem comes, however, when you're offered a job while you're still waiting to find out if you're going to get a better offer from someone else. You don't want to say yes and then miss out on the better job. But you don't want to say no if you might not be offered the other job. Hmmm.

Your first response in this situation should be to play for time. Say you're delighted to be offered the job and please can you get back to them in 24 hours. It's not going to be reasonable to leave it that long, but they'll guess what's going on if you ask for several days to decide. No one wants to be second best, so don't let them know you're hoping for a better offer. If they ask why you need time to decide, you can say that you want to talk it over with your family. Or simply say that taking on a new job is a big decision and you don't like to rush big decisions. They can't argue with that.

It's perfectly reasonable to get in touch with your preferred employer at this stage and explain the problem. They'll be pleased to be your first choice, and if they think everyone else wants to employ you too, that makes you look like an even better prospect. Don't expect an instant answer from them, but ask if they could get back to you by tomorrow. They can always say no.

If this sounds like a good technique for getting an offer out of your first-choice employer even if you haven't really been offered another job, it isn't. Don't go there. If they were going to offer you the job anyway, it may well persuade them to offer fast before they lose you. And it may work if they were tossing up between you and one other candidate. But if you were a borderline choice, it is as likely to bounce them into saying no to you if they don't want the time pressure. But at least a firm 'no' now leaves you free to accept the other offer, rather than wonder whether to turn it down and then risk ending up with nothing.

All sorts of circumstances, of course, can get in the way:

- It may be that your first-choice employer is nowhere near making a decision.
- Perhaps you haven't even been interviewed yet, or maybe they're still drawing up a shortlist for second interviews.
- Or maybe your first choice is internal promotion and you're reluctant to tell your boss that you've been applying for jobs elsewhere.

In any of these cases, I'm afraid there is nothing you can do but gamble. You'll have to weigh up how much you want this new job, how much you'd mind staying in the job you're in now, your chances of getting the job you really want, and so on. But remember – you're obviously employable and you can give a good interview. The fact that this interviewer has offered you the job is a very good sign.

▶ Negotiating a deal

You should aim to leave any negotiations – on salary or other terms and benefits – until you've been offered the job. Once they've admitted that you are the candidate they want, it puts you in a much stronger negotiating position. So, as we've seen earlier, you should resist any attemps made by the recruiter to persuade you to talk about money at interview stage.

You should expect to negotiate the contract rather than simply saying yes to whatever they first offer. It shows that you have a strong sense of your own value, and that you are no pushover. While this may mean they have to give more ground than they might want, in broader terms these are good qualities in an employee. In any case, they will expect to negotiate and they usually have some leeway to do so.

You should expect to negotiate
the contract rather than
simply saying yes
to whatever they first offer.

However, there's no point trying to get more than they can afford – you'll end up with stalemate and you'll lose the job at the last moment. Unless you only want the job at a certain salary level, make sure your salary demand falls within their budget. So how much can they afford?

- If a salary range has been quoted – or is quoted now – you can reasonably expect to get the top end of the range provided you can demonstrate that you're worth it.
- If an approximate salary has been quoted, you can assume that there is about a 10 percent leeway.
- If the job is one of those where there is a set pay scale which is inflexible, you can still negotiate over other benefits.

The more valuable you can demonstrate that you are, the better chance you will have of pushing the employer up to the higher end of their range. So if your qualifications or experience exceed what they asked for in their recruitment ads, that gives you a way to show that you're worth more than the average for the job. You need to prepare justifications for asking for the top end of the salary range, such as:

- 'I've not only gained my 706/1 qualification, as you specified in your recruitment material, but I also have my 706/2 and 706/3.'

- 'You were looking for two years' experience in computer programming, and in fact I've been programming computers since I was at school, and I've done it professionally for nearly four years now.'

- 'In addition to the experience and qualifications you asked for, I also speak French and Spanish fluently, which will be an important advantage since you have so many foreign clients.'

You've been offered this job because you can bring more to it than the other candidates, so presumably you have greater than average strengths. All you have to do is identify them, and use them as a negotiating tool.

You still haven't begun negotiating yet, but you're getting somewhere:

- You've established your leverage for asking for a higher salary than their opening offer – that's all the ways in which you can demonstrate that you're worth more, from extra experience to useful additional skills.

- You know what your bottom line is – the level below which you would turn down the job rather than accept the offer.

The principle of good negotiating is that everyone should come out of it feeling like a winner. A negotiation alongside a job offer should be less confrontational than most – you're both on the same side after all – but if you're dealing with a naturally competitive negotiator, they will still want to feel they've found the best person for the job, and at a knock-down price.

Top Tip **Negotiating your salary**

Before you start your negotiations, you must know how much money you're looking for as a minimum. It might be the least you can afford to live on, or it might be the least you feel you are worth – any less and you'd rather not take the job. However you choose to define it, you must go into negotiations knowing your bottom line. If you don't, you're likely to be negotiated down below it.

Finding variables

There's one more thing you need to do before you start talking. You need to identify all the variables. In other words, all the other items you can negotiate over in addition to your salary. If you discuss money only, you're left haggling as if you were in a marketplace. You start a few thousand higher than they do and you each keep giving ground until you meet in the middle. But a salary negotiation can be far more sophisticated than that, and it's in your interests that it should be.

The principle **of good negotiating is** that everyone should come out of it **feeling like a winner.**

The variables are all the other factors you can bring into play to balance up with your salary. So if they offer you less than you wanted and seem unable or unwilling to budge, you can ask for extra holiday entitlement, or a home computer supplied by the employer, or share options. The more variables you have to play with, the more scope you both have for negotiating.

Have a look through this list of variables – there's room for you to add more at the end. In the middle column you can jot down what the offer is (if you know), and in the right-hand column you can write down what you want to negotiate for. Just remember, no one's going to give you everything. If you hold out for more commission, you'll have to concede something else such as a reduction in your basic salary. So fill this list in according to what you think is fair, reasonable and plausible, not according to some fantasy ideal.

Variable	Current offer	Target
Salary		
Bonus		
Commission		
Overtime		
Profit sharing		
Holiday entitlement		
Personal leave days (dentist appointments, kids are home sick, etc.)		
Medical/other insurance		
Pension contribution		
Stock options		
Childcare contribution		
Relocation costs		
Company car		
Company computer		
Mobile phone		
Travel allowance		
Accommodation expenses		
Health club membership		
Start date for the job		
Others:		

Once you've established what the variables are, you don't have to negotiate on everything. You may only negotiate on the ones you're really concerned about. But you know the others are there to bring into play if you start getting to a stalemate. If they simply won't move any further on salary or holidays, that may be time to ask for a computer or childcare allowance.

Employers can be very sensitive about paying you more than other comparable employees, in case word gets out. So they're much happier agreeing a salary no one's going to object to and making up the difference in other benefits. Equally, your salary is a straight cost, but it will cost them far less to provide you with a computer than it would cost you to buy one for yourself. You'll judge the value of the computer by the money it saves you buying your own, but the actual cost to them is far lower. So there are several reasons why you will often find it much easier to get them to concede benefits than salary.

Don't forget that if you can't agree the starting salary you want, you may still be able to get the employer to agree to a salary review or even an agreed raise after a fixed period. It's not unreasonable for them to want to make sure you're as good as you seem. Get them to agree a specific salary raise at the review if you meet pre-agreed targets: 'How about £30,000 now, with an understanding that if I increase productivity by at least 3 percent, that will go up to £32,000 at my six-month salary review?'

▶ Negotiating techniques

The first rules of negotiating we've already covered:

- Establish your leverage.
- Know your bottom line.
- Find all the variables you can.

Once you're actually in conversation, there are three more rules you'll need to follow:

- Get all the cards on the table.
- Never give free concessions.
- Agree to all or nothing.

Get all the cards on the table

If you're dealing with a tricky kind of negotiator, keen to negotiate the best deal they can for their company, there's one ace they'll be holding up their sleeve. You have to find out what it is. They may well have concessions they want from you before they will agree to a particular salary. They might want you to agree to start on a lower salary, or to take on extra responsibilities as well as those originally agreed. And if they are an underhand dealer, they will wait until the last minute to spring this on you. In other words, they'll wait until you've pretty well agreed on the salary.

And then out of the blue: 'Oh, and I'd also like you to deal with your colleague Philippa's accounts while she's on maternity leave.' Now, it's not that you don't want the opportunity to show that you can take Philippa's accounts in your stride. It's just that if you do, that will increase your value even more, and with it the size of starting salary you deserve. But hang on, you'd almost finished negotiating, and your future employer knows that you were about to accept a salary somewhere in the middle of the advertised range. It's much harder now for you to backtrack and insist that you want a salary close to the top of their range. And they know it is.

Ask them to put all their cards on the table, and do the same yourself.

The way to prevent this is very simple: ask them to put all their cards on the table, and do the same thing yourself. That way, you can balance all the issues against each other. All you have to do is to say, for example: 'We need to talk about my salary, and I'd also like to discuss my holiday entitle-ment. Are there any other issues we need to discuss at the same time?' You've made it extremely difficult for them to keep back the fact that they want to talk to you about covering for Philippa while she's away. If they don't mention it, and then spring it on you later, you have the moral high ground and will find it much easier to insist that you go back over the other points you've agreed and revise them in the light of the new information.

Never give free concessions

This is a simple but critical rule for negotiating. All it means is that if they ask you to lower the amount you're asking for, or concede that you will wait six months before getting a rise to the salary you want, you don't simply say yes; you trade the concession for a matching concession on their part:

- If they say, 'I can offer you a salary review after only three months', you don't simply say, 'OK, then'. You say, 'So long as my salary increases by at least £1,000 if I successfully complete the probation period.'

- 'When they say, 'I can only offer you a 5 percent commission' you say, 'If we do it that way, the commission would need to be at least 5 percent of gross.'

- 'When they say, 'The holiday entitlement is only 4 weeks,' you say 'In that case I'd need at least 5 personal leave days a year.'

You've got the idea. This principle is crucial simply because it means that you end up with a better deal. Every time you lose something, you also gain something. Just make sure the concessions you gain roughly match the value of those you are giving.

Make sure the concessions you gain
roughly match the value of
those you are giving.

Agree to all or nothing

The way you reach a final settlement in your negotiation is by moving all the variables around until they balance. So, for example, if the salary is lower than you wanted, you will insist on a childcare allowance as well. Of course, you could manage on a lower childcare allowance, but only if you get more personal leave days. And so on. It's as though all these factors are on sliding scales, and you are sliding one up as another goes down, keeping them all in a balance which produces a settlement you're happy with.

The one thing you mustn't do is to agree to any one variable before you agree to the rest of them. It would mean one of your sliders was stuck fast, and you couldn't adjust it to bring the whole thing into balance This makes it far harder to agree on a final deal, and you may have to give more ground than you wanted on one of your other sliding scales to get a balance.

So you want to outlaw from the negotiation any comment such as: 'Right we've agreed the basic salary. Now let's talk about the fringe benefits. Don't agree any such thing, and if they try to railroad you with a comment like this just say, 'We haven't finalized the salary yet; I'm still considering it. But I'm happy to go on and discuss the other benefits.'

Top Tip Talking tough ...

When you don't give free concessions, your future employer will soon learn that you're a tough negotiator. They'll think twice about asking concessions from you when they realize that every time they do, they have to give up something themselves. And in the long term, it's a good thing if they know you are no pushover when it comes to negotiating.

▶ The offer letter

Once the deal is finalized, you can expect an offer letter from your new employer. This should outline clearly:

- the position that is being offered
- the remuneration and any other benefits
- the date of commencement of employment (if agreed)
- the location
- any conditions to which the offer is subject
- the timescale and procedure for acceptance/rejection of the offer.

Assuming all this tallies with what you've agreed, you're on your way. Technically, your new job isn't guaranteed until you have been offered it in writing, with a contract stipulating pay and conditions, and you have returned a written acceptance. So don't hand in your notice until this process is complete, otherwise you could end up with no job at all. As a condition of accepting the job, you may wish to mention if you already have booked a holiday in the next six months or so. Technically, you may not be entitled to take paid holiday for several months but most firms will respect any pre-existing holiday arrangements. It's far better to sort this out up-front, and also whether they will pay you for the time you're on holiday.

Before you accept the job, get the company **to agree to respect** pre-existing holiday arrangements.

This is also the time to sort out notice periods with regard to your former employer. If your new employer would like you to start as soon as possible, tell them what your contractual notice period is with your former employer

– one month perhaps. Then add that you will try to persuade your employer to let you leave earlier if at all possible and get back to them.

If you decide to decline the offer for whatever reason (perhaps the terms weren't as good as expected, or a more interesting job came up in the meantime, or you opted for a job that didn't entail a house move), you'll still need to write a letter. Explain in brief terms that the offer did not match your needs/expectations at this time but reaffirm your appreciation for their consideration. Who knows, you may have dealings with the company at some later stage in your career, so it pays to be be courteous.

Chapter twenty

Preparing to
resign

By the time you reach this stage of the job-hunting cycle, you should have received and accepted your job offer in writing and have a confirmed start date with your new employer. If you have not received an offer in writing for whatever reason, do not, repeat *do not* resign from your current role until it has arrived.

Only resign if you've received
a job offer in writing and you have signed and returned the contract.

You can expect to experience a change in how your co-workers and supervisor relate to you as soon as you submit your resignation, so it's wise to prepare yourself.

As soon as you submit your resignation, your employer will be watching you with a close eye, especially if your notice period extends to two weeks or more. I would recommend that prior to resigning, you take some precautions to gather or remove any personal files from your computer or workspace, especially those that could be used against you. When removing personal items prior to your resignation, take care to do so in a subtle manner so as to not arouse any suspicion. Your method and manner of resignation should stay under your control for as long as possible.

Some companies have a policy in place that requires you to be removed from your office immediately. Your indicator on whether this is likely to happen to you should be based on what has happened to colleagues who resigned in the past – how were they treated?

▶ The resignation meeting

Approach your boss directly, preferably in his or her office and always privately before you hand in your official notice. No matter what your reasons are for resigning from your job, it's important to keep a cool head and behave in a courteous and professional manner. Many people use the resignation letter or meeting to air all their grievances – bad idea! It may make you feel better in the short term but could have future implications on your references or final salary, so whatever your reasons keep them short, simple and professional. Remember that difficult interview question we looked at in Chapter 13: 'Why do you want to leave your current job?' In the resignation meeting, as in the reply to that question, it's a good idea to focus on the positive elements and opportunities that you hope your next job will offer you in terms of personal development rather than airing any personal grievances connected to your current job.

Don't use the resignation meeting or resignation letter as an opportunity to air **old grievances.**

Prepare for your resignation meeting by writing your letter (an example is provided at the end of this chapter), bearing in mind that it should be short, sweet and straight to the point. Consider what information you feel is necessary to share with your boss during the meeting. It is to your advantage to play your cards close to your chest and impart as little information as possible about your new role, especially when your boss may be tempted to slander your future company and put doubt into your mind about the merits of your decision. Some unscrupulous bosses have even been known to attempt to destroy a job offer before a candidate has started! Play it safe and don't take any chances you don't need to.

Hand your boss the letter accompanied by a short statement such as, 'After a great deal of consideration I have decided to resign my position' and let them take it from there. It is advantageous to you to remain friendly and polite during the resignation interview, no matter how hostile your boss may become.

◗ Notice period

Your notice period is usually stated in your employment contract. On average, for clerical staff it is generally around one month (if you are paid monthly). Normally you will be expected to work your notice period, although there may be reasons why you or your current employer would want to shorten or even waive this.

Some employers insist that an employee leave the premises on the same day as they hand in their notice, and the employee will be asked to surrender office keys etc. on the spot. If this happens to you, don't take it personally as it may well be general company policy. IT companies, major advertising corporations and stockbrokers, for example, need to safeguard their interests and will be anxious not to lose clients or confidential information. This may not be as bad as it sounds, as the company would still have to pay your notice period, even if you are no longer working for them.

Your new employer may wish you to start as soon as possible; however, you should always let them know at the time of your acceptance of the job offer what your official notice period is with your current employer. The best way to handle this is to state what the official notice period is, but add that you will try to persuade them to let you go earlier if possible (assuming they want you to start sooner).

However, if you are in the middle of a major project or campaign, it may be difficult to persuade your boss to release you early. This may be a point of discussion either at the resignation meeting or later, once your boss has had time to take in the news.

▶ Dealing with counter-offers

A counter-offer is simply an inducement from your current employer to get you to stay with them after you've announced your intention to take another job. Mention of a true offer carries an actual intention to quit and is often the time when your boss will make you a counter-offer to persuade you to stay.

Whatever your employer's reaction or reasoning, a counter-offer is very rarely made for the good of the employee. Whenever an employee resigns, irrespective of the reasoning behind it, it is a direct reflection on the boss; their gut reaction in most cases is to persuade you to stay until they can regain control of the situation.

A counter-effect **is very rarely** made for the good of the employee.

While your boss is mentally summarizing the effects your resignation will have on the company and, more importantly, on them at a personal level, their response to you will normally sound something like this:

- 'We have plans for you scheduled to take place next month. I should have told you about them before now.'
- 'We'll match the offer; your raise was supposed to take effect next quarter but because of your great service I will bring it forward to next month.'
- 'You're going to work for who? I've heard bad things about them.'
- 'I'm really shocked, I thought you were happy here, what can I do to persuade you to stay?'
- 'You've picked a fine time to land this on me. Who's going to finish the project?'

Before you are swept along by the tide of flattery and emotion surrounding a counter-offer, take time to consider the following important factors:

- Counter-offers are only made in response to a direct threat to quit. Will you have to consider this approach every time you deserve a rise in salary or better working conditions?

- Your reasons for leaving and embarking on the job-hunting cycle still exist; conditions may seem more tolerable in the short term but will they really improve your satisfaction levels over the long term?

- Counter-offers are usually nothing more than stalling devices to give your employer time to replace you – at a timescale to suit them!

- No matter what the company says when making its counter-offer, your loyalty to the company will now be questioned; consequently your status and promotion prospects in the organization will diminish.

It's important, prior to any resignation discussion, to consider that a counter-offer may be made and mentally to prepare yourself to ward it off. By entering into counter-offer territory you will make the whole process of changing jobs a much harder one that it needs to be, not to mention the wasted investment of your and your present company's time and energy.

It's a natural emotion to avoid change and minimize disruption. For this reason many people fall into the trap of feeling guilty and find it hard to say 'no' to their employer when entering the counter-offer phase. Remind yourself why you have chosen to resign and stay strong and committed to your decision. You are making this move for the good of your career and your future. No one is indispensable and your employer will get along fine without you.

No one is indispensable and your employer will **get along fine** without you.

◗ Resignation letters

Resignation letters come in a variety of guises but the most important factor to consider is to keep it simple. As previously discussed, do not be attempted to put anything down in writing that you may later come to regret, especially when you require references or have a final salary to

---

25 Glebe Street
Manchester M2 5BB

Mr P. Brown
Smith and Brown Engineering
22 Brown St
Manchester M2 4LL

17 July 2003

Dear Mr Brown

This letter is formally to give one month's notice of my resignation from Brown and Smith Engineering with effect from 17 August 2003, which will be my last day of employment.

Please let me know if there is anything I can do to ensure a smooth handover of duties during my final month with the company.

Yours sincerely

(Your signature)

Paul Smith

come. There is no need to go into great detail about your reasons for leaving as these may be open to misinterpretation and could lead to difficulty when your references are applied for, for example:

> 'While I enjoyed the job at Smith and Brown Engineering I found that my daily tasks had become repetitive.'

This could easily end up in a verbal or written reference as:

> 'Janet Smith was easily bored by repetitive tasks.'

It is sufficient simply to state that you are formally submitting your resignation. Mention the official period of notice required (as stated in your terms of employment) and what your final working day will be.

▶ You're on your way!

So you've accomplished what you set out to do and are on your way to what we hope is an exciting new career. Good luck and remember the Chinese proverb:

They must often change,
who would be constant
in happiness or wisdom.

Confucius

Index